Crucial Issues
in Caribbean Religions

Martin Luther King, Jr. Memorial Studies in Religion, Culture, and Social Development

Mozella G. Mitchell
General Editor

Vol. 10

PETER LANG
New York • Washington, D.C./Baltimore • Bern
Frankfurt am Main • Berlin • Brussels • Vienna • Oxford

Mozella G. Mitchell

Crucial Issues
in Caribbean Religions

PETER LANG
New York • Washington, D.C./Baltimore • Bern
Frankfurt am Main • Berlin • Brussels • Vienna • Oxford

Library of Congress Cataloging-in-Publication Data

Mitchell, Mozella G.
Crucial issues in Caribbean religions / Mozella G. Mitchell.
p. cm. — (Martin Luther King, Jr. memorial studies in religion,
culture, and social development; v. 10)
Includes bibliographical references and index.
1. Caribbean Area—Religion. I. Title.
BL2565.M58   200.9729—dc22   2006022454
ISBN 0-8204-8191-2 (hardcover)
ISBN 0-8204-8863-1 (paperback)
ISSN 1052-181X

Bibliographic information published by **Die Deutsche Bibliothek**.
Die Deutsche Bibliothek lists this publication in the "Deutsche
Nationalbibliografie"; detailed bibliographic data is available
on the Internet at http://dnb.ddb.de/.

The paper in this book meets the guidelines for permanence and durability
of the Committee on Production Guidelines for Book Longevity
of the Council of Library Resources.

Map of the Caribbean

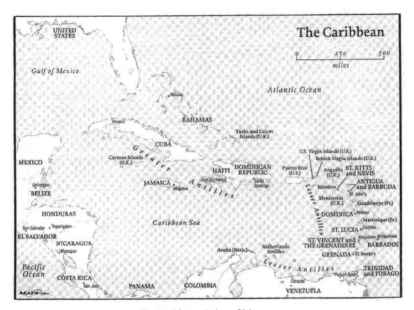

By special permission of Maps.com

Contents

Preface

Throughout history religion has always played a distinctive and defining role in the shaping and formation of cultures and national groups. Just as Catholicism, Protestantism, Judaism, and other religions were foundational to the various European national groups before the age of exploration and migration to other lands such as the Americas and countries in Africa, and Asia, so religious groupings became the pattern of settlement in the new worlds to which Europeans migrated. For instance, Puritan New England became a major force in North America, serving as a dominant influence on the shaping of the society and government and culture of that area of the country and even spreading its influence to the rest of the U.S.A. as the country grew into a nation. In the developmental stages, the country was dominated in certain sections by other religious groups, such as the Catholics in Maryland, the Quakers in Pennsylvania, and the Anglicans in the South. So even today, long after the disestablishmentarianism of the Constitution era, these areas of the country and their cultural distinctiveness still bear the defining marks of those religious associations. And as American religious historians know so well, the national character of the U.S.A. today is very much determined by its Anglo-Saxon Protestant Christian cultural foundations and influences. This is the case in spite of the numerous other religions and national groups within the country of both Eastern Asian, African, and Western and Eastern European, and other cultural, religious, and national origins.

It must be noted that these immigrants came to lands that were peopled by hundreds of national groups each of which were known for their distinctive cultures and religions, governments, and ways of life. The Native Americans were and remain a strong and enduring influence in the Americas because of their distinctive civilizations and cultures, buttressed by powerful religious foundations.

Similarly, the peoples of African and Asian nations who came to the New World either as slaves or as migrants came from strong religious orientations and foundations. Whether of indigenous religious origins or from Islamic, Buddhist, Hindu, Christian, Jewish, Taoist, Confucian, or other religious roots, these peoples' lives and contributions on the continents of North and South America are of distinctive and remarkable proportions.

This book concentrates on the effects of intersections in the Caribbean of major world religions such as Christianity and its various forms (both Catholic and Protestant), Judaism, Islam, and Hinduism, with indigenous religions such as Caribs and Arawaks, African-derived religions such as Lucumi (Yoruba/Santeria/Regla de Ocha), Regla de Palo, Vodun, Obeah, Rastafari, Orisa or Shango in Trinidad, and others. Various problems and issues have arisen historically as a result of the religious and social encounters of the various peoples from whom these religions stem. And the attempts of the various peoples from different parts of the world (countries in Europe, Africa, Asia) to form workable relationships and to build community have been very difficult. Conflicts, greed, exploitation, violence, wars, rebellion, revolution, struggles for liberation from slavery, wars for independence from colonialism have all complicated the efforts of people to build a reputable, peaceful, and productive life in these Caribbean lands, mainly of Cuba, Haiti, Jamaica, Puerto Rico, and Trinidad and Tobago, and to some degree the Dominican Republic, Bahamas, U. S. Virgin Islands, and others as they relate to and further clarify issues being discussed. While taking into account the effects of these various encounters and interactions, the book will deal in depth with the issues that are reflected and grappled with in the various religions in many different ways. Closely examined are the social and economic problems and issues of exile, slavery, economic oppression, racism, sexism, ethnocentrism, cultural dominance, issues of religious diversity, syncretism, popular religiosity, religious and spiritual imperialism, religious continuity and change, survival techniques in face of attempts at eradication by religious powers, interreligious dialogue and engagement, and the quest for universal spirituality.

Much interest has developed in the these religious issues due to the rapidly increasing population of immigrants to the U.S. and Canada from the Caribbean and South and Central America who have been exposed to these religions, and many of whom are practitioners of one or more of these religions. All of these religions may be encountered in this country, where they are largely misunderstood and berated, causing practices to be carried out under secrecy and camouflage. There is a need to openly explore and clarify Caribbean religious practices in all their complexity and diversity and to dispel the misconceptions and fears that have long been built up concerning perfectly legitimate and healthy religious manifestations.

The premise on which I base this study is that the religious diversity and mixture of the Caribbean is strongly based on the issues that are the basis of Caribbean life. Many of these religions and religious practices have been under attack historically, and attempts have been made on the part of government authorities and established religious officials to eradicate many of them. In many cases, this is still taking place. But such attempts have been unsuccessful, I contend, because the strong issues driving these religious practices are keeping them very much alive. And they are transmitted to other parts of the world as their proponents migrate to other countries such as the U.S., Canada, England, France, the Netherlands, Ghana, Nigeria, and other African and European countries. There needs to be a better understanding and appreciation of these religions, and exploring the issues keeping them alive is one way of achieving that.

None of the many books and films that I have encountered and used in my teaching and research approach the subject from the issues perspective, although at some point they do incorporate some issues in the content of their writing. Their basic perspectives are mainly from the standpoints of the history of the development of the religions and their character, make-up, and practices. Such is the case with Dale Bisnauth's *History of Religions in the Caribbean,* 1989; M. Fernandez Olmos and Lizabeth Paravisini-Gebert's *Creole Religions of the Caribbean: An Introduction from Vodou and Santeria to Obeah and Espiritismo,* 2003; George Brandon's *Santeria from Africa to the New World,* 1993; and Barry Chevannes's *Rastafari and Other African-Caribbean Worldviews,* 1995.

The present work is a socio-cultural and religious analysis and interpretation. The religious issues are examined and interpreted, elaborated and explored against a backdrop of historical, social, political, and economic settings, but the author does not attempt to use the technical methods of historical, economic, and political investigation, expertise and analysis. However, sources with such expertise are used for understanding, validation, and corrective. The author's position is from a descriptive, comparative, interpretive, and critical religious standpoint. Books, films, travels to various countries of Africa, the Caribbean, the U.S.A, Australia, South and Central America, Canada, direct observations and gathering of data, and personal interviews are used for this study. The author makes use of films taken, pictures, artifacts, and data collected during live research in various countries among religious practitioners and audiences. Much use is also made of interviews with students from the Caribbean who have taken the author's course in Caribbean Religions, as well as materials gathered from student papers and projects, especially from those who have encountered or practiced the religions in question.

The book is divided into five parts and will consist of nine chapters dealing first with how the various peoples and cultures and religions came to exist in this part of the world, then with the nature and character of their encounters with one another, how they are presently constituted and related, with the crucial issues facing each of the religions as they seek to exist in this diverse and often complex setting, and finally, presenting a concluding section that attempts a comparative analysis and interpretation of the issues in the various religions and searches for universal spiritual perspectives that may be seen in the religious manifestations.

Acknowledgments

I am much indebted to numerous persons and entities for the conception, research and study, and the publication of this work. I must first recognize the University of South Florida for granting me the Sabbatical which allowed me the time to devote more or less exclusively to travel, research, study and writing. I am grateful to the members of the Department of Religious Studies at the University for their encouragement and assistance, including the Chairman Dr. Danny Jorgensen and the rest of the Faculty, the Administrative Assistant Mrs. Linda Thompson, Assistant Tori Lockler, and other staff and assistants. A number of graduate students have assisted in the research and development of my thinking and approaches including Leo Hackett, Adetokunbo Borishade, Raul Canizares, Max Griffin-Maya, and Teresa White. Max Griffin-Maya deserves special mention for his generosity in allowing the observation and filming of the Santeria ceremony in his home, as well as the permission to use the pictures for illustrations in the text. Also, I am deeply indebted to the numerous undergraduates who have been enrolled in my classes in Issues in Caribbean Religions over the years and have challenged me and added to my knowledge and understanding of the almost endless varieties of experiences and cultures in Latin America and the Caribbean, areas to which many of them were native. Among those are Celia Rubi, Dane Vernon, Julisse Maya, Maguene Jerome, Toni Hinchcliffe for carefully proofreading the manuscript, and others too numerous to name. I am truly appreciative to Mrs. Sharon Ostermann for patient assistance with the production revisions.

I owe a debt of special gratitude to Nasio Fontaine for permission to use lyrics from the CD *Reggae Power*, and to his assistant Melissa Bardfield, who secured the permissions.

I am truly grateful to all the administrators and personnel at Peter Lang Publishing Company for their generous work with me on this project, but most especially to my Acquisitions Editor Heidi Burns, who has encouraged and inspired me as well as struggled along with me in getting everything together, following procedures and technicalities, putting things in perspective and rendering invaluable assistance in all kinds of ways. I must express deep appreciation to persons who have assisted me in doing research in their countries of residence and hosting me in such generous ways: Robbie Benjamin of San Juan, Puerto Rico; Miriam Rodriguez of Tampa Florida and her daughter Miriam Enid Castro and family in San Juan Puerto Rico; Iya Amoye in Princess Town, Trinidad and Tobago; Dr. Althea and Mr. Eddie LeCointe, Iya Patricia McCleod, Baba Sam Phills, Baba Erin Folami, Iya Pearl Springer, Professor Rawle Gibbons and Mrs. Gibbons, Chief Ricardo Hernandez, and Iya Kambiri Osunreyeke, Ministers Colin Sampson, Noble Khan, and Cyril Paul, and many others all of Trinidad and Tobago who made my journey and experience there rich, rewarding, and highly productive. Finally, to my family and friends and religious colleagues in Tampa, Florida, I give thanks for moral support and encouragement: especially daughters Cynthia Woodson and Marcia Miller, granddaughters Zahra D. Brown and husband Kendrick Brown and Jamila A. Woodson; as well as the Presiding Elder of the Tampa District of the A. M. E. Zion Church Rev. George Bolden and all my fellow clergy, district officers and workers; Bishop Richard K. Thompson and Bishop James E. McCoy.

Chapter One

The Encounter of Religions in a New World

"Nation Dance" is the paradigm Patrick Taylor aptly uses to reflect the great diversity of peoples and cultures and religions in the Caribbean.[1] Adopting the phrase from different sources, especially from the Eastern Caribbean ancestral ceremony "in which a community pay their respects to their ancestors and retrieve from them the knowledge of the past that will sustain the present and the future,"[2] Taylor finds the "dancing of nations" typical of the wider Caribbean religious experience. There the African national groups such as Ibo, Cromanti, Congo, Arada, Moko, are able to join with Europeans and celebrate their unity and diversity.[3] Taylor's conclusion and interpretation of this terminology is instructive. He asserts:

> The modern nation, whether in the Caribbean or outside of it, is the site of difference, plurality, and transformation. In the Nation Dance, the dispersed nations dance their separate dances in the same yard. They borrow from and influence each other, but the dancing of the different nations does not stop. The dance of nations is not ultimately about the dialectic of ethnicity on the stage of History; nor is it simply the immanent expression of a monotheistic God's strange and polymorphous ways. It is about spirit as it manifests itself in the individual community; and it is about the relations between living communities in a modern globalized world….The ability to invoke the emergence of a Caribbean person as a voyager in an international world, a person who can dance the terrestrial dance with an identity that is at home with difference—this is one measure of the contribution of Caribbean religions to Caribbean and world culture.[4]

Taylor is reflecting on the present situation in the Caribbean context, which is the result of long years, centuries, of historical, cultural, political, economic, social, and religious development among ethnic and national groups much too numerous to name, who gathered here in this region for various reasons and purposes, and whose encounters with one another have produced much hardship and suffering, as well as the joys of learning, understanding, and adapting to their environments and situations. In this chapter, we will explore who these diverse groups are and how they came to be situated and associated in this area

of the world, as well as the encounters and conditions under which they have
had to make their adjustments to these lands they inhabit.

The Indigenous Inhabitants: Caribs and Arawaks (Tainos)

The earliest known inhabitants of the Caribbean Islands are the Caribs and
Arawaks, both of whom were migratory peoples who, having lived in South
America, migrated from place to place in the Caribbean areas hundreds of years
before the coming of Columbus, especially in such lands as Cuba, Hispaniola,
Jamaica, the Bahamas, Trinidad, and Puerto Rico.[5] These indigenous peoples
were and are similar to other indigenous peoples across the earth from Australia
to India to Africa, from Europe to the U.S.A., Canada, and other parts of the
Americas. Before their ways of life were interrupted by outside immigrants, explorers, and invaders, they possessed significant culture, language, and satisfactory economic, social, and religious structures. Although the numerous
indigenous peoples around the world belong to different ethnic groups, speak
different languages, have differences in social organization, and display certain
differences in the religions they practice, there is a context in which we should
view indigenous peoples and their religions and cultures in order to see the
meaning and significance of them. And this common perspective is important
in our consideration of the Caribs and Arawaks (Tainos) whom the Europeans
and other ethnic groups encountered in the Caribbean.

Before looking at the nature of the religion and society of indigenous peoples, we might consider the essential characterization of religion in general.
Concerning the question of what religion is, no definition exists that is completely satisfactory. We do know that it is a powerful, dynamic force in the lives
of peoples all over the world. It is something that is believed and practiced
which tends to elevate humans above ordinary life to connect them with what is
called the "holy," the "sacred," however this may be defined. Some of us may
take such words for granted, but that doesn't say that we really know what they
mean. Whole books have been written simply to try to begin to define such
terms.[6] William James in *Varieties of Religious Experience* more or less affirms the
legitimacy of religion in discussing it from the standpoint of the "reality of the
unseen." He says that one may say that religion consists of the belief that there
is an unseen order (the invisible) and that our supreme good lies in harmoni-
ously adjusting ourselves to it. He asserts that all our moral, practical, emo-

tional, and religious attitudes are shaped by the "objects" of our consciousness, the things we believe to exist, whether really or ideally. We may have a sense awareness of them or only think them, but the reaction is the same. We have just as strong a reaction to what is only in our thought as we do for what is present to the senses. The more concrete objects of most peoples' religion, the deities they worship are known to them only in idea, but it's powerful idea, James asserts.[7]

Michael Barnes in his book, *In the Presence of Mystery*, has some interesting insights into religious characterization. He uses the "stages" approach, which may be problematic for some, or overly simplistic. But it is helpful in many ways. He sees religion as the "story of how we have responded to the dimension of mystery in human life" (William James' "the unseen").[8] Religion, he says, is a way of relating to mystery as a sacred or divine reality. "The religions of humankind are all manifestations of a kind of courageous faith in the meaningfulness of life in the face of the mystery that surrounds us."[9] As such, using Robert Bellah's model, Barnes sees religion as having come through three stages in human existence and is entering upon a fourth: the primitive, the archaic, the historic, and the modern. Looking at the first three will be helpful in our consideration of indigenous religions as religions in their encounter with the so-called developed and established religions. Barnes asserts that each of the stages is repeated in each individual life. Each of the stages blends with compatible stages of human culture. Primitive culture lives in a relatively small world populated by various spirits and strange powers (mana), no gods. Archaic cultures perceive a larger world with powerful gods at work (this is the polytheistic practice). Historic cultures conceive of a universal Power or Being that exerts its influence everywhere. The mystics and modern religiousness emphasize the infiniteness of the Mystery, called by the name that has an equation with the term "God."[10]

This categorizing serves a good purpose for understanding, basically. It can distort the picture, but Barnes handles it well, even admits its limitations, throughout the book. Every subject in religion is treated from these four standpoints, but he makes it clear that later "stages" do not exclude earlier ones. It is useful in the consideration of indigenous religions such as those of the Caribs and the Arawaks to examine Barnes's contrasts of the ways in which the "primitive" and "archaic" cultures confront, interpret, and relate to the numinous or mystery in their surroundings. First, the characteristic practices and beliefs of the "primitive" cultures involved luck, magic, good and bad omens, divination (reading of omens by some means such as casting pebbles, bones, cowrie shells, and the like), the existence of an impersonal power (mana, a Melanesian word, also taboo, tabu, tapu), and the existence of all sorts of spirits rather than gods (nature spirits, demons, personal attendant spirits, spirits of the dead, ancestral spirits, and other lesser beings such as gnomes, leprechauns). All of these are phenomena that supposedly represent how primitive peoples perceived, interpreted, and related to their surroundings. They enhanced their lives by trying to deal effectively with the "spirits" that were everywhere in their environment. A characteristic term used for these beliefs and practices by some scholars is *animism*. With no structured social hierarchy, no kings, no priests, no landlords, but simply families, clans, tribes, organized around simplified daily activities of necessity, supposedly, these peoples lived by hunting and gathering what nature provided, and herding of cattle.[11]

Second, the transition from the "primitive" to the "archaic" culture is dated to some 10,000 years ago, occasioned by the invention of agriculture, wherein villages grew into towns and social class distinctions arose (upper and lower). Cities came into being, bringing on a larger society, necessitating even greater social stratification: landowners, military, merchants, peasants, chiefs or kings. Religiously, the functionaries of priests and prophets developed. And the existence of spirits was relegated to a kind of secondary status, as a higher manifestation of the numinous was recognized in the form of gods, with greater power. Among the gods, a power hierarchy was determined, with a high god, such as Zeus among the Greeks, and Marduk among the Babylonians, Olorun among the Yoruba of Nigeria, West Africa.[12]

What Barnes calls the archaic religions, some other modern scholars such as Mircea Eliade refer to as Traditional Religions, Primary Religions, which also still exist in some form among indigenous peoples of the U.S., South America, Alaska, Canada, Central America, the Caribbean, and Africa in the still predominantly agrarian societies. Some people refer to these as primitive. Barnes mentions the problem of the sometimes fuzzy distinction between what is considered "primitive" and what is considered "archaic." Using another scholar's viewpoints, Barnes admits to a legitimate issue of dispute. "The most primitive societies of today do not exhibit beliefs in extremely powerful spirits. (This is a disputed point. Many still agree with Wilhelm Schmidt, an early 20th century German scholar, that even primitive societies tend to believe in the existence of a high god, even though this god might be distant or inactive as to merit little attention from them.)"[13]

With this examination thus far of the nature and character of religion, I believe we are better equipped to view the indigenous religions and cultures of the Caribbean encountered by the European explorers and to understand the consequences of that encounter. First it must be granted that sources are not extensive regarding descriptions of the pre-Columbian Caribs and Arawaks and their religions and culture. But much work is being done by scholars and the surviving remnants of these peoples to retrieve such.

One source describes the Arawaks as a "group of linguistically related but culturally diverse Indian peoples who inhabit the tropical forests of South America, especially north of the Amazon River, extending from the Andean foothills to the Antilles. The Antillean Arawak or Taino were agriculturalists who lived in villages and practiced cultivation of cassava and corn. The people were arranged in social ranks and gave great deference to theocratic chiefs. Religious belief centered on a hierarchy of nature spirits and ancestors, paralleling somewhat the hierarchies of chiefs."[14] The same source describes the Caribs as "American Indian people who inhabited the Lesser Antilles and parts of the neighboring South American coast at the time of the Spanish conquest. Their name was given to the Caribbean Sea, and its Arawakan equivalent is the origin of the English word cannibal.[15] Carib groups of the South American mainland lived in the Guianas, and south to the Amazon River. Some were warriors and they lived in small autonomous settlements, growing cassava and other crops and hunting with blow-gun or bow and arrow."[16]

We can see from these brief descriptions that both the Caribs and Arawaks fall roughly into the category of archaic religions as described by Michael Barnes and his sources, with some characteristics of the primitive category. However we may categorize them, their religions and culture were a very strong presence in the Caribbean area before any other peoples arrived, and in spite of efforts carried out to eliminate them, they still survive in numerous areas and are working at restoring and maintaining their religion and culture. They are very evident in the mixture of peoples and cultures in the Caribbean of today. We will thus explore briefly the religions and cultures of these peoples and what happened to them in their encounters with the newcomers to their territories.

The Caribs are famous for their warring tendencies, their bravery, and determination to succeed against their enemies and to maintain their way of life and productivity. At the top of their social structure was the war leader or *ubutu*, under whom came the priests and elders, followed by warriors and hunters. Only in times of peace did the district elder or headman (called a tiubutuli *hau-the*) have a leading role, which was limited to supervising the fishing and the cultivation of crops. The war leader made all the decisions and plans regarding time, place, procedures, and leaders of war campaigns. He was chosen by the elders of his village based on his record as a warrior. The training and initiation of boys was carefully and effectively centered on their fulfilling successful roles as warriors, except for those few who were trained and initiated for the role of priest or *boyez*. Men and women had well-defined roles. Males could practice polygamy. Marriages were arranged for girls in their mid-teens. The basic social unit was not the family but the community. Men lived separately in their carbets or houses, and the women lived in huts. Men were supposed to be warriors, priests, leaders, builders of houses and boats, craftsmen and hunters. Women were supposed to fulfill the roles of domestics, raising children, collecting firewood, bartering produce, weaving, hammock-making, and cultivating the land.[17]

In regard to religion, the main focus of the Caribs was the *maboya*, which they felt controlled everything. Each person had his or her own *maboya* to ward off evil. Besides the *maboya*, each person had also his or her own good god or *chemmen*, thought to be stronger than the *maboya*. In case of sickness or defeat or death, a hex had been placed on one by an enemy *maboya* (spirit). A ceremony was held to get rid of the evil, which was performed by the *boyez* or priest, involving (in case of sickness) cleaning the house, offerings of fruit and cassava to the *maboya,* engagement of family members, incantations calling upon the patient's good god, blowing of tobacco smoke, and the prescription of a mixture of herbs for the patient and for the family to take revenge on the evil *maboya.* The *boyez* or priestly initiation was performed with boys who were apprenticed to an older priest for several years, during which time they underwent fasting and abstentions. Investiture was concluded when the boys successfully passed certain procedures and the priest's *maboya* entered and possessed the initiate. Finally, in regard to life after death, the Caribs embraced the notion of an afterlife and conducted elaborate burial rituals. But their focus was centrally on this life here and now, trying to remain healthy and strong and to enjoy what life had to offer. They had great respect for the sea and carefully regarded the ocean spirits.[18]

By way of contrast to the Caribs, the Arawaks were characterized as being gentle and peaceful. But Kim Johnson takes issue with this as a misconception as well as with the name "Arawak" and rather prefers the name Taino.[19] According to Johnson, the Arawaks living in Guyana today call themselves "Lokono," a word which means "the people" in their language. The Arawaks encountered in the Caribbean proper have been described by most other scholars as peaceful, gentle, friendly, sedentary, preferring the practice of negotiation and commercial exchange to war.[20] Johnny Dahl in a conciliatory way gives praise to the Arawaks for having a rather admirable culture: "Before the Spanish conquest [at Hispaniola] the large-island ecosystems [offered] bountiful harvest and abundant fish. It was a well balanced culture, in perfect harmony with the forces of nature. The compact and stable island populations permitted the development of an elaborate political and social structure."[21] This statement does fit well the descriptions of the Arawak culture as presented in most accounts. The Arawaks were indeed the first indigenous people the expedition of Columbus encountered when they landed by mistake in the Bahaman Islands in 1492. He and his crew members found a friendly welcome there among these people who indeed had established a complete and satisfactory way of life.

Their society was organized and socially stratified with a paternal hierarchy. Each group comprised a small kingdom headed by a king or chief, designated by the title *cacique*. In their practice of polygamy, the average male was allowed up to three wives, but the king or chief could have thirty. They employed a mild form of temporary enslavement for captives as a means of assimilating them into their social and work structure. Men and women played different roles. A clear division of labor existed between men and women. The men cultivated the land while women did the rest of the needed agricultural work. Men made products such as woodworks, armaments, basket weaving, and did hunting and fishing, of course. Women did weaving as well, such as making the hammocks, and the cooking and preparing the staple food of cassava.[22] Bob Cobert makes the comment that this was virtually a work-free agriculture, making for a materially simple social system and leaving an abundance of time for engaging in games and recreation and developing elaborate religious rites.[23]

The way the typical village was laid out gave vent to such activities, which consisted of a "flat court in the center of the village which was used for ball games and various festivals, both religious and secular. Houses were around this court."[24] Spirituality and religiosity were built into their styles of life and artistic creations, such as religious artifacts as a part of stone-making, religious symbols from the belief system placed on woven baskets, carvings, and ceramics, and the uses of tobacco smoke in both social life and religious ceremonies.

The religious system was a completely functional one integrated with their economic, social, and political life. The Gods and Goddesses of their religion were many, the highest being the Creator God, the supreme being, called by the name Yocaju or Yucaju, who shared the creative powers with his mother, the Goddess Atabex or Atabeira. The Mother Goddess has other manifestations, one of which is Guabancex. Other Gods included Bayamanaco or Yaya, God of fire; Boinayel, God of rain; Juracan, God of power and strength, the storms, and the like. He was to be feared for the destructive force he could bring. He was somewhat the opposite of Yukiyu, the good God. These are a few of the many deities who had power over everything in nature. The tutelary divinities who ranked below Yocaju in power were known as the Cemi (or Cemies, Kemi, as variously called), who were in closer contact with humans and were very significant in assisting them in living in balance and harmony with nature. For they were in control of the forces of nature.[25]

Religious practices included specifically worship and service of the Cemi; participation in festivals in honor of the spiritual realities, ritual consultation of the Cemi through the medium of priests or the bojique (bohita, some say), who was a healer who had great knowledge of cures of all kinds stemming from the use of plants and sacred traditions. There were religious feasts and ceremonies for agricultural purposes; the use of carved figures of Cemi in the forms of toads, turtles, snakes, alligators, and various distorted human faces used in ritual; drumming and dancing; the ceremonial serving of cassava in hierarchal manner, first to the Cemi, then to the Cacique, and finally to the average persons (similar to the Christian Eucharist). Another important festival practice was the ceremonial singing of the story of the village in honor of the Cacique and his ancestors. This certainly has parallels in other indigenous societies such as the African griot tradition, the Macedonians, the Greeks, and other cultures. The belief in the afterlife was centered on a place of reward for the good, where one would meet dead relatives and friends, especially for women, for some reason.[26]

The Encounter of the Indigenous Caribbean Inhabitants with the Spanish

History has recorded that Christopher Columbus in his explorations in search of a new route to the East (India in particular) under the sponsorship of King Ferdinand and Queen Isabella of Spain wandered off course and landed by mistake on an island in the Bahamas, one that came to be called Hispaniola (now divided into the two nations of the Dominican Republic and Haiti). There Columbus and his crew of the three well-known ships (the Nina, the Pinta, and the Santa Maria) first met the indigenous Arawaks. Various views as to the character of this initial encounter are put forth in literature describing it, as well as to the subsequent interactions with and treatment of these indigenous inhabitants of the Caribbean by Columbus and the Spanish conquerors who would later follow him. But little disagreement exists over the fact that the Arawaks welcomed what must have seemed to them these strange visitors. And it is clear that the visitors, thinking they had landed in India, took them to be Indians and labeled them such, a label that has stuck to this day. How the Arawaks, as well as their neighboring Caribs, were treated by the invaders and the cultural and religious consequences of the encounters of the Spanish, as well as other European colonialists, with these native peoples is described somewhat differently in the history and literature of the different countries of the Caribbean, and also by scholars studying the situations in various nations. It is evident by all accounts, however, that the history of these encounters is not an admirable one, to say the least. It is in fact an ugly, hostile, violent, bloody, and inhumane one. Notwithstanding, there is much knowledge, insight, understanding, and mature perception to be gained from careful observance of the actions and reactions of human beings in very complex and almost unimaginable circumstances of cruelty and misunderstanding, and then to see how they have come through such conditions and somehow endured and prevailed against the odds.

The Spanish came to this New World bringing their culture, consisting largely of economic and political power, and their religion of Catholicism. Dale Bisnauth sums up well the purposes, actions, and consequences of the Spanish conquests. "As explorers, discoverers, *conquistadores* [Spanish government-authorized leaders in the conquest in the Americas] and traders sought to open up the region for economic exploitation, missionaries and priests sought to introduce what they considered to be the blessings of European civilization to the

indigenous peoples and to incorporate them into the fold of Catholicism."[27]
With total disregard for the legitimacy of the culture and religions of these host
peoples, these conquerors imposed their ways and wishes on these natives in
most brutal ways. The "friendly" Arawaks were the first to feel the savage blows
of the intruders, even though they strongly resisted. Their resistance was easily
overcome by contrast with the long-lasting campaigns of resistance of the warrior groups of the Caribs. Bisnauth cites an example of the reprisals for resistance suffered by the Arawaks: "In Hispaniola…even when resistance had been
quashed, the conquistadores vowed to massacre twelve Indians daily in honor
of the twelve apostles. A thirteenth was to be immolated in honor of Jesus
Christ! Such was the ruthlessness with which the Spaniards treated the Aara-
waks that by 1520 their subjugation was complete."[28]

After a futile attempt to find accurate accounts of the number of Arawaks
in Hispaniola at the time of Columbus' landing there, Ben Corbett describes
their treatment and seeming demise:

> Whatever the number, what happened to them is extremely tragic. They were not im-
> mune to European diseases, especially smallpox, and the Spanish worked them unmer-
> cifully in the mines and fields. By 1507 the Spanish were settled and able to do a more
> reliable job of counting the Arawak/Tainos. It is generally agreed that by 1507 their
> numbers had shrunk to 60,000. By 1531 the number was down to 600. Today there are
> no easily discerned traces of the Arawak/Taino at all except for some of the archaeo-
> logical remains that have been found. Not only on Hispaniola, but also across the
> Windward Passage in Cuba, complete genocide was practiced on these natives.[29]

Corbett is speaking of Hispaniola and Cuba, two of the main places in the Caribbean the Arawaks made their home. Today Arawaks have managed to survive
and revive their cultures to some extent in the South American country of Guyana (some 30,000), in French Guiana, in Suriname, and in Puerto Rico.[30]

The encounter of the Spanish with the Caribs was more complex, involved,
difficult, and sustained than that with the Arawaks, and the result, we will see at
some point, was quite different. In the Lesser Antilles the Caribs put up vigor-
ous resistance to being dominated by the conquering Spanish powers. They
were not easily subdued nor decimated. Dale Bisnauth points to a reason for
their being spared subjugation in Cuba at the same time as the Arawaks other
than that of their resistance. "In the final analysis," he says, it "was because the
interests of the Europeans had swung away from the Caribbean to the mainland
of Central and South America" where gold and silver were found.[31] But the

bravery and resistance of the Caribs continued, as they were able to survive the onslaught of the Spanish in Cuba and Trinidad and Tobago, and lasted well into the late eighteenth century, as they waged wars on other European colonizers such as the French, the English, and the Dutch in order to keep their culture and their lands. And St. Vincent is one place where these fierce battles were waged. They carried out many campaigns and won and lost a number of battles in their relentless struggles before they were finally forced into surrender in 1797. [32]

The struggles of the Caribs in Dominica, where today their descendants number about 3,000 living in Carib Territory, established in 1903 and consisting of 3,700 acres of land owned exclusively by the Caribs; are also documented.

> The weakening of their hold on Dominica began from the time of the first Spanish caravelles dropped anchors in Prince Rupert Bay, shortly after the second voyage of Columbus. From then on, ships of all nations came regularly to collect wood and water and to trade with the Caribs for fruit and cassava flour. For almost two centuries, contact was limited to trading and skirmishes, by the mid seventeenth century Dominica had become a refuge for Caribs retreating from the other islands where the surge of French, English and Dutch colonization was sweeping [them] from off their ancestral lands. The rugged mountains, thick forest and iron coastline provided a natural citadel for the final retreat. From this base they made attacks on the fledgling European colonies and suffered at least two massacres in retaliation; one at Anse De Mai in 1635 and another in 1674 at the village which is still called Massacre today.[33]

Attempts to Christianize the indigenous peoples were not often very reputable and did not meet with much success. Forced conversion was the initial tactic supported by the colonial power. The first missionaries to get involved were those belonging to the Catholic orders of Franciscans and Dominicans, followed by the Jesuits and others. Admittedly, there was seriousness in the religious commitment of the missionaries, for they established schools and agencies by which to do a good religious work according to the best in their traditions. However, their religious expressions and activities were a part of a system and institution which was not free of corruption and was limited by its connection with a politico-economic establishment which was interested in self-perpetuation and expansion of power and control. The governmental system that was employed to undergird the religio-economic program was called the *repartimiento-encomienda*, under which "the Spanish Crown gave or 'commended' Indians to Spanish conquistadores and gentlemen with the understanding that these encomenderos would have the right to exact labour or tribute from the

Indians. In return for this favour, the encomenderos were to provide religious instruction for their Indians and to offer them protection, presumably from their fellow Indians."[34] It is clear that this system was designed to exploit the indigenous peoples and enrich the Spanish citizens. The Indians did not respond well to nor understand the Catholic training, practices, and teachings to which the religious trainers attempted to expose them. And there were scant results to the Christianizing efforts, even though the Catholic Church and its traditional institutions were being well-planted in the Spanish territories for the benefit for the Spanish themselves. What did begin to happen in a rather natural way in terms of religious interaction and understanding between the indigenous peoples and the Catholic religion, however, was that that the Indians began to understand and appropriate Catholic beliefs and practices by correlating them with parallels they could make with their own religions. Bisnauth states: "God the Father, of Catholic belief, [the Arawaks] identified with the creator-god, Wamurreti-Kwonci, whom they otherwise knew as the benign Jocahuna [Yocayu]. Sometimes they identified Jesus Christ with Jocahuna; at other times they believed him to be the son of Jocahuna…and the Virgin Mary, whom they confused with Atabei [Atabex, Atabeira], a Goddess of Arawak belief."[35]

Other natural parallels included identifying the Holy Spirit with Hurakan [juracan], the Mighty Wind; the role of the bohito [bojique] or priest was seen as more or less identical with that of Catholic priests; the spirit of kanaima was easily identified with Satan, and the heaven of Christianity was identified with Arawak Coyaba.[36] This is a reflection of what took place between African religions and Christianity, especially Catholicism, and is referred to as syncretism.

The Encounter with Other Europeans and Their Religions

Other European explorers, conquerors, colonialist, immigrants, religious enthusiasts, and missionaries followed the Spanish in pursuit of economic, political, social, and religious goals. Thus there was naturally a mixture of different European cultures to take root in this new world. The major settlers and adventurers were the Portuguese, the French, the English, the Dutch, and these contended with one another in staking their claims to and competing for resources in various portions of these new lands as well as in spreading their religions and cultures to its inhabitants and the African slaves who were soon brought in to boost the labor forces and economic production of the areas. Through wars, trade agreements, and political truces, the various European powers, mainly in the 16th century, were able to establish their colonial domination, with one power replacing another in some areas. For instance, the French finally won control of the western portion of Hispaniola (a name given the Island by Columbus meaning "little Spain") in 1697 after many decades of struggle with the Spanish over this gold-producing area.[37] Dale Bisnauth points out:

> It was primarily the desire of France, England, and the Netherlands to benefit economically at the expense of Spain that motivated those European nations to poach on Spain's preserves in the Indies. The Dutch had an additional motive for fighting Spain related to their struggle for political independence. But religious factors were not without their significance in the challenge to Spain's supremacy in these parts. Up to 1559, this was more the case with the English and the Dutch than it was with the French.[38]

With the Spanish the areas had been Catholic domains, particularly Spanish Catholic. But now with these other nations came the exposure to and planting of other religions such as the French variety of Catholicism and the many Protestant denominations such as the Hugenots, Anglican Protestants, Dutch Reformed, Lutherans, Quakers and others. Jewish groups also settled in the Caribbean along with Christian religious groups.[39]

The colonial possessions of the Islands more or less established in the 16th and 17th centuries resulted mainly in French occupation of Guiana, St. Christopher (St. Kitts), Martinique, Guadeloupe, Tortuga, and St. Domingue (Haiti); the English domination of Barbados, Jamaica (taken from the Spanish in 1655), Trinidad and Tobago, Antigua, Nevis, and Montserrat; the Dutch assumed control of Curacao, Bonaire, Aruba, Saba, St. Martins, St. Eustacius; among those retained by the Spanish are Cuba, Puerto Rico, eastern portion of Hispaniola. The character and cultural mixture of peoples of these lands was highly influenced by the religions which their occupants embraced and those they encountered in interactions with other peoples. Although each European people's religions were destined to undergo transformation and adaptation in this New World, the same conflicts and battles for supremacy and power they underwent in their European settings followed them to the new situations. The struggles between Catholics and Protestants persisted; differences and divisions within the Protestant groups such as German Lutheran and Swiss Reformers remained prevalent; battles within the Church of England over Catholic elements (Puritanism and Calvinism, especially) and the like did not go away easily. Also the problems of church-state connection and conflict were at issue.[40]

The Spanish Catholic Church in the Caribbean operated fairly closely with the Spanish government and Catholic Church authorities in many ways. The French also worked in conjunction with French Catholic Church authorities and the French government authorities (such as expressed in the *Code Noire* regarding Christianization of slaves, though not followed for long), although the French were highly intolerant toward the Caribs and sought to annihilate them, as well as also persecuting Jews and Protestants in the French colonies of Martinique, Guadeloupe, St. Lucia, and Grenada.

An interesting and revealing example of the experiences of an attempt to perpetuate church-state relations in the Caribbean is seen in the problems encountered by the Church of England. The examples of Barbados and Jamaica Bisnauth describes will suffice in summary.

With a strong perception of the Caribs as heathens and infidels worthy only of slaughter, English settler John Powell in 1625 claimed Barbados in the name of James I of England for both the state and the Church. The island was divided into parishes five years later by the English governor, Sir William Tufton. In like manner in 1634, in Nevis, Antigua, and Montserrat, Archbishop William Laud, Primate of England, with an order from Charles I, "extended the jurisdiction of the Bishop of London over English congregations and clergy abroad." This state-church union met with modification under the governor of Barbados, Lowther, who opposed the intrusion of religion in the state affairs when the rector of St. Michael's wanted to erect a spiritual court, which the governor said would "clash with the laws of Barbados, embarrass the government, impoverish the larger free-holders and ruin the common people." The governor believed the church ought to be subordinate to the state though not divided from it: "the former was but the latter at prayer." And this was the practice that was adopted that eventually led to some unhappy results and consequences. For instance, the church in Barbados became loyalist and slavishly capitulated to the state. In the Jamaica which was conquered from Spain in 1655, religion was simply an arm of the political machine dominated by the wealthy. Though government acts were passed that encouraged tolerance, Jamaica having become a sugar-producing island, church dissents and attitudes of cynicism grew among the people. Members of the Church of England were "either indifferent or hostile to the authority of the church or they were lax in the practice of their religion.

These attitudes in turn were to harden into a tradition which was to plague the Church for a long time to come." There developed therefore a lack of religious inclinations among the English in Jamaica and a moral licentiousness of white men with their female slaves.[41] In a nutshell, the Church of England was tied to the state, which owned it, and the church's doctrine, beliefs, liturgy were settled and established by Parliamentary law, and the church in the Caribbean adhered to the same. But there was a low level of clergy sent to the Caribbean due to scarcity of committed clergy, and it was not until 1825 that bishops were appointed there.[42]

The Quakers (Society of Friends) were among the Dissenters who were transported to the Caribbean in 1665, to Barbados, Jamaica, and Nevis, having developed in England between 1640 and 1660 under the leadership of George Fox. They believed in the truth stemming from the light within, not from outward religious authority, as such. The Quakers therefore had little or no use for the Church of England.[43] They rejected all creeds, sacraments, and established religions, and war. They were conscientious objectors. Bisnauth comments that:

> The refusal of the Friends to participate in maneuvers was, in the eyes of their fellow whites, tantamount to a betrayal of the Englishmen's cause and of the plantocracy. That betrayal was complete when the Friends began to encourage slaves to attend their meetings. In Barbados, in 1676, the Assembly passed an Act forbidding Quakers to bring Negroes to their meetings. The Quakers in 1755 forbade their members to trade in slaves, and... they were among the first people in the Caribbean to agitate for the abolition of the slave trade and the emancipation of slaves.[44]

Other important religious groups came to the Caribbean and have had and still have tremendous impact on its culture, such as the Moravians, the Methodists, and the Baptists, and others Evangelicals. We shall look briefly at these later. But now we must consider other groups of peoples who were brought to these islands as slaves, have a profound imprint and are highly intertwined with the cultures there. From them also stem significant religious and social issues crucial to the Caribbean, to all the Americas, and to the world beyond. We shall look at the influx of the Africans and then at the coming of the Chinese and the Indians and other world religious groupings.

Entrance of the African Peoples into the Caribbean and Their Religious Influences and Interactions

The massive entrance of Africans into the Caribbean began in the early 16th century by means of the African slave trade, instigated by the Portuguese in the late 15th century. African slaves were brought to the Caribbean in 1510. After 1517 large numbers were brought to Hispaniola, Jamaica, and Puerto Rico. It was the development of the sugar plantations that created dire need for laborers and encouraged the massive importation of African slaves to Brazil, where the first sugar plantations were developed by the Portuguese, and afterward to the Caribbean. Hundreds of thousands of slaves were brought in to work the plantations, although some enslaved Indians were at first used alongside the African ones. By 1580 Brazil was the most important source of sugar for Europe. In the 17th century (especially between 1630 and 1654) the Dutch took control of the sugar trade and the slave trade (by way of the Dutch West India Company). They gained control of northeast Brazil and excelled over the Portuguese in naval warfare, capturing the Portuguese slave-trading ports of the African Gold Coast, Arguin and Goree Islands. Not interested in developing sugar plantations of their own but rather in dominating the trading industry, the Dutch passed on their expertise in sugar technology to the English and French in St. Kitts, Barbados, Martinique, and Guadeloupe.[45]

Between 1640 and 1655 the Caribbean Islands were transformed into sugar colonies, with sugar superseding tobacco production by far. African slaves were brought in droves, with small farms being ousted to make room for the slaves. The English from 1651 to 1808 excluded the Dutch and carried out their own slave trade in their colonies, bringing approximately 1,900,000 Africans to the Caribbean. The French also conducted their own slave trade from 1664 to 1830, bringing approximately 1,650,000 into their colonies. The Dutch brought some 900,000 to the Guianas (later called Guyanas), Curacao, Aruba, Bon Aire, and St. Eustatius. Many of the African slaves were brought from Senegambia, Sierra Leone, the Windward Coast, the Gold Coast, and the Bight of Benin, coming from several different tribes and speaking different languages. Those from the Windward Coast and Sierra Leone were mostly Mandingoes. Those from the Gold Coast (now Ghana) included Koromantyns. From Whydah on the Bight of Benin came Papaws mostly. There were numerous other ethnic groups who were brought in, all of whom were to have a thoroughgoing effect on every facet of Caribbean life, including that of religion.[46]

The Europeans, as they did with the indigenous Caribs and Arawaks, promoted and perpetuated grossly mistaken and distorted notions of African religions from the very beginning of contact with these peoples. Some denied that the Africans "knew" any religion. English planters denied that they had a system of beliefs that could be described as religion and denounced their beliefs as heathenish superstition. Their claim was that Africans were incapable of religious sentiment. The reality of the situation to dispel such myths is that the very lives of the Africans (in contrast to Europeans, who reserved religion for special days and occasions) were permeated with religion. Africans had very complex, sophisticated religious systems. Religion among the slaves was brought with them from their several homelands and included their traditional religions and Islamic religion, though Islamic practices did not long survive the rigors of the Middle Passage, as there were no structures to facilitate them such as Imams, the Qur'an and other necessities. But indigenous or traditional African religions could and did survive the difficulties of plantation life. Though these religions underwent changes in the New World, they remained recognizable in structure and form. And they proved to be adaptable to the new situations.[47]

Leonard Barrett has some further clarifications on this issue of religion and culture. He asserts that, though Africa contained high cultural development expressed in institutions of agriculture, trade, economics, belief, art, morals, law, social and government bodies, religion is the most vital institution of Africa. "Religion for Africans was, is and ever shall be the source of life and meaning. It is in religion that they live, and move, and have their meaning."[48] And this is the best way to understand the ethos of African culture in the New World. Since everyone (all scholars, Black and White) see that their religious worldview contributed most to their survival in the New World, that worldview must be understood if there is to be any real perception of Africans. Barrett cites characteristics of the traditional worldview and cosmic economy. He refers to the traditional worldview as the vision of cosmic harmony in which there exists a vital participation between animate (God, humans, animals) and inanimate things—vital relationships of being between each individual and his/her descendants, family, brothers and sisters in the clan, antecedents, and also one's God—the ultimate source of being. God is seen as the source of all power, the lesser deities function to see that the world works smoothly, ancestors see that their descendants act morally, heads of families are next in authority (nearest to ancestors), and other members of the family fit into the hierarchical scheme in the order of their age and importance.[49]

We shall see in examining the African religious expressions in the Caribbean that the three most powerful influences of African religious traditions on New World Africans were the Fon-speaking people of Dahomey; the Yoruba of Nigeria, and the Akan of Ghana. Through the continuing exercise of these traditions and others we see that the soul and spirituality of Africa has been retained and has served as a strong resistance to the dehumanizing influences of European powers. In encounter with Christianity, the Africans took the essence of the Christian religion and united it with their traditional practices and beliefs and created new religions, syncretistic ones, appropriate to the needs and demands of their New World identities and cultures.

Being frowned upon and banned by governments, the religions were practiced in some form in secret, underground, clandestinely. An example of resistance to these restrictions is that of the response to the ban of obeah in Jamaica after 1760 (making the practice punishable by death). In response the Koromantyn slaves on an estate in the Parish of St. Mary staged an insurrection, the Tacky Rebellion. Resistance was not the only response, however. Something referred to as *creolization* took place as well, wherein Africans began to adopt some of the ways of the Europeans and neglect some of their traditional practices. But the strength of the African religions to survive principally in spite of the odds, bans, prohibitions, and the like was due to the makeup of these religions with solid religious and cultural foundations and their ability to adapt to new situations.[50]

There were common characteristics in the African background among those religions that survived such as their beliefs regarding the creation and maintenance of the world, the relation of humans to both God and nature and to other human beings (their cosmology), and their systems of worship and ritual practices and beliefs. In general, Africans believed in an almighty God, known by different names among different peoples. *Nyame* or *Nyankopon* is the name used among the Akan-speaking Ashanti, Fanti and Barong peoples. For the Yoruba of the lower Niger, central Dahomey and Togoland, *Oludumare* or *Olurun* is the name of the supreme being. *Mawu-Lisa* is the name used among the Ewe-speaking Fon of Abomey, Allada of Porto Novo, the Ge of Togo and the Ga of the Gold Coast (Ghana). *Chukwu* is the name used among the Igbo, of Nigeria especially. Though referred to by different names in their various languages, this Supreme Being had the same general characteristics. This God is the author and preserver of all creation, who is almighty, omnipresent, omniscient, infinitely good, transcendent. Only among a few was the Supreme Being actually worshipped (such as among the Akan). Worship, however, was accorded the lesser deities, who were closer to humans in existence. The Yoruba worship rituals, for instance, were devoted to lesser gods (Orishas) who were powers in control of various aspects of nature and existence and could thus assist them in their daily living. Major ones included Obatala (the sky god), Ogun (god of war, iron, etc.), Shango (god of fire, thunder, etc.), Ifa (god of divination, etc.), Eleggua (god of the crossroads, etc.), Oya (goddess of the cemetery, etc.), Ochun (goddess of the river, female beauty and power, etc.), Yemaya (goddess of the Ocean, mother of the gods, etc.).[51]

The Akan also worshipped the lesser gods, children of Nyame, but the Ewe, like the Yoruba, had a pantheon of lesser deities whom they worshipped, called vodu (spirits), Sakpata, So or Xevioso, and Legba (Messenger of Mawu, who was female and was worshipped in conjunction with her male partner Lisa). In all these cases, the lesser gods were functionaries, agents of the Supreme Being, who had absolute control of the universe. They were derivatives, lesser manifestations of the Supreme Being, placed in charge of various areas and operations of nature (earth, sky, thunder, sun, fire, water, agriculture, the forest, etc.). They were *mediators* between humans and the Creator. Trained priests and priestesses presided over the worship at shrines, temples in villages or compounds. Characteristics of African religious worship included elaborate ceremonial dances by priests and devotees of gods, spirit possession of worshipers, communication of the gods by way of devotees who under their powers became the spokespersons of particular deities.[52]

Although all aspects of the African religious content and practices did not survive in the New World setting, because adaptations had to be made to the various locales and environments, African worship practices survived to a great extent in the Caribbean. For instance, dancing and spirit possession are very much a part of the Yoruba worship in Trinidad, known as Shango or Orisa, and the Yoruba deities such as Ogun, Eshu, and so forth are retained. Also the same is the case in St. Domingue (Haiti) where the Dahomean (Benin) deities Damballa, Legba, Shango, and others remain functional.[53] Many of the gods surviving in the Caribbean countries have undergone name changes.

Largely, what contributed to the survival was the adaptability of these religions to the new environments and the blending of their religious beliefs and practices (syncretism) with Roman Catholic beliefs and practices, such as in Trinidad, Haiti, Cuba, Brazil, and other places. There was also the combining and blending of the gods and divinities of different tribal groups as they were made to live and work together on the same plantations. In cases such as these, stronger divinities (with a well-developed pantheon) subsumed other weaker ones (with little if any pantheon). Such was the case with the Yoruba domination. The slaves were able to use the strong African powers to their advantage in a hostile world in this life (such as in the slave revolts). Also very significant to their survival are the beliefs and practices regarding the ancestors' roles in their society and religious life; their beliefs and practices concerning the afterlife, and the like. Overall, religion encouraged and strengthened these peoples to bear adverse circumstances and to prevail in a harsh context. They were able to bond together with varying groups from different ethnic groups, using geographical criteria for distinguishing peoples rather than tribal origins. In Cuba, for instance, they identified themselves as either Lucumi or Congolese, depending on where they boarded the slave ships for passage to the New World. Haitians likewise described themselves as Aradas or some other designation stemming from Allada, most likely.[54]

Leonard Barrett notes the African genius for amalgamation and inclusion prevailing in the New World wherein some fifty or more tribes included in the slave trade were blended into a few.

> The numerically dominant tribes established the cultural mold to which all other tribes contributed their religious practices and beliefs as needed. Thus we find Vodun (a Dahomean word for spirit) as the base or mold in which the spirits known as *loa* (a Congo word) operate. In the Vodun temple there are altars to a Nago divinity, an Ibo divinity, a Dahomey or Arada divinity and a Congo divinity. In a Vodun ceremony, one may distinguish a Nago, Congo and Dahomey drumbeat all in one polyrhythm. In the Trinidadian Shango ceremony we have the "drum of the nations," which means a drum on which all the tribal rhythms are played.[55]

Barrett further describes the African slaves' process of "indigenizing" the New World:

> The Africans in the New World fell into two separate groups. The first were those with a highly developed pantheon, in which the deities played a dominant role. In this category are the Fon people of Dahomey and the Yoruba, generally called Nago, of Nigeria. Wherever these people were represented in large numbers, their religion with their pan-

theon of numerous deities predominated. Examples of this are found in Haiti, Brazil, Cuba, Trinidad and New Orleans. The second group of Africans emphasized a religion with a strong ancestral cult, but a weak pantheon of gods. This group seems to have blended their form of ritual with the dominant Fon- and Nago-speaking peoples. Thus we hear little of the Akan and Bantu gods, but much of Shango, Ogun, Damballa and Vodun.[56]

The Interactions of Africans and Indigenous Arawaks and Caribs

Arawaks, Caribs, and Africans in the Caribbean, as in other parts of the Americas in colonial times had much in common as indigenous peoples from different cultures and religions and coming from different parts of the world. For one thing they lived close to nature and had a high regard for the natural world. Religion and spirituality were an intricate part of their existence. Their worship and rituals honored the spirits and divine powers in creation. Though the make-ups of their religions were different and their ritual practices varied, there were some basic parallels, such as perception of humans and the divine and the relations of humans to one another. Their religions would fall roughly under the category of archaic described by Michael Barnes. Whatever their similarities and differences, the Europeans they encountered in the colonial set-up had similar regards for them as a people and for the nature of their religions. They all were considered to be heathens or savages with little if any religion, and worthy only to be exploited as laborers for the benefit of European economic and political enterprises. To make them suitable for this role, they were to be forced to abandon their native religions and take on the "civilized" European Christian religion. And any resistance to this process was to result in extermination.

George Brandon speaks of the situation of the intermingling of the mixed labor force in Cuba which also included whites. "This mixed labor force of whites, Indians, and Africans—all interacting and influencing each other—formed the basis of the racially mixed population which evolved out of Cuba's early days and from which the elite strove to isolate itself. Parallel to the mixed work force, then, was intermixture at the level of sex, marriage, and biological reproduction."[57] Brandon is speaking of a period under the Spanish in Cuba wherein this mixed labor force was controlled by the Spanish.

But in the face of the hostile and destructive colonization process, the indigenous Caribbean peoples and African slaves were able to make common cause with each other where possible. They managed to find common ground. There are numerous cases in which runaway slaves were accepted into indigenous societies and united with them in their efforts of survival and resistance. Although there were cases in which the Arawaks and the African slaves made connections in Haiti (Hispaniola, St. Domingue) and shared religious and cultural elements (such as the Vodouisants' adaptation of Azaka from the Taino or Arawaks),[58] the cases of Carib and African alliances and ethnic and religious intermixture are much more numerous. The best examples of this are seen in the Maroon communities and societies. Rebecca B. Bateman refers to this in her comparative study of Black Caribs and Black Seminoles. She refers to the more numerous Black Caribs on the Island of St. Vincent, more numerous than the Island or "Red" or "Yellow" Carib.

> The natural increase in their population was augmented by a steady influx of escaped slaves from the neighboring islands of Guadeloupe, Barbados, and Martinique. By the early eighteenth century, the Black and Island Carib formed two territorially and politically distinct groups, the former occupying the windward side and the latter the leeward side of the island. As the century progressed, conflicts with one another and with Europeans increased as the French and English played the two Carib groups against each other to further their colonial objectives.[59]

The history of the Garifuna reveals a mixture of Carib, Arawak, and African cultural groups in St. Vincent. The Garifuna are a mixed African and Carib people mainly in Belize who claimed never to have been enslaved as Africans and fought bravely to maintain their freedom against domination by the British. It is reported that slave ships in the seventeenth century bound from the Bight of Benin to Barbados wrecked near St. Vincent Island. The slaves escaped to the Island, which at this time was inhabited by a mixed people of Carib and Arawak stock who spoke mostly Arawak language and were known as Calinago or Island Caribs. "With the addition of runaway slaves, the African population grew and finally outnumbered the Caribs by 1735. An amalgamation of West African and Calinago traits followed, and the Garifuna (Black Carib) culture developed."[60]

These people thrived here for a number of years developing their own culture and economy and fighting off encroachment from the Europeans.

> Women marketed their produce and cassava bread (*areba*) and men sold their skills as seamen. From the Calinago, cultural traits such as language, the cassava complex, canoe technology, features of the shamanic cult, song styles, dances, and even head binding

were adopted. These traits served to mark the free status of the Garifuna during the en-
suing century when European settlers with thousands of African slaves attempted to
build a sugar economy in St. Vincent. Contested by the territorial claims of the French,
British, and Garifuna settlers, St. Vincent lapsed into a period of bitter warfare in which
the Garifuna maneuvered and fought to defend their autonomy. In 1797, after the British captured St. Lucia, the Garifuna lost their main source of French military support
and were deported by the British to the Island of Roatan, off the coast of Honduras.[61]

Mixed Maroon communities of Africans and Caribs, especially, were and
are found in other places of the Caribbean and Central and South America.
Kamau Brathwaite cites six main areas of maroon activity of great importance
in the Caribbean and the Americas where significant African and Amerindian
alliance, consensual intermixture and/or cooperation took place: Dominica,
Hispaniola (including both Santo Domingo and Haiti), Palmares (in Bahia, Brazil), Jamaica, the Suriname/Guiana, and the Garifuna (of Belize/Honduras).[62]

Hindu and Islamic Encounters and Interactions in the Caribbean

When the emancipation of slavery began in European colonies in the Caribbean (the English and French in 1838, the Dutch in 1863, Spanish and Portuguese colonies had much later emancipation), the demand for labor led the
colonist in a new direction, toward the Asian continent, especially India. Numerous indentured servants were brought in from India, most of them of the
Hindu religion and culture, but also many of the Muslim faith. With these new
arrivals, whose status as indentured laborers was often not considered much
different from that of slaves, came the problems and issues of integrating new
cultures and religions into the Caribbean mixture, as well as their struggles to
survive in the new environment and to maintain their religions and cultures. As
with all other ethnic and religious groups, adjustments and adaptations had to
be made as these East Indians encountered each other in this New World and
all the other cultural groups they found here.

Today Guyana, Trinidad, and Suriname have populations of 45 to 51 percent East Indian, while in Jamaica, Bermuda, and Martinique, their percentage
amounts to 5 percent.[63] Petronella Breinburg stresses the intermixture of peoples in certain Caribbean areas.

Though the image often presented to the general public and to students of Caribbean Studies is an African-Caribbean one, in reality the Caribbean, certainly Surinam, Guyana, and Trinidad and Tobago, is a multi-racial, multi-religious, and multi-lingual territory, Surinam, in particular, is perhaps one of the most complex areas of the Caribbean. People of Asian descent, for example Indians, Chinese, Indonesians, and Javanese, form about 50 percent of the population. There are also the descendants of Africa who had freed themselves from slavery and went to live in the bush....Among these people are the Nduka (formerly spelt Djuka), the Auka, the Saramakaners, the Paramakaners, and the Malawi Maroons.[64]

Abraham Khan makes it clear that although the Muslims in the Caribbean come mostly from India, many Muslims in Cuba and some other areas of the region come also from the Middle East.[65] Also he takes note of socalled "free" Arabs: "Some groups arrived as neither colonial adventurers or outcasts, nor slaves, nor indentured workers. Arabs, for example, constitute one such group. Their arrival, which began in the 1860's, became a major flow thirty years later. They are predominantly in countries such as Jamaica, Dominican Republic, and Haiti, making significant contributions to the economic, social, and political life of the Caribbean region."[66] The cultural and religious interactions and cooperation of the religious groups will be dealt with more fully in Part Two of the book.

Chapter Two

The Present Setting of Caribbean Religious Interactions

Expansion of Protestant Christianity in the Caribbean

A great variety of Christian groups or denominations began to develop and spread in the Caribbean during the international evangelical focus of the Christian Church in the eighteenth century and really took off in the nineteenth century. Powerful evangelical and missionary zeal began to grip religionists in Germany, England, North America, France, and other places in Europe and the Americas, stirring in them a competitive desire to spread the gospel (the good news of Christian salvation) to the rest of the world. A special focus of this Evangelicalism was the African slaves and the indigenous peoples of the New World. This movement was known as the Great Awakening, which took hold in the United States in 1740, engaging the efforts of most Protestant groups. The Moravians, under the strong influence of German and European Pietism, were the first of the Evangelical groups to arrive in the Caribbean, initially St. Thomas, in 1732. The Moravian missionaries had an enormous impact in a matter of decades, gaining thousands of converts to Christianity with their focus on the suffering of Christ, his scourging, the crown of thorns, the crucifixion, the nail prints in his hands, the wounded side. This was especially appealing to the slaves who were suffering greatly under the heavy bonds of slavery and dehumanization. Their ability to convince the plantation owners that the conversion of the slaves made them more useful in slavery helped to contribute to their success, such that they made great headway in establishing bases in St. Thomas, St. Croix, St. John, and from these to move on to other areas such as Jamaica, St. Kitts, Tobago, and other places.[1] The Moravians were no threat to slavery in their teaching and preaching. In fact, they even owned slaves themselves.

The Methodist missionaries also had great successes in evangelizing in the Caribbean, following on the heels of the Moravians, though not as immediately as the Moravians. Not officially established as a denomination until 1784, the developing Methodist movement under the leadership of John Wesley, initially an ordained minister in the Church of England (himself having come under the influence of the Moravians both aboard ship en route back to England from the U.S.A. and in England), had missionaries in the Caribbean in the 1770's, such as John Baxter and Thomas Coke. And by 1824 the Methodists had bases of operation in several Caribbean Islands such as St. Vincent, St. Kitts, Barbados, Dominica, Jamaica, Bahamas, Haiti, Guyana, and Trinidad, among others. Unlike the Church of England, which was the church of the Whites, the Methodist missionaries built a largely Black body of both slave and free congregants.[2]

The Baptists were also well-planted in the Caribbean during this period, especially in Jamaica, led by the ex-slave from North America, George Liele, who had been a thriving slave pastor in South Carolina. During the Revolutionary War he sided with the British and with their help was able to facilitate his escape and travel to Jamaica, where he founded the first Baptist organization there in 1782. Also the Baptists were established in the Bahamas under the aegis of Blacks escaping North American enslavement who were aided by Loyalists between 1776 and 1783. Prince Williams, another Black, had been the first to come to the area of Nassau and had done mission work much earlier. Congregationalists started in Guyana in 1808, Presbyterians established a base in Jamaica in 1814,[3] and many other Christian groups proliferated and have been growing until this day, including varieties of Pentecostalism.

During all the religious fervor in the Caribbean in this period of history some very important social and political events were also taking place which would impact religion and be equally impacted by it. In this period the slave trade was to be abolished by the British, several slave revolts were to take place both in the Caribbean and in North America. The Christian churches were challenged to take an ethical stand in regard to slavery and its abolition. Different ones lined up on either side of the issue, as did the churches in North America. But only the Quakers came out flatly against slavery, while some brave Methodists, at the urging of John Wesley, took a stand against it.

Dale Bisnauth sums up a crucial aspect of what was taking place during this time and the reflection on the churches in their missionary zeal.

> The sugar industry in the British Isles reached the peak of its development and then began to decline during the American War of Independence. The slaves in St.

Domingue revolted in 1789—an event that was not without its effects on the attitude of planters to missionaries in other islands. The British colonies were involved in such important issues as the abolition of the slave trade, amelioration, and the emancipation of slaves. These issues agitated public interest in Britain as much [as] in the Caribbean. One would expect that missionaries who had recognised the humanity of blacks enough to work for the salvation of their souls and whose work was primarily among slaves, would support the movements for abolition, amelioration and emancipation which so crucially affected the welfare of their converts. In fact, one looks in vain for a positive, uncompromising declaration on the part of the evangelical missionaries in the Caribbean against the institution of slavery.[4]

It would be left to the African slaves themselves to carve out of their religious backgrounds and their religious appropriations and encounters in this New World an adequate response to the challenges and conditions facing them as human beings.

Africans' Appropriations of Christianity in the Caribbean

Dale Bisnauth refers to this process as "The Africanisation of of Christianity."[5] Leonard Barrett has a somewhat different perspective on it. Barrett describes the Afro-Caribbean religions as redemption cults, which, within the context of the reactions of the slaves to captivity, offered sustained resistance (resentment, hostility) that continued throughout the slave period, with collective aggression carried out. They invoked their African Gods (as Jews and any other people being so oppressed), especially Ogun and Shango, respectively, Yoruba god of war and god of lightning and thunder (greatest hero-god). They used their own culturally approved techniques of resistance by practicing deception, by reinterpreting their native folklore, esp., the "trickster lore"–which has lengthy descriptions of escape by disguise and trickery. They used the psychic forces, employing the sorcerers against the powers of oppression. These redemption cults resulted over a long period in the mixture of Christian ideas and African traditional beliefs. In other words there was a grafting of Christian ideas onto the traditional African roots. The Christian God became an African God who was perceived to be at least as powerful as the African God. The Christian angels were identified with lesser deities of Africa. The Christian message of salvation included deliverance from oppression (which was seen in Christ as liberator but also as a carryover from the Exodus story). It had a millennial flavor, Jesus as Redeemer.[6]

Redemption cults have been found in New Zealand, Melanesia, Africa, North America, and the Caribbean. Most developed in the 19th century as a reaction to the false messages of the missionaries, of abundant life, equality, justice, love. These messages of the missionaries "became a haunting mirage to the people in these primal societies as they came to realize that their lands were gradually being appropriated, their prestige destroyed, their ancestral religion proscribed, and that a new economic system was being introduced which left them in what they felt was a deprived condition in their own ancestral homeland."[7] As a response, nationalistic interests and efforts began to develop among these peoples, buttressed by strong religious orientations bent on restoring their cultural and religious roots and using whatever other religious resources found among them as foundation for their human quest. So political, economic, and cultural nationalism was, as usual, grounded in religion and religious restoration.

These take on many forms, including revivalism and nativism. Classic forms of the redemptive cults are found in Haiti and Jamaica as revivalism. Haiti had one of the most impressive mixtures of African peoples of all the Caribbean Islands. From Senegal were the Yolop, Bambarras, Foulas, Poulords, Kiambaras, and Mandingos. From West Central Africa were the Aradas, Makis, Hanassa, Ibos, Yorubas, Binis, Takwas, Fanti, Agonas, Sobos, Limbas, and Adjas. From Angola and the Congo were the Solongos, Mayombes, Mosombes, Bumbas, and Kangas (according to Moreau de Saint-Mery).[8] These were in addition to those from Dahomey. All had their own indigenous religions. The Dahomey Vodun religion, however, was the most powerful of the religions and flexible enough to incorporate all the religious beliefs within its rituals. It is a mixture of various African divinities along with the Christian Trinity and the roster of Catholic saints–a prime example of the African propensity for assimilating other religious forms. This is seen also in Macumba in Brazil, Santeria in Cuba, and Shango in Trinidad.[9] Adroitly, it leaves no power outside its orbit.

Barrett reviews what he sees as five periods in the development of Haitian Vodun. The first he designates the period of gestation (1730–1790), in which there was forced indoctrination of the slaves into Catholicism and baptism. The second involved the expansion and self-assertion (1790–1800), in which Vodun grows and a fusion of religious elements takes place as Vodun becomes the life force of the Haitian Revolution (under Touissant L'Oeverture). A third period involved Black rulers' suppression of Vodun (1800–1815), especially Dessalines and Christophe, for fear of its power. The fourth period involved a diffusion of Vodun among the masses (1815–1850). And the fifth is the era of Papa Doc (Francois Duvalier), who strengthened his reign by boldly extolling Vodun and claiming to be the African Messiah, a reincarnation of the dead heroes who fought for the Haitian liberation.[10]

Though there are many Gods, Damballah-Weda, god of fertility, bringer of rains, is the highest, and is symbolized by one or two snakes. (Weda or Ayida is a West African country.) The loa most frequently called upon is Legba, however. Omniscient and omnipresent, the mediator between the world of humans and the spirit world, he is the one who opens the door for other loa, who breaks all barriers. All Vodun ceremonies invoke his presence. Maya Deren said of Legba: "As principle of life, as initial procreative whole, Legba was both man and woman.... As navel of the world, or as its womb, Legba is addressed in prayers at childbirth with the phrase which signals him: 'Open the road for me...do not let any evil spirits bar my path.'"[11]

Goddess Erzulie-Freda, of femininity and fertility, is the African counterpart of the Catholic Virgin Mary, and represents love, beauty, and luxury. These three gods mentioned (Damballah, Legba, and Erzulie) are among the gods of Dahomean origin and part of a variety of ones used under the Arada rites (benevolent rites). Also there are the gods of the Yoruba and Ibo pantheon such as Obatala, Ogun, Shango, and others. There are also the Petro rites (considered magical, malevolent, and demonic).

> The same divinities...appear in the Petro rites but with hyphenated names indicating their different manifestations. Erzulie-Lemba, Legba-congo, Damballa-ossange. The most powerful loa in the Petro series is Guede, or Ghede, the god of death. The difference between Arada and Petro rites is not always clear, but it is generally believed that the spirit of Haitian revolution was precipitated in Petro rites. It is also believed that in Petro rites blood sacrifice is performed, while in Arada rites it is rare.[12]

Bisnauth believes that it was in Haiti and Trinidad that the accommodation of Christian ideas and practices within the framework of African beliefs was greatest. In Haitian Vodun, he points out that the Supreme God, *Le Bon Dieu* (Good God) or *Le Grand Maitre* was all good and did not need to be worshipped. But the loas, who numbered in the hundreds, were and are spirits or lesser divinities *(vodous)* that needed to be appealed to in worship and ritual for assistance and protection. They were mostly African in origin, but some were of

Amerindian derivation. The African ones were fairly easily identified with Catholic saints. Examples are:

Legba—   St. Anthony
Damballa—St. Patrick
Erzile—   Mater Dolorosa (Mother of Sorrow),
the Virgin Mary
Papa Pie—St. Peter

Bisnauth surmises that what "might have happened is that the peasants [under whom the practice of correlating saints with African spirits started], at first, added the Catholic saints to the host of African spirits which they worshipped. Then, as some saints came to be perceived as resembling some spirits in function and in other characteristics, the former were identified as the latter."[13] However the practice developed, certainty is that "the Catholic saints had been given the status of divine intermediaries between Le Bon Dieu and the vodunists."[14]

So what appears to have taken place here is that the saints were turned into *loas,* as the characteristics attributed to the saints were not taken from any Bible sources or Catholic tradition, but rather drawn from the African traditions. For instance, "St John was regarded as a rather stern, nervous loa, who was always on the move" and "credited with a thirst for champagne and fine liqueurs and an appetite for the meat of black cattle and white sheep." Also there was a mixture of worship paraphernalia on the altars in the *humforts* (temples) with both African and Catholic items used: crucifixes, rosaries, holy water, chromoliths of Catholic saints, along with thunder stones, flags, flowers, foods and liquors that the gods preferred, all from the African ritual practices. Also elements of Catholic practices, words, and prayers were integrated into the ceremony. These ceremonies were highly elaborate, involving extensive dancing to sacred drums and the entrance of the gods into the service to possess certain participants (hougans—priests, mambos—priestesses, or serviteurs), special requests of the spirits, and other facets. Most vodunists were also members of the Catholic Church, but their Weltanschauung (cosmology) was vodun. Ancestral traditions also played a major part in their rituals and daily living, as well as in their beliefs and practices in regard to death, burials, views of which also combined Catholic and African elements.[15]

Although the major practice of vodun in Haiti involved the Dahomean religious rite, called Rada (probably from the Dahomean town of Allada) and this rite integrated Catholic Religious elements within it and principally benign, another religious rite in Haiti was derived from the New World situations of escaped slaves who dwelled in the mountains (who belong to the category of maroons), and this rite is more aggressive and threatening, and has been very effective in the slave rebellions and ultimately the Haitian Revolution of the 1790's. This rite is known as the Petro rite. Some of the deities are said to derive from the indigenous Arawaks. Bisnauth states: "These included Dan Petro, Baron Samedi, Simbi and Azacca. Simbi was originally the local Amerindian god of rain and Azacca the Indian deity associated with the maize. Samedi and zombie might well have been derived from the Arawak *zemi*; both were related to the spirits of the dead. Obviously, Indian ideas were assimilated into the African framework of beliefs."[16]

As to the idea of the Africanization of Christianity, Leslie Demangles's summary of the most commonly held Vodou beliefs in a creed certainly can be seen as exemplary of the process.

> I believe in Bondye [Le Bon Dieu], the Almighty Father of the sky, who manifests his spiritual nature in me; in a large number of spirits; and in all things visible and invisible.

> I believe in the lwas [loas], the gods of Africa, and all the saints of the Catholic Church. Masters of the universe, they are manifestationsof Bondye, who see all things and direct the course of all things; that some have made themselves known to us through our ancestors in Africa, and that others we have come to know, emulate, and serve in our new home in Haiti; that these lwas are potent enough to mount us, their children, in spirit possession; and that through their mounting, they can inspire us as to the needs of our community; that our moral duty is to faithfully serve them; that the lwas are capable like us, of gentleness and mercy, but also of anger and revenge.

> I believe in the power of ancestors who watch over us and serve us before the lwas; that they must be remembered and served faithfully.

> I believe in the right granted us by the lwas to interfere through magic in the normal flow of events as established by Bondye's will; in the efficacy of the medicines derived from the local fauna endowed to us by the lwas. I believe in the Holy Roman Catholic Church, in the communion of saints, and in life everlasting.[17]

In close similarity to Vodun, which derives from the Fon of Dahomey, Shango of Trinidad, though Yoruba in origin, assimilated the Catholic elements into their religion. Bisnauth states:

Two Yoruba gods, Elephon and Obalufon , are regarded as "Eternal Father" and Jesus respectively. But it is to be doubted that either of them is held in the same regard as Olurun [Supreme Being of the Yoruba who did not seem to survive the Middle Passage to enter into Trinidad] is held by the Yorubas. For all practical purposes, Eternal Father and Jesus are just Christian names that have been assigned to Elephon and Obalofon who, in spite of those names, retain their "African" characteristics. Thus, Elephon is regarded as the "head man" in shango ceremonies and rituals.[18]

The correlation of Catholic saints and African spirits among the shangoists or Orishas (as the people refer to themselves) includes identifying Shango as St. John, Shakpana as St. Francis or Moses, Obatala as St. Benedict, Ogun as St. Michael. Some saints are identified as independent powers with no identification with African divinities. Such are St. Agatha, St. Rose, and the Virgin Mary.[19]

The African peoples not only absorbed Catholic beliefs and practices into their African religious practices, beliefs, and traditions, but also Africanized Protestant branches of Christianity. Raboteau takes note of the fact that several Jamaican groups like Revival and Pocomania represent "nonorthodox synthesis of Protestant and African beliefs." He notes that the establishment of the Baptist faith in Jamaica, led by George Liele, was not simply a triumph for the Christian denomination but another chance for Christian and African synthesis. He states, "By the middle of the nineteenth century, African Baptist beliefs had begun to fuse in the Native Baptist movement, the precursor of present-day Revivalist groups in Jamaica."[20] Also in Trinidad the synthesis succeeded among Protestant groups.

In Trinidad, the Spiritual Baptists, or Shouters, are especially interesting because of their subtle interweaving of African religious customs with a rigidly orthodox Christian creed. Strict Fundamentalists, the Spiritual Baptists subscribe to the five-point platform of the early twentieth-century Fundamentalist movement in the United States. The five points of the fundamentalist platform are biblical inerrancy, authenticity of Gospel miracles, the Virgin Birth, the physical Resurrection of Jesus, and the satisfaction theory of the Atonement. At the same time there are affiliations between Spiritual Baptists and Trinidadian shangoists. Some leaders of *shango* cults mix ritual elements from "Yoruba work" with those of Spiritual Baptist worship; others conduct services in both rites at separate times.[21]

Bisnauth describes the intermingling of Christian practices in Jamaican Revivalism. He asserts that Revivalists believe in a "high god who is the creator and ruler of the universe," who is the same as the Christian God the Father, who is not involved in their worship services. He does not possess a worshipper, and neither does Jesus Christ, God's Son, "trump" (special spiritual dance) in the service, though he shows up. The Holy Spirit does come to every service and is the chief spirit and trumps with the worshippers. Trumping with the worshippers are Bible prophets, evangelists, archangels, and apostles such as Elijah, Moses, Daniel, Isaiah, Mark, Luke, John Gabriel, Peter, and the like. Possession by the spirits is primary and contributes to personal spiritual growth and development. "The whole purpose of the revivalist service is to induce the spirits to possess the worshippers. Possession itself is held to be desirable because it is by this means that the worshipper comes to apprehend the truth of spiritual realities. The initial possession is felt to have a cleansing effect on the individual; subsequent possessions help him to grow into spiritual maturity."[22]

Besides the appropriation of Christianity in African religions in the Caribbean, other religious mingling with African religious manifestations has taken place, such as the mixture of Hindu, Christian, and Jewish elements along with African ones in the Jordanite religion found especially in Guyana, Trinidad, Jamaica, and Grenada. Mention has already been made of indigenous appropriations within Afro-Caribbean religion. There are also the appropriations of indigenous perspectives, Christianity, Judaism, Hinduism, and Muslim elements, along with African traditions and perspectives found in the Rastafari religion, which began in Jamaica in the 1930's and now is spread in numerous parts of the world today. Barry Chevannes shows clearly how this religion grew out of Jamaican Revivalism and is still connected to its Revival past.[23]

Problems in the Encounters and Interactions of Christianity with Non-Christian Religions and Perspectives in the Caribbean

Life in the Caribbean for the numerous ethnic, racial, cultural, and religious groups always involved interaction and interweaving of different worldviews and religious beliefs and systems, which was a difficult social process, to say the least. And all the groups who came to exist there were forced to alter their original ways of functioning, thinking, and acting to some extent in order to blend in as well as possible with the other people and the natural requirements of this New World environment. The problems of this adjustment are seen as an ongoing process that has been going on for centuries. And although progress has been made over the centuries in the building of community among these various peoples who have struggled to maintain their identities and basic aspects of their original cultures while at the same time sharing meaningfully in and contributing to the establishment of a new Caribbean culture (or new cultures), serious problems continue to exist and efforts are continually being made to remedy the situations and deal with the issues. Abraham H. Khan delineates the problems conceived in trying to express and determine a "Caribbean identity."[24]

After considerable analysis of such issues as race, ethnicity, religion, personhood, he concludes that "Any proposal for a Caribbean identity would have to accommodate as much as possible the experiences of all who make up the cultural *chiaroscuro*—from the Aboriginal peoples to the latecomers of the Caribbean region."[25] Before stating this conclusion, he determines that it is not race but cultural hegemony that is the problematic factor implicit in what he rejects as the "eulogized Caribbean identity."

> It affects not just Muslim and Hindu communities, but also the Christian community with its missionary zeal. This latter community, another source of input to the region's cultural texture, expresses its ideals in the form of western or European values and social practices. Though it counts among its adherents a large percentage with African ancestry, its religious outlook no more provides, it seems, a framework for the desired Caribbean identity than does Islam or Hinduism. Its outlook too will have to give way in the contrived geopolitical cultural identity formation to an outlook that is reflective of "the people from below" and proffered by Rastafarianism (Nettleford 1993:125–26, 168).[26] Christianity as a form of socio-cultural interaction is therefore subject to displacement even though it defines itself differently.[27]

Similar issues and problems were discovered and voiced extensively in an ecumenical conference held in Lelydorp, Suriname, in May, 1994. The conference was sponsored by the Caribbean Conference of Churches (C.C.C), assisted by the Moravian Theological Seminary and the Roman Catholic Catechetical Centre. The topic of the conference was "Popular Religiosity," which really had in mind the relationships of Christianity with other religions in the Caribbean. Assembled at the conference were participants from Guyana, Suriname, Cuba, Venezuela, Trinidad and Tobago, Barbados, England, Jamaica, North America, and other places. Among the religious groups represented were the Moravians, Presbyterians, the Roman Catholic, Hinduism, Islam, the Rastafari, the Methodists, Cuban Santeria, Trinidadian Shango or Orisa, and Winti religion of Suriname. Christian ecumenical organizations represented were the World Council of Churches (WCC), the National Council of Churches, U.S.A. (NCCC), and the Caribbean Conference of Churches (CCC). Papers presented and dialogues that took place were published in the volume edited by Burton Sankeralli, titled *At the Crossroads: African Caribbean Religions and Christianity* (St. James, Trinidad and Tobago, WI: 1995).

Strategic questions raised by one of the presenters at this conference, Dr. Hesdie Zamuel, concerning the identification of the Afro-Caribbean religions and their assimilations of Christianity into their structures, may also be applied to other religions in the Caribbean which have a dual origin—meaning that they were first developed in their motherlands of, say, countries such as those in Europe and Asia, North America, and the like, and had a somewhat different origin in the Caribbean rendering them somewhat different from their counterparts back home. This is certainly true of Islam and Hinduism, as well as of the different branches of Christianity. The questions Zamuel raises are this: "Are we talking about a form of Christianity that, in confrontation with the African way of thinking and believing of the slaves and their descendants, has come to this specific composition, or have we to do with an African religion which has accommodated itself to the Caribbean situation? Or must we perhaps presume that these religions are Caribbean creations, which cannot simply be reduced to religions of Africa or to Christianity?"[28] Zamuel does not give answer to these questions but leaves the matter open. However, I do believe that similar questions can be applied to most, if not all, the religions developing in the extremely diverse setting of the Caribbean Islands and their surrounding areas.

To be more exact, the forms of Hinduism and Islam that developed in the Caribbean are not the same as their more classic or orthodox forms found in Asia of the nineteenth century. Hinduism is thought to be the most ancient religion in the world. And the enormous diversity within the religion itself and the great propensity it has for inclusiveness of other gods and religions would naturally render it impossible for relatively few indentured laborers from the Indian sub-continent to bring with them the whole of this extensive religion. Likewise, these bearers of the faith would hardly lose the religion's character of openness to other faiths. So what turned up among the workers from India who were Hindus are Hindu sects, the first of such being the "Sieunaraini (or Sri Narayana) Panth. In Guyana, the Sieunarainis were called Ramanandis or Kabir Panthis; in Trinidad, the three groups were regarded as three different sects."[29] They had basic or traditional Hindu beliefs and beliefs distinctively their own. They held to beliefs in reincarnation, the law of karma, the Vedas (Hindu Scripture), and were devotees of Vishnu. They did not look to the priestly class of Hindu Brahmins for the leadership but rather to certain gurus or teachers. In their struggles to establish and maintain themselves in the Caribbean, they made adjustments. "Practices were suited to life on plantations in distant lands in a way that other systems of Hindu beliefs and practices were not." Having no buildings or other sacred place, they worshipped wherever they chose. There were no dietary restrictions or ban on mingling with other peoples or castes. "Above all, they could (and did) proselytize; this was unheard of among 'orthodox' Hindus."[30]

Other groups of Hindus came near the end of the nineteenth century bringing in other established practices and spiritual aspects of the faith. For instance, temples of worship appeared in Trinidad and Guyana, prayer flags (*jhandi*) used in *puja* (worship) of the gods. Hindu festivals were instituted such as the *Dasserah* or *Durga Puja*, which was held in honor of the Goddess Durga's (Kali's) victory over the demon giant Maghisan.[31] Nevertheless, Hinduism in the Caribbean did not remain pure and unaffected by the other religions which it encountered there. Their beliefs in spirits brought them in proximity with similar beliefs among Africans, especially Obeah, for one thing.[32] And their contact with fellow Muslim countrymen from India also made impact on the Hindus, as well as their interactions with Christians.

Muslim indentured workers, who were much fewer in number than the Hindus, sought to follow their religious practices, such as the Five Pillars (reciting the Shahada, prayers, the zakat tax, observance of Ramadan, though the fifth, the Mecca Hajj, was not within their realm of possibility); and they did establish mosques as early as 1891 in Suriname, Guyana, and Trinidad. However, their celebration of their festival of *Tadjah* or *Tazia* led them into violent clashes with the Hindus celebrating their Dasserah in some colonies.[33] There were also some clashes between the two opposing groups of Muslims, the Sunnis and Shi'ites, in the celebrations of their festivals. There was a special Caribbean development in the Caribbean among Muslims, known as *kitab*, which was the reading of the Qur'an in the homes of devout Muslims. "On this occasion, relatives, friends and neighbors are invited, gifts are made to the poor, *sherni* is distributed, and the guests are treated to a meal. The Kitab might have developed in imitation of the Hindu puja."[34]

Both being East Indians in this New World of mixed cultures, the Hindus and Muslims were not at first perceived as being of different religions; in fact,

Islam was regarded for a time as a Hindu sect, especially since there were different sects of Hinduism in the area. And both groups came to be regarded as "barbarous aliens" by the Christian society such that their assimilation into the larger society was made difficult, as membership in the Christian Church was considered the mark of civilization.[35] These religions joined the indigenous and African ones in becoming labeled "popular," "pagan," and the like.

In the encounters of Christianity with other religions and cultures in the Caribbean, certain issues were and are dynamic influences in the struggles of the Caribbean peoples to find common ground. Principally, those are issues of color, race, class, and ethnicity. Bisnauth cites the fragmentation of the Trinidadian society as exemplary. Quoting H. O. B. Wooding describing the situation in 1914, he says:

> The French in Trinidad represented an urbane and distinguished segment. They were a people who were ever mindful of their aristocratic origin and ever watchful to preserve their cultural and economic dominance. The British saw themselves as benevolent administrators. They remained aloof from the rest of Trinidadian society. The Africans had not forgotten the humiliation of slavery; they chafed under the disadvantage of social inferiority to which that institution had doomed them. The Portuguese and Chinese (who came originally as immigrant labourers) and the Syrians and Jews (who came as traders and entrepreneurs) contented themselves with their associations and showed little concern over the difficulties of others. The coloureds pirouetted upon the stage and convinced themselves, but nobody else, that they were "*la crème de la crème.*" The East Indians lived as outcasts in their new home.[36]

This situation was repeated to some degree in all the colonies of the British West Indies, and the Christian churches merely perpetuated the social set-up, for church membership was stratified and organized and structured hierarchically on the basis of race, class, color, and ethnicity.

Bisnauth gives the example of Jamaica where ex-slaves and descendants of slaves were at the bottom rung of the society, and on the next level up the social ladder were the mulattoes, "the offspring of members of the white managerial class and black slave and ex-slave women." Racial bias was shown in church membership, wherein the Anglican and Presbyterian churches were the prestigious ones, wherein the membership was white. The members of the urban Methodist churches were almost exclusively "coloured," while the urban membership of the Baptist churches were almost exclusively black. And the Baptists gained the reputation of being a church for the poor. Similar situations existed in the Bahamas, the Cayman Islands, and Bermuda. Except for the Baptist churches, clergy leadership remained in the hands of whites in the nine-teenth century.[37]

The French islands of Martinique and Guadeloupe and the Spanish islands of Puerto Rico and Cuba, which were officially Catholic, were similarly domi-nated by a color caste system in their own ways. In Martinique and Guadeloupe the lighter complexioned coloreds held the blacks in contempt and refused to mingle with them. In Puerto Rico and Cuba, there was some degree of mixing between the mulattoes and the whites, resulting in more mixed racial features. Mixing between the coloreds and the blacks was highly discouraged. Bisnauth states, "Mulattoes avoided marrying blacks because it was generally felt that while the possession of caucasoid features increased a person's chances of up-ward mobility, the possession of negroid features had the opposite effect." In-terestingly, the Catholic Church in these islands, having displayed a more human attitude toward the slaves than the Church of England displayed in the British colonies, did not discourage discrimination and inequality among its membership after emancipation. The result was that the same color caste men-tality persisted in the Catholic Church membership and practices.[38]

The Sephardic Jews, who first came to the Dutch island of Curacao around 1650 and prospered well, were wealthier than the Dutch Reformed Protestants (the leading class of the society here), but they were regarded as alien and infe-rior. At the bottom of the social ladder, of course, were blacks, who during slavery outnumbered the whites. They were evangelized by the Catholic mis-sionaries, who were permitted to do so by the opposing Dutch Reformed body as a preference to having the social barrier between blacks and whites breached by the existence of any such evangelizing by Dutch Reformed missionaries. "Such evangelizing would have led to blacks becoming members of the 'white' church."[39]

Christianity had an impact on the assimilation of other immigrant groups into the social structure of the Caribbean, especially in the colonies of Guiana, Trinidad, Jamaica, and Suriname. After the period of their indentureship Chi-nese easily established themselves in urban centers and undertook business and commercial enterprises. Socially, they enhanced themselves in general by joining the Anglican and Catholic churches. The Portuguese assimilated easily, as they were already of the dominant Christian religion, though they had some clashes with urban blacks in Guyana. The East Indians encountered many serious problems, however, in trying to assimilate into the society. Being Hindu and Muslim, they were despised by both Black and White Christians. Bisnauth states:

> From the standpoint of the coloureds and the educated Negro classes—people who subscribed to the social consensus—as well as from that of lower class Negroes, the East Indian appeared uncivilized and contemptible. A Methodist missionary declared that the Indian immigrants in Guyana were a low and filthy lot with dissolute and immoral habits. This same missionary remarked that 'of several of them it may be said that they are more fitted to be the associates of wild animals than of humanized—if not even civilized beings.'"[40]

Similar negative attitudes of creole Blacks toward Indians existed in Trinidad, looking upon them as barbarians, the same as their enslaved African forebears had been perceived. Bisnauth states: "The Negro in the post Emancipation period, having been inculcated with the blessings of the Anglo-Saxon civilization, now came to regard the Indian from the standpoint of that much vaunted civilization as barbarous. It was perhaps only in Jamaica that the attitude of Negroes to the immigrants was different." Missions of such Christian groups as the Presbyterians and Moravians to the Indians resulted in the switching of some Indians to Christianity, which was not difficult for Hindus, and the change in their predicament, at least, was achieved. But the acceptance of Christianity was actually a synthesis of Hindu and Christian beliefs and practices.[41]

When the United States became a colonizing power in the Caribbean in 1898, assuming control in such countries as Cuba and Puerto Rico, whose independence from Spain was achieved, missionaries from numerous Protestant Christian churches in the U.S. flooded the Caribbean areas wherever they could find entrance, making headway even in predominantly Catholic countries such as Cuba, Haiti, and Puerto Rico. So far as the social stratification and racial and ethnic discrimination are concerned, these churches simply spread their North American brand of the same to these islands.[42]

Chapter Three

Challenges of Non-Christian Spirituality to Christian Spirituality in the Caribbean

Encountering a plethora of religions and religious viewpoints in the spiritually rich and varied world of the Caribbean, the different branches of Christianity, both Catholic and Protestant, have faced and still face one of the greatest challenges of Christian religious history. Having a long history of Western European domination and intricately interwoven with Western culture and economic and military imperialism, despite its turbulent character of internal religious and political friction and factionalism throughout that history, Christianity encountered the other religions with an attitude of superiority and triumphalism. With the claim and conviction of being the only true religion, proponents of the Christian faith tended to condemn every other world religion to paganism and idolatry, or to obsolescence in the case of Judaism, to say nothing of their regard or non-regard for or non-recognition of the religious manifestations of indigenous and African peoples encountered in the Caribbean, as well as, of course, in Africa, Asia, Australia, and all other places in the world where colonialism stretched its tentacles. First came the shock that all the peoples encountered did actually have genuine religions which they had believed and practiced for centuries and that served as the foundations of their societies and existence. They were not only not lacking in religion and religious foundations, as the Western interlopers into their ways of life deemed, but they were determined to hold on to their religions and cultures, even to the point of preserving them in some sort of blending, if necessary, with encroaching religions and cultural manifestations they encountered. This took place often to the anathema of orthodox Christian leaders and authorities in what is referred to as religious syncretism.

Syncretism and Christianity in the Caribbean

Many disagreements exist among scholars and religious practitioners as to the meaning of the term *syncretism* as well as to whether or not it can be accurately applied to what I am referring to as the mixing and intermingling of different religions and religious elements and practices that took place in various ways among different religious groups. So I must acknowledge that there are different types and degrees of syncretism and that in some cases other terms than syncretism would be more appropriately applied to certain formations or processes that occurred. Patrick Taylor entertains some of the various terms that have been selected by different interpreters to describe the intermingling process. They include *mestizaje*, suggested by Roberto Fernandez Retamar; "creolization," preferred by some; "symbiosis," preferred by Leslie Desmangles.[1] Taylor concludes: "The idea of symbiosis helps pull together two apparently opposing schools of Caribbean social and cultural thought: the creolists and pluralists. Whereas creolization focuses on the developing unity of the new formative nation, pluralism emphasizes the social and cultural differences that divided and continue to divide a conflictual Caribbean region."[2]

Margarite Fernandez Olmos and Lizabeth Paravisini-Gebert prefer the term "creole religions," as used in the title of their text,[3] but they too respect the preferences others put forward as alternatives. They state, "The complex dynamic of encounters, adaptations, assimilation, and syncretism that we call *creolization* are emblematic of the vibrant nature of Diaspora cultures."[4] The authors use Roger Bastide's terms in distinguishing three types of syncretism. The first one is morphological or mosaic syncretism which has to do with the "juxtaposition and coexistence African-derived elements and Catholic symbols—the Vodou *pe*, or altars, with stones, wax candles, crosses, the statues of saints, and pots containing souls of the dead, for example." The second is institutional syncretism, "which combines prescribed religious observances by reconciling Christian and African liturgical calendars." The third is syncretism by correspondence, the same as Desmangles's "symbiosis"—in which case "an African deity and a Catholic saint become one on the basis of mythical or symbolic similarities."[5]

It should be made clear that although African religious syncretism is the most prevalent and pronounced form to be found in Caribbean religions, other religious expressions of such also exist in the region as well. Also, it should be clear that African religions in the Caribbean did not simply incorporate Christian elements in their religious practices, but other religious elements, such as indigenous Carib and Arawak elements, East Indian, Islamic, and Jewish components.

Olmos and Paravisini-Gebert take note of the historic debate on the term "syncretism" dating from the seventeenth century, its application to Christianity in earlier years and its broadening to apply to all religions at some points in their development. They also alert us to the derogatory use of the term to refer to non-European religions. They point to the dynamism in the syncretism of creole religions and acknowledge the "guided syncretism" practice of the Catholic Church in the colonial period, "tolerating the existence of a polytheistic idolatry that could be identified with Catholic saints and considering it a necessary evil—transitional state that would eventually lead the conquered peoples to the 'true' faith and elimination of such beliefs." But this expectation did not materialize. "The old gods refused to disappear (and still do)....The conquered peoples embraced Christian forms but with new meanings they themselves had refashioned at times appropriating them as tools of resistance." Finally, these two authors acknowledge Andrew Apter's assessment of religious syncretism as "yet another form of empowerment, another modality of revision and popular resistance."[6]

Adaptations and Syncretic Challenges of East Indian and Other Spiritualities in the Caribbean

Althea Prince poses some interesting questions and makes some revealing points regarding the acceptance of the religious mixture and the multi-religious conception of the Divine in Caribbean thinking.

> What meanings lie unspoken, but are given purpose in their usage? What lies layers-deep in the collective unconscious that enables some Caribbean persons to embrace or reject Rastafari at the same time that others hold steadfast to Hinduism, Buddhism, Islam, Catholicism, Protestantism, Shakerism, Vodou? The obvious link between these questions and the patchwork creations of my mother, with her tolerance for composite manifestations of the Divine, is not lost on me. The patchwork demonstrates an appreciation for many fabrics, in terms of texture, color, weave. Thread links them, and a unifying border gives them definition and clarity, allowing for continuity. As a small

child and throughout my teenage years, I accompanied her to what Antiguans call "Wayside Churches"; they were in small spaces—in one instance, above a rum shop. I also went with her every Sunday to High Anglican Mass in the eighteenth century English cathedral. At the same time, I listened spellbound to her stories of the power of Obeah rituals, healings, and curses that she had witnessed. Yet she took pride in the fact that she had never used the services of an *Obeahman* or *Obeahwoman*.[7]

Prince speaks of this experience of moving between two worlds as a Caribbean person's spiritual quest of trying to make sense of her/his place in the cosmos, of being there; shifts they make in the conceptualization of the Divine between Africa, India, and Europe. She further asks the questions and answers them:

What do Indian people feel when they sing together, listen to the drum, together? What does the African do in response to the drum? How is that creation different from the Lord's Prayer or the Twenty-third Psalm in terms of usage, impact, meaning, feeling? How can we sing the Lord's song in a strange land? "The land is strange no longer and the people sing their own definition of the Lord's song." For their Gods are creolized, the Divine is their Divine.[8]

"Their Gods are creolized" seems a perfectly appropriate phrase to begin this discussion of the ways in which the spiritual challenge is made by the non-Christian religious mixtures of the Caribbean and their challenges to Christian spirituality.

When the East Indians in the Caribbean who were practicing Hindus were struggling with situations of challenge from a predominantly Christian society that did not respect and acknowledge the legitimacy of their Hindu faith but rather condemned them as "heathens" of "pagans," many of them, especially in Trinidad and Guyana, accepted Christianity when appealed to by the Presbyterian missionaries. And owing to the propensity of Hinduism for openness to other faiths and other gods, it was relatively easy for these immigrants to accommodate themselves to Christianity within the beliefs and practices of their own Hindu traditions. Hinduism is a much more ancient religion than Christianity, and in India it was accustomed to assimilation of other religious tradition. For in this faith there exist many ways and sects by which one may travel the path to salvation, the major three being Jnana Yoga, Bhakti Yoga, and Karma Yoga. The first is the way of knowledge, inner withdrawal and meditation. The second is the way of devotion to a God, whatever divinity one chooses. The third is the way of full action in the world, political, social, and otherwise. The way of devotion to a God, Bhakti, is one way in which the Hindus can accept other Gods such as Jesus and the Son of God, or an avatar, God manifested in human form.

Bisnauth states that many of these Hindus in the West Indies could easily accept *Yisu Masih* (Jesus Christ) as an *avatar* (incarnation) of Brahma (the Creator God in the trimurti of deities, the other two being Vishnu, the Preserver, and Shiva, the Destroyer). Bisnauth describes the syncretistic manner in which the Hindus in this region assimilated Christian beliefs within their own religious ones regarding the *Nishkalanki Avatar* (Spotless Incarnation) of popular Hindu belief:

> The one who would appear in the last *yug* (era) —the *kala yug*—to reveal the right way to Brahma. Representing Brahma in his more personal aspect as *Ishvara* (Lord), [Christian] catechists made out that Jesus Christ was the incarnation of Ishvara in such a way that Yisu Masih, Ishvara and Brahma came to be regarded as one and the same deity [what has been called "syncretism by correspondence" or"symbiosis"].[9] It did not enter the consideration of the preachers that the Nishkalanki Avatar was but the last in a series of Brahmanic incarnations which included Krishna and Rama; that he was but the reappearance of these avatars in another guise. But if this theological point eluded the catechists, the presentation of Yisu Masih as the avatar of popular Hindu expectation put Jesus Christ within the tradition of Hinduism and made him acceptable to those Hindus who could be convinced that they lived in the kala yug.[10]

According to Bisnauth the greatest degree of Hindu-Christian syncretism came about in Martinique within the context of French Catholicism, where some of the Indian immigrants easily accommodated certain features of Hinduism and Catholicism. Some worshippers were able to identify certain deities with Jesus Christ (Madeyan, Vishnu Maldevidan—who was "the Nishkalanki Avatar whom Hindu mythology spoke of as coming on horse-back, sword in hand, to purge the world of its sins"); the Virgin Mary (Mari-Eman, "sometimes called Mari-amma (Mother Mary"), regarded as "the queen or the maid servant of Maldevidan," also as "the goddess who controlled certain diseases."[11] This trend also continued in the French island of Guadeloupe, where "Mari-Eman was worshipped…as Mali-Eman," with attributes exactly as those of Kali Mai, the Black Mother. And so Kali also became identified with the Virgin Mother.[12]

We see parallels in the Indian Hindu syncretism and the African syncretism, which was and is much more widespread and inclusive not only of Christianity but also of Hinduism, indigenous religions, and others. It should be noted that, as in the Afro-Caribbean religions, the Hindus also identified certain of their gods with the Catholic saints—Katarai with St. Michael, for instance. And as with the Afro-Caribbean religions, the Hindu cultists mixed their worship practices with Catholic ones and sacrificed animals to propitiate the spirits, as well as became possessed. Bisnauth asserts: "Maldevidan cultists went to the Roman Catholic church to be married. Their babies were baptized and their dead buried by Catholic rites. In their temples they crossed themselves piously in the name of the Trinity. But their temple worship service was not unlike Kali Mai puja in which the sacrifice of a sheep or a goat was made to propitiate the deities, and the advice of the gods was given through *l'abbe coolie* who became possessed."[13]

Frederick Ivor Case's brilliant analysis of Obeah and Kali Mai in Guyana,[14] in particular and in some respect in Trinidad, displays extensively the deeply spiritual qualities and contributions resulting from the intersections of these two religious traditions stemming from the respective countries of Ghana, West Africa, and India with each and with Christianity and other religious manifestations in the Caribbean setting. They are seen clearly to be a challenge to Christian spirituality in many ways. He refers to their interactions as "intersemiotics" rather than syncretism, which he defines at points as "positive acknowledgment of otherness and its adaptation" (p. 48), or "the active acknowledgment of otherness and the tendency to interact and produce innovative semantic and mythical systems" (p. 43). The author is concerned in the article more with the integration of Kali Mai puja elements into Obeah than the other way around, but the opposite has taken place. His fieldwork was done in Berbice, Guyana, where Obeah encountered a diversity of spirits. Here Obeah reveals the unambiguous spiritual presence of "Dutch" spirits. Historically, all of Guyana was at one point a Dutch colony, and the spirits that manifest themselves may be Aboriginal, African, Indian, European, Jewish, Christian, or Muslim. However, Berbice shares a common Border with Surinam, and there is frequent movement of individuals from one country to another. Historically, in order to survive on the plantations, African systems had to be versatile and to put in practice their ability to be inclusive."[15]

Case shows how the intersections of the codes of Obeah and Kali Mai puja—two different cultural and spiritual traditions, contribute to creation of a dynamic ritual and belief. He stresses the fact that the people of these traditions have social and political status in common—they are united in their poverty and political impotence. "Obeah in Guyana remains the spiritual resource of the dispossessed seeking inner and physical healing as well as the experience of nearness to God." And similarly, "The literature of Kali Mai Puja confirms the same social class bases of those who practice this form of *din* [service to God, spiritual service]." Both systems having been stigmatized and ostracized, they have "fulfilled similar social and psychological roles and have sustained the inner life of those who, in their quest for God, adhered to their beliefs."[16]

Both systems have been impacted by Christianity in meaningful ways that have contributed to enrichment of their spirituality in ways that make it a challenge to Christianity. One example Case elaborates on is merging of Jesus' mother with Kali Mai in Trinidad, evidenced by Kali Mai's versatility at the shrine of La Divina Pastora in Siparia. "The creative imagination of Kali devotees who have recognized in Mary, Mother of Jesus, their own Mother Kali is a transcendence of La Divina Pastora. The Hindu devotion in Siparia is not merely an acknowledgment of the universal principle of motherhood; it is the recognition of Mary as a principle of mediation and a deepening of her experience as benevolent shepherdess of a vastly diverse flock....Mary claims Kali and Kali claims Mary. In the creative imagination of the Kali worshippers, there is constructive dialogue of Mary and Kali to the point that they enunciate one discourse." The distinctive difference in the Catholic spiritual conception and that of the Kali worshippers indicates a broader and more meaningful perception on the part of the latter. "The discursive path of Kali worshippers is not the same as that of Catholic worshippers. However, for Kali worshippers, the two paths converge since the Kali myth is inclusive and the other is exclusive in its adherence to Catholic orthodoxy."[17]

Case analyzes the two systems of Obeah and Kali Mai in their oral beliefs and practices, use of magic and metaphor and successful communication with the spirits. And he makes clear that Obeah, earlier associated with evil practices, has evolved through interaction with Myalism (a benign Ghanaian religion) and Christianity in Jamaica. Transformations are seen as having occurred in Kali Mai. "In the social and cultural readjustments of [slavery] slavery and indenture respectively, both systems have adapted elements from other *din* of their respective regions of origin, and in Guyana, both have come into conflict with Christianity and its diverse orthodoxies." But both traditions have survived the clashes and present an openess and liberating spirituality that is a positive challenge to Christianity in its narrowness. They impose "few daily constraints on adherents. Persons of all ethnicities and religious affiliations present themselves for consultations in either *din* and participate in their rituals.....This set of mobile semiotic codes is particularly appropriate to the volatile cultural and demographic context of the Caribbean."[18]

Finally, Case stresses the fact that Guyanese Obeah incorporates Christian and Hindu elements and shows spiritual strength in doing so. It becomes for adherents a corrective to misleading Christian interpretations of Scripture.

> Guyanese Obeah relies heavily on the Christian scriptural tradition. It is generally acknowledged by a number of African Guyanese Obeah practitioners and believers that Europeans deliberately misled entire populations in the interpretations of the Old and New Testaments. Mother M. [one of the author's interviewees), in her annual ceremony of the Planting of the Ensigns, commemorates God's giving of the *jhandi* [Hindu flags] to the African Moses during the exodus from Egypt. The Africanization of the Christian scriptures is accompanied by the discursive inclusion of Hinduism in the narrative of Obeah. The *jhandi* were given to each of the twelve tribes so that God could identify each tribe from above (Num. 2:2; Isa. 10:11, 30:17). Hence the integration of *jhandi* within the iconographic code of Obeah. Kali's *jhandi* occupy a logical place in the mythic structures of Obeah. They underline the legitimacy of Kali as a divinity deriving spiritual strength from God of the Old Testament.[19]

Personal experiences shared by practitioners and participants in the Caribbean religious mixtures reveal tremendous insights in regard to the present setting of religious interactions. Students of Caribbean and Central and South American origin in my classes in Issues in Caribbean Religions have ranged all the way from those who are not in any religion in particular or who are of strict Catholic or Protestant affiliation and condemn the socalled cults in their homeland, to those who themselves have never actually been active participants in any of the syncretic religions but who have witnessed with interest parents and other relatives do so, to those students who are presently active participants in or clients of these religions, to actual initiates and priestesses of the especially Afro-Caribbean cults or other religious mixtures. I will share some of those student insights later in the book. But for now, I would suggest that some of them fit the category of Marta Moreno Vega[20] initially, an Afro-Puerto Rican born and raised in New York City without much religious orientation, who, in growing up having seen evidence of her parents and relatives' involvement with both Catholic and Afro-Caribbean religions (the latter more in secret), in her adult years embarked on her own religious journey to discover her Afro-Caribbean religious and cultural roots. What she found and how it influenced her life thereafter is very enlightening as to the present Caribbean religious mixture involving the African, Eastern, and Indigenous, as well as Christian religious manifestations.

Vega grew up in her family home in New York City, where her parents and grandmother openly embraced the Catholic religion and secretly practiced Santeria and Espiritismo,[21] three religious varieties found in both Cuba and Puerto Rica and which are a part of and stem from the multi-religious encounter found in both those Caribbean countries. Her *abuela* (her father's mother) lived in her own apartment in the apartment building where the family lived in conjunction with other families of African American, Puerto Rican, and Italian background. There had developed a close friendship among these diverse groups, a sense of family, really.[22] Although her *abuela*, grandmother, camouflaged her African beliefs behind Catholic images and did not share her religious practices with Marta, Marta was able to have access to her grandmother's sacred room where she could view her *boveda*, her ancestral altar table, on which were water, flowers, statues of Catholic saints, an Indian chief, a Gypsy woman, and African men and women. In later years she was to understand the significance of her grandmother's altar, on which there were seven glasses of water, each dedicated to the memory of an individual spirit energy (guardian angels and spirits that continued to protect the family and its racial and cultural identities). Vega states, "One glass was filled for the Yorubas, one for the Kongos, one for the Native Americans, another for our guardian angels, one for relatives, one for loved ones, and finally, a last for unknown spirits."[23]

Marta, her sister Socorro, and her brother Alberto were provided no formal training in religion by their mother and father, nor by their grandmother. Marta embarked on her own religious search, exploring many faiths and attending a number of different churches, including Protestant, Catholic, and Pentecostal ones. The mother and father pretended to be Catholic and never displayed any of the symbols of the *orishas* as the grandmother did.[24] However, the parents did practice the traditional rituals and kept them secret from the children, two occasions of which Vega discusses in her book. These involved a healing ritual for her mother during a heart ailment from which she was cured, and the healing of her niece by an *espiritista* possessed by her guardian spirit.[25] After her *abuela's* death in 1959 and her mother's death in 1964, Marta intensified her religious search while trying to organize her life around marriage, building a family, establishing a career. Becoming Director of the community's Puerto Rican cultural center known as El Museo del Barrio was a turning point in Marta Vega's life. She embarked on a search for her roots and became immersed in the study of Puerto Rican culture. Researching her African heritage, she had to deal with the conflict of her double heritage—Black and Puerto Rican. Her travel to Black towns in Puerto Rico helped her with this problem, however. Her search finally led her in 1979 to Cuba, after her development of the Caribbean Culture Center and travels to a number of the Caribbean Islands (including Trinidad, Tobago, and the Dominican Republic), where she became irresistibly drawn to the Orisa religion and culture, as well as Espiritismo rituals.

There in Cuba she began to see and experience the religious and cultural dialogue and blending that is common in Cuba and evident in most Caribbean religious and cultural experiences, especially Chinese, other Asian, Native American, and East Indian encounter and involvement with Orisa religion. Three striking incidents and situations stand out in the book. The first is that of the eighty-year-old Santera, Ma Mina, priestess of Oya, whose home Marta and her godmother (*madrina*), Zenaida, visited. At the time widowed for ten years, Ma Mina had been married to a Chinese who was initiated as a Santero of Oya. As an Afro-Cuban woman, she had come to a perceptive understanding of the relationship between the two religious traditions. She stated, "The divinities of the Chinese community are very similar to the *orishas*. People like to argue about the Chinese divinities. For me, they are different roads to the same destination." Her husband apparently shared her insights. She explained that he was even more devoted to the *orishas* than she was. But he did not abandon his cultural and religious heritage. The two of them united the two traditions. He decorated their home with artwork from his homeland. She explained that, "His family was brought to Cuba as indentured workers during the abolition of slavery. The Chinese were treated like slaves. They suffered the same treatment as we did." It appears that their marriage and mutual experience in the Orisa and Chinese religious and cultural realities played a role in their achievement of wholeness and serenity in life. Even in death their bond had not been broken. She stated, "His spirit visits me almost every night. He wants me to join him. I know we will soon be together. For now, I have placed his Oya and mine next to each other as a symbol of our unending marriage and love."[26]

Vega experienced another Asian santero and diviner during her initiation procedure. It was El Chino, the *oriate* who presided over her *ita*, the special divination session necessary which determined her new African name and the course of her future life as an initiate and servant of the orisha. Vega described him and the process.

> A tall, thin Asian man nicknamed El Chino welcomed me into the room....El Chino was surrounded by the elder santeros and santeras. I sat on a low stool facing him, with my bare feet placed on the straw mat. When he began to move the sixteen cowrie shells

in his delicate hands, everyonestopped talking and focused their attention on him. El Chino began sprinkling drops of cool water on the ground, reciting the prayers calling the ancestors and then Ellegua to guide his hands.[27]

The session proceeded wherein Vega was given messages of guidance from major Orishas (Ellegua, Oya, Ochun, Yemaya, Shango, and Obatala). It is notable that the whole initiation process is conducted within a family group of initiates, and the different ethnic origins or religious backgrounds of the participants do not make a difference. El Chino was fully accepted and honored in his role. When the session was finished, he collected his divination paraphernalia and advised Vega: "Make certain that you follow the instructions of your *orishas* for life; in helping yourself, you also protect your family. Having these sacred powers in your possession will radiate in everything you do. I wish you the very best."[28]

In Trinidad Vega encountered an East Indian Yoruba priest who included Hindu gods on his altar, along with the Yoruba ones. Amit, an initiate of Shango, headed a large family of initiates in the Shango religion that included Trinidadians of all racial groups. Vega described Amit and her experiences in the in his setting. On his altar she says, "The ornate beauty of Shango resided alongside Shiva, the East Indian warrior divinity, as members of the same family." She described Amit's blending of the two religious and cultural traditions. "When I visited his home with Mother Sheila, Amit was comfortably dressed in the traditional clothes of West Africa, designed with East Indian red, white, and golden cloth." Vega further asserts that, "Amit's home...reflected the unification of two religions, as the double-headed ax of Shango was surrounded by the golden, red glitter of exotic silk cloth.[29]

Vega's visit to the temple of Shango priestess Mother Gabby in the mountains of Port of Spain, a thin, dark-skinned young woman, led to some revealing insights regarding unity among Indian and Yoruba religiosity. Speaking of Mother Gabby, she says,

> Walking back toward the room where she kept the Catholic saints, she motioned for us to follow. "Let me show you a portrait of a saint I recently purchased in Venezuela; it is an image of Maria Lionza. According to the blacks in Venezuela, she is the representation of an Indian goddess. The Catholic followers of Maria Lionza are spiritualists who, like us, work with natural elements of nature. Air, earth, wind, and fire, tobacco and candles, call the spirits in a similar way to our practices."[30]

Vega comments that, "Once again, the cross-cultural connections emerged, affirming that the American Yoruba belief systems are inclusive, embracing many traditions, yet maintaining the philosophical foundations, the fundamento, of the original African philosophies. In every temple I visited, I found testaments to the power of faith and religion in keeping a community unified."[31]

Patrick Taylor in the beginning of his book, Nation Dance, includes a real life story of the Afro-Cuban Spiritualist Eva Fernandez Bravo, a 70-year old great grandmother with six children, thirteen grandchildren, and eight great-grandchildren, who participated in a scholar-practitioner conference on Caribbean religions held in Canada in 1996. What she has to say of her multi-religious experience sheds much light on how the intersections of religions in Cuba affect the people and the culture.

> My "head saint" [santo de cabeza] is blessed Santa Barbara and my ritual, after, is of the spirits. My humble mission is to be a missionary and to help my neighbor. But today my neighbors are divided: one has faith and the other doesn't. So the path that we must walk is more difficult, but we are going to carry on and we will prevail. As part of my mission I have a lot of contact with Lazaro, who is a missionary of health and cures many; he's very miraculous. I have Yemaya, the Virgin of Regla, as mother of the deep sea, mother of the spirits. When we gather at the altar we first count on her so that spirits arrive and put us into a trance. I spoke of Santa Barbara, but my protector spirit is man, and when I pass through my protector spirit and my guiding spirit, then I can work African, Chinese, French, all spiritual fields. So that woman is not an idol. No. All the spirits, male and female, when we invoke them, a man or a woman may come down. Now I adore Santa Barbara because she is my "head" [cabeza], but my protector spirit is a man, and my guide is a nun. I have no church of my own. My church is Catholic and my home is my center. On Sundays we gather there. That is what we call a spiritual Center. Then we work, trying to find faith because the other side is selfishness, evil, envy. These two parts cannot unite. So we must try with faith to clean this part, to purify it so that we can unite and live better.[32]

Finally, in respect to the intersections of religions in the Caribbean in the present setting, Rastafari must be mentioned, for it is one of the clearest cases of creolization in the region. Patrick Taylor describes Rastafari as "hybridity at its grandest, narrated as dispersion and return, Africa and Europe mutually implicated, pushing meaning of the other to its limits, transforming, humanizing."[33] This religion folds into its structure and practice indigenous and cultural perspectives, African, Islamic, Jewish, Christian, and East Indian religious elements and traditions. To begin with the founding of the movement in the 1930's, one of the founders, Leonard P. Howell, is said to have taken the ritual name "Gangunguru ('Teacher of Famed Wisdom') Maragh ('King'), a title given to him by his Hindu adviser, Laloo." And the Rastafari adopted the smoking of ganja "(sometimes called 'Kali' after the Hindu Goddess)" as part of their ritual and created their own version of the Hindu belief in reincarnation.[34] Basically, however, the Rastafaris have developed their own adaptations of Judaism and Islam from the Jewish Bible and the Christian New Testament mixed with Marcus Garvey's beliefs in Pan-Africanism. In summary, the newly crowned Emperor of Ethiopia, Haile Selassie, in 1930 led initiators of the movement to consider the "prophecy" seen in the Bible passage of Psalm 68:32 ("Princes shall come forth out of Egypt; Ethiopia shall soon stretch forth her hands unto God") now fulfilled. In the ancient Ethiopian epic Kebra Negast (The Glory of Kings), "venerated by the people as containing the final proof of their descent from the Hebrew Patriarchs, and of the kinship of their kings to the Solomonic line with Jesus Christ, the Son of God,"[35] was found the root of the trend of equating divine kingship to Ethiopian emperors. The lore centered around Haile Selassie ("Power or the Trinity"), being dubbed "Ras Tafari" ("Prince of Peace"), "Conquering Lion of Judah," "King of Kings," "Lord of Lords," led to fixing on him as God, "Jah" (Jahweh), as well as Jesus Christ, the Messiah returned. In the messianic and millennial themes, combining both Judaism and Christianity, Ethiopia became the Promised Land, Heaven, to which Africans, the true Jews, were to be repatriated.

Rastafari has withstood the test of the time, surviving through all manner of assaults and persecutions and becoming entrenched in the Jamaican society socially, religiously, and politically, as well as economically. It has spread to other areas of the Caribbean including Cuba, the Bahamas, Grenada, Guyana, and Trinidad, among others. And with the spread of Reggae music, its religious mouthpiece, it has made inroads into many parts of the world in North America, Europe, and Africa and gained proponents among other races, ethnic groups, and religions, including Jews and Christians.[36]

Chapter Four

Issues of Religio-Social and Cultural Manifestations Found in Caribbean Religions: Cuban Santeria and Haitian Vodou, Brazilian Candomblè and Trinidadian Shango

The religions of the Caribbean thrive on the crucial life issues that have kept them alive and vital to this day. All of them, whatever their origins and whatever the struggles they have undergone, serve vital life needs and contribute to the ongoing life of the region. The issues are expressed in the religions themselves as they are practiced and conceived in response to the contexts in which they exist and search for continuing relevance, meaning, and vitality of their adherents. These issues are social, cultural, economic, and political, having to do with such phenomena as race, ethnicity, cultural validity, gender, syncretism, cultural and religious continuity and change, social dominance, cultural survival, resistance to efforts of elimination by the dominant culture, appropriation and accommodation. At many junctures in previous chapters we have had occasion to touch upon such crucial issues as they related to other discussions. But in this section we will be dealing with them as we see them being incorporated and reflected in the structure, concepts, spiritual realities, rituals, and practices of different religions. In this chapter we will examine Cuban Santeria and Haitian Vodou, Brazilian Candomblé and Trinidadian Shango. These four Afro-Caribbean religions have much in common in so far as their use of African cosmology is concerned; the origins of their divinities in the same or similar West African sources; their synthesis of Catholic saints, symbols, and other religious elements; as well as their tendencies to be inclusive of other religions encountered in the region. However, though there are similarities in their reflections of these issues, each of these religions differs greatly in most ways in which these issues are dealt with in them. And the differences are due in part to the socio-economic, cultural and political settings of the countries in which they have developed and presently exist, as well as to other circumstances.

Crucial Issues in Cuban Santeria and Haitian Vodou

These two Afro-Cuban religions developed under different colonial governments and social systems, but they share in common an exposure to Catholicism within the framework of their African worldview and they share African divinities in common, especially from the Yoruba traditions of Nigeria and Dahomey, while some of their African deities were from other sources, such as the Fon-speaking peoples of Dahomey (present-day Benin), the main source of Haitian Vodun. Both of these religions were developed by the African slaves in their respective colonial countries of Cuba and Haiti and had to be practiced in secrecy for the most part owing to governmental restrictions on the practices of their African religious traditions. They both struggled in ways available to them in their particular settings to maintain their cultures and establish their religions in this new context and keep them alive and functional. And they were quite successful in doing so even though changes and modifications had to be done in order to adjust to the different situations in their particular Caribbean areas. To be more precise, both Cuban Santeria and Haitian Vodun are based upon the belief in an African pantheon of deities, known as Orisha in Santeria (Lucumí, Regla de Ocha) and Lwa (Loa) in Haitian Vodun, head of which is the Supreme Being who is Creator and has power over the lesser gods or spirits. In Lucumí or Santeria, this God is a trinity whose names are variously Olorun, Olofi, Olodumare; in Vodun this God is referred to as Le Bon Dieu, Bondye, Grande Maitre (the Good God, the Almighty, respectively). The Supreme Being is not worshipped, however, but rather the lesser gods and spirits, who have been given powers over certain natural forces and elements and certain domains of life, are closer to the humans and can assist them in their daily living. Therefore, they are appeased and appealed to for aid through worship and ritual practices, including the very important practice of spirit possession wherein the deity possesses the priest/priestess's or devotee's body and speaks and communicates through her/him for the benefit of the community.

Many of the deities in Santeria and Vodun are the same but are called by different names. Therefore, in order to discuss issues clearly and concisely, we should take a look at a chart which shows the major deities, their West African derivation, those they share in common with each other and with the Catholic saints and divinity; for both established and maintained their religions through a similar form of syncretism with Catholicism. And this relates to the first major issue, that of Syncretism. (Table 1)

Table 1. Religious Synthesis in Cuban Lucumi/Santeria and Haitian Vodun

Yoruba	Lucumí /Santeria	Vodun	Catholicism
Olodmare /Olorun/Olofi Supreme Being	Olodumare /Olorun/ Olofi	Fon deity: Mawu-Lisa—Bondye	God the Father, Creator
Obatalá	Obatalá	No parallel seen	Our Lady of Mercy
Eshu/Elegba	Elegguá	Legba	St. Anthony, St. Martin de Porres
Ogun	Ogun	Ogu	St. Peter, St. James
Shango	Changó	No parallel seen	St. Barbara, Virgin Mary
Yemoja	Yemayá /Olokun	Agoue	St. Ulrich, the Virgin of Regla
Oshun	Ochun	Erzuli, Ezili Freda	Mater Dolorosa, Virgen de la Caridad del Cobre
Oyá	Oyá	No parallel seen	St. Teresa
Orula/Orunla/ Orunmila/Ifá	Orunmila/Ifá	No parallel seen	St. Francis of Assisi
Obaluaye	Babalu Ayé	No parallel seen	St. Lazarus
Osanyin	Osain	No parallel	St. Joesph, etc.
		Damballa, Dahomeyan origin	St. Patrick, Moses
		Baron Samedi, of Arawak origin, Zemi, Guede	St. Gerard

The practice of syncretism became in both Cuba and Haiti the major means of cultural survival and resistance to efforts of dehumanization and absorption into alien cultures on the part of African slaves. As Olmos and Paravisini-Gebert express it: "In the crucible of the plantation—amid relationships based on European power and African powerlessness—the slaves' very survival depended on their ability to manipulate and resist their complete absorption into the core values of the plantation masters.…African religions merged in a dynamic process with European Christian and Amerindian beliefs to shape syncretic theologies that provide alternative ways of looking at the world 'in a certain kind of way.'"[1] But the process took place somewhat differently in each country.

The Process of Syncretism in Cuban Santeria

George Brandon defines Santeria as a New World neo-African religion with a clear dual heritage," including Spanish folk Catholicism, Traditional African religion (Yoruba orisha worship), and Kardecan spiritism, "which originated in France in the nineteenth century and became fashionable in both the Caribbean and South America."[2] When African slaves were brought to Cuba and pressured under threats of violence to abandon their African religious beliefs and practices and to accept the Catholic religion of their slave masters and white surroundings, they complied by combining what they could comprehend of the Catholic faith and practice within their African worldview and belief systems and practices, which resulted in a dual religion on their part. For the most part they learned to conceal their African worship behind the practices they observed in Catholicism. To see how this was possible, it is necessary to understand what the religious background was like in the Old Country. For one thing, Traditional Yoruba religion was not an organized, institutional religion like the Catholic religion they were to encounter on this side of the Atlantic. Yoruba was not a body of beliefs, doctrines, and rituals, but a way of life based on mythology, legends, proverbs, religious rites, symbols, organized family and community life that involved interrelatedness of ancestors, the living, and the coming generations, interacting with natural and divine realities to maintain unity, control, and cohesiveness in a harmonious and productive existence.

The African religious setting was reconstructed in the New World so far as the situations and conditions would permit. In the African setting worship was done in temples and shrines, houses, other outdoors and indoors spots, where altars were decorated with the sacred paraphernalia, and priests and priestesses performed the necessary rites. Each temple was dedicated to one of the numerous deities amounting to 409, only about 30 of which survived the Middle Passage to be included in the Cuban pantheon. "Although some of the altar images were in the forms of human icons, most of them were not. Instead they were usually common ordinary objects, such as pots, cowrie shells, pieces of iron, gourd bowls, stones, tree limbs, and branches. These were selected because of their symbolic association with the deity or function they were to serve." Worship was organized in hierarchical manner with levels of priests and priestesses serving in certain positions and different rankings within temple groups, and great respect for elders. "The temple priesthoods all came under the responsibility of a village or town priest, who was in turn responsible to the priesthoods of the national or royal cult....Worship took place in a daily, weekly, and annual round, with daily worship centered for the laity in their compounds. Weekly worship gathered together those who worshiped the same deity. The annual celebrations, commemorating each major deity worshiped in the area, were communitywide festivals."[3]

Important to understanding how the Yoruba system was capable of absorbing and syncretizing the Catholic beliefs and practices is taking into account their religious worldview or cosmology. Central to that perspective is the ashe, the all-encompassing power or energy permeating the entire universe. Clyde Ford cites one myth of the creation which begins with a force, a plenitude from which the orisha come into existence.

> Before the pantheon came the plenitude; before the archetypal forms came the primordial formlessness; before the many gods and goddesses came the one godhead, known as Orisa-nla. In the beginning there was only this godhead, a beingless being, a dimensionless point, an infinite container of everything, including itself; and this uncreated creator was serviced by a slave known as Atunda. As Arisa-nla toiled away on a hillside garden, Atunda—rebelled, rolling a massive boulder down the embankment, smashing Orisa-nla into a multitude of fragments. These fragments—the number varies from 200 to 201, 400, 401, 600, 601, 1001, or more—became the Yoruba gods and goddesses, known as the orishas.[4]

This "plenitude" seems to be equated with the ashe which surrounds all.

At the top of the hierarchy of existence is the Supreme Being Olodumare/Olorun/Olofi, the the Orisha, followed by the Egungun (ancestors), the humans, plants and animals, and at bottom are the non-living things. Olodumare is the creator and sustainer of the universe, remote from humans, for whom they build no temples nor dedicate any priesthood. The orisha emanate directly from Olodumare, being either beings from heaven or humans who for special reasons after their deaths were metamorphosed into orisha. "The orisha are the guardians and explicators of human destiny. It is they to whom people turn for help, and advice in the great and problems of life." The city of Ife is the Holy City, the place of the birthplace of most of the gods, but many gods or orisha are associated with the former Yoruba city-state of Oyo, such as Shango, Oyá, Yemoja. Orisha worship is not the same as ancestral veneration and ritual practices, the egungun, concerned with the moral and social order of society and with adherence to public norms. "The role of ancestors was not to ensure individual achievement and satisfaction, although they remained interested in the fates of their descendants; it was to undergird the continued existence of society and a just social order at all levels." Humans were related in responsible ways to the plants and animals and non-living things. Plants and animal were relished as a part of the environment providing means of survival and nourishment and depending on humans for care and protection. Things like rivers, clouds, stones, have a 'life' of their own. They too possess ashe. Finally, "it is ritual which allows humans to traverse all categories of being through the manipulation and communication of ashe. The various forms of divination allowed people to have access to the accumulated wisdom of the deities and the dead as the paradigms for solving current problems. Offerings of food, objects, song, money, or blood of animals in sacrifice all revivified the ashe of the orisha and directed it toward specific ends. In ceremonial spirit possession, the link between the orisha and its descendants became palpable as, in ceremonies held in its honor, the immaterial being came down from on high and took over the body of one of its children, communicating to the assembly in a visible, physical human form....It is the ashe in the priestess and the herbs, in the blood of the animal and the chants of praise and supplication, that heals the sick and forestalls death in rituals of affliction." It was a humanocentric universe, though humans were not masters of that universe, but were could create and sustain the harmony and balance of it. There was an ecology, an interdependence of creation.[5]

Within this Yoruba framework, it should not be difficult to see how the African slaves were able to fold in Catholic beliefs and practices. They already possessed basic structures within which Spanish folk Catholic practices and beliefs could be folded, such that they could give the impression of following Catholicism while in reality worshiping their own orisha and carrying out their own ritual practices and forms of religious participation. Brandon summarizes the Catholic perspectives as they may relate to the Traditional religious ones.

> Spanish Catholic religious manifestations can be grouped under two headings. One is the basic cult, which consists of the seven sacraments of baptism, confirmation, matrimony, extreme unction, the eucharist, penance, and holy orders. The other is a cult of personages. These are the specialized cults of Jesus Christ, the Virgin Mary, and the saints. From the cult of personages arises a vast array of religious phenomena: legends and miracle stories elaborated into folk dramas, the yearly cycle of feast days, the festivals of patron saints....While the basic cult and its sacraments were definitely the domain of the priests and official Catholicism, the cult of personages (especially Mary and the saints) were open to folk interpretation....As potent intermediaries between humans and God, ones who would respond to pleas and offerings and imitation, saints eclipsed the other forms and objects of worship. Among folk Catholics it was the saints who received the greatest adoration. Saints were venerated at domestic altars as well as in church. The official church could no more completely control the worship of these saints among the folk than it could control the distribution of the saints' images upon which much of folk Catholicism depended. Attendance at mass paralleled, or was replaced by the erection and tending of a home altar containing religious icons.[6]

Recognizing the well-known trend in African religion of being "amenable to accepting the 'foreign' gods of their neighbors and enemies" and the history of Catholic "popular piety" of being open to syncretism with 'pagan' beliefs and practices, Albert Raboteau notes the compatibility of the Catholic and African practices.

> No fundamental contradiction existed between veneration of the Virgin Mary and the saints in Catholic piety, on the one hand, and devotion to the orisha and vodun in African religions, on the other....Catholic notions about the role of Christ, Mary, guardian angels, and patron saints as intercessors with the Father in heaven for men on earth proved quite compatible with African ideas about the intervention of lesser gods in the day-to-day affairs of human life, while the supreme god remained benevolent and providential but distant.[7]

In Cuba the syncretism developed in a unique way, principally by means of the urban cabildos, which was a system of socalled guided syncretism undertaken by the Catholic Church, using the practice stemming from Spain called the cofradias or fraternities, social clubs, or essentially mutual aid societies. In Cuba these organizations were organized according to African ethnic groups and were intended to be used by the Church to teach and train the Africans in the Catholic religious practices and beliefs, as well as to serve as mutual aid societies. Under the watchful eyes of priests, the Church allowed for the accommodation of African religious customs to the Church's worship, hoping that eventually the participants would abandon their old religious ways and assimilate completely into the Catholic religion. But the opposite apparently took place as the Africans seized this opportunity to keep their deities alive and functional by deliberately disguising them as Catholic saints. Brandon states, "By the nineteenth century at least fourteen African nations had their own cabildos." The dances were performed according to the character of the nation each represented. "The cabildo dances bore the names of the drums which played for the dancing, and the drums themselves were ethnically significant symbols of the different nations." The songs, music, language, and drum rhythms were distinctive for each nation. "The most important dances occurred on the Catholic religious holidays, but the dances performed remained African in origin and style." Each cabildo was headed by an elected overseer called *el rey* (king) who was held responsible for any problems that developed. These clubs are seen as the most likely source out of which Santeria developed, where no doubt the dances turned into religious ceremonies in which spirit possession took place.[8]

More or less pure Yoruba religion called Lucumí in Cuba (one source says it stems from the Yoruba greeting Oluki mi (my friend),[9] another, that it could derive from the port of Ulkami or Lucumí in southern Nigeria from which slaves were taken[10]) developed among slaves in the countryside, unmingled with Catholic religion. Here worship took place out in the open where trees, hills, and fields served as shrines, and the orisha was invoked and offerings and sacrifices made, and the like. But in the urban setting the cabildos brought together the worshipers in community, and even the homes were used to set up temples. Here it was possible to have set up permanent shrines and altars, even though they had to be concealed. "The cabildo and the home took the place of the temple and became known alternately as ile ocha (Yoruba, house of the orisha) or casa templo (house temple). When permitted, the great religious processions…were the major public venues for Lucumi worshipers, but temporary wayside shrines could be put up in parks and near large trees." Generally, not communal but private worship was done in the countryside (except for the palenques—communities of cimmarones or Cuban maroons), whereas the urban cabildos were communal.[11]

The name Santeria was attached to the religion because of the reverence for the saints of the Catholic Church, of course. And the priests and priestesses were referred to as santeros and santeras, respectively. An elaborate ritual has to be undertaken to initiate one into the priesthood of any particular orisha or saint, referred to as kariocha or asiento (making Ocha or seating of the god in the head of the priest), comparable to an ordination. One becomes the "bride" of the santo, one who serves the santo daily and through whom the spirit manifests to the community. Olmos and Paravisini-Gebert summarize the santera/santero's function.

> Followers celebrate the spiritual entities, offer sacrifices, consult their will   in divination, follow their advice, attempt to control them, and, if possible, incarnate them in their bodies in possession—the intimate communion with the divine—in quest of assistance in coping with human problems and the challenges of everyday life. Spiritual growth is manifested by stages of initiation, complex and symbolic ceremonies of death and rebirth that are the sources of ritual knowledge, development, and evolution. Those who require balance and harmony in their lives due to physical or emotional illness or a life crisis seek out the help of a priest of Ocha who will undoubtedly consult the oracle to hear the spiritual solution proffered by the deities.[12]

Divination is central to the practice of Santeria/Regla de Ocha/Lucumí, as all rituals, sacrifices, and initiation rites require the practice of consulting the divine will and direction. The god of divination is Orunmila/Ifá/Orula. "Devotees consult the oracle for guidance and counsel at the beginning of every important transition in life and at critical moments."[13] Olmos and Paravisini-Gebert give a simple description of the three principle methods of divination and the necessary requirements of each in terms of practice and practitioners. The three,

> the coconut or Obi, the sixteen cowries or dilogun, and Ifá (in the form of the ekuele chain or the Tabla de Ifá)…are practiced differently and by a sort of ranking in terms of difficulty and prestige. The Obi can be practiced by all believers; the dilogun by all priests and priestesses of Ocha; Ifá, considered by some the most complex and prestigious form requiring years of study, is only practiced by the babalao. Divination is not limited to the above, however: messages from the gods are also communicated in states of possession.[14]

The Process of Syncretism in Haitian Vodun

Albert Raboteau cites anthropologist Michel Laguerre who says that Haitian vodou as a syncretism "between Catholicism and Afro-American cults has largely been a syncretism of material and magic. Blessed objects (candles, pictures, holy water), gestures, and prayers have been appropriated from Catholicism for use in the cults because they are believed to possess magical power. To add the power of Christianity to that of African cults made sense, for 'it is better to rely upon two magics instead of one.'"[15] Raboteau also asserts the distinctive character of Catholic syncretism in Haitian vodou, which distinguishes it from that in Cuban Santeria and all other forms of syncretism in the Caribbean.

> Perhaps nowhere in New World slavery did the revolutionary potential of this syncretism between African and Catholic magic emerge as clearly as it did in Haiti. The Code Noir of 1685 legislated that all slaves brought to the French possessions in America must receive instruction and baptism within eight days of arrival. Baptism was not difficult but instruction was another matter. Thirty-seven years later, Fr. Jean-Baptiste Labat objected that the slaves used Christianity to disguise their African beliefs. "The Negroes do without a qualm, what the Philistines did; they put Dagon with the Ark and secretly preserve all the superstition of their ancient idolatrous cult alongside the ceremonies of Christianity." In a decree of the Conseil du Cap of 1761 the clergy were still complaining that the slaves were guilty of mingling "the Holy utensils of our religion with profane and idolatrous objects" and of altering "the truths and dogmas of religion."....The preservation of African cults alongside Christianity in Saint-Domingue (as Haiti was formerly called) could not be taken lightly by civil authorities either.[16]

Clearly the circumstances under which syncretism took place in Haiti was quite different from those which were experienced and described as "guided syncretism" of the cabildos of Cuba. The whole atmosphere was quite different. So was the background of vodun stemming from Dahomey (Benin) into which the other religions of the Yoruba and Ewe and others were inculcated. And the fact is that vodun in the New World was a syncretism of much more than Catholic magic but also of indigenous Arawak and other combinations.

Among the slaves brought to Haiti from West Africa (Dahomey, Angola, etc.) were many different religious and cultural groups including, Yoruba, Fon, Ewe, Congo, Ibos, and many more.[17] These were all accustomed to intermingling of religious beliefs and traditions. Being more powerful in its pantheon of gods and spirits, and possessing flexibility and openness to cultural incorporation, the Dahomeyan vodun system became dominant in the Haitian setting. Leonard Barrett speaks of Vodun as "a conglomerate of various African divinities with the further addition of the Christian Trinity, plus the roster of saints of Catholicism," leaving "no powers outside its orbit."[18] All sources agree that Vodun is a religion that developed in the heart of the revolutionary spirit of resistance to the institution of slavery and dehumanization on the part of those Africans who found themselves in this particular Francophone area of the New World. They felt strongly that the way to free themselves was through the preservation of their religion and culture. And one group among them who was devoted to this purpose was the maroons, those Africans who had resisted enslavement by escaping to the mountains. "In the public square south of the presidential palace in Port-au-Prince stands the statue of a muscular Maroon, kneeling on one knee, blowing a conch shell, known in Haiti as lambe. This statue commemorates a special breed of Haitian Black who, like the Jamaican Maroon, fled to the mountains and from there harassed the French."[19]

Desmangles describes how focused the maroons were on the preservation of the African traditions in their strong resistance to African enslavement. It turns out that the preservation of religious traditions and therefore the New World creation of Vodun was done, not under the eyes of Catholic and government officials in the cabildos as was often the case in Cuba, but pretty much in the secret societies called confreries, as noted in his book.

> The vivid millenarian message of the leaders [of maroons] gave the maroons and slaves a more than ephemeral hope of escaping servitude—a hope that kept them from falling into despair....Marronnage also played a significant role in preserving whole enclaves of religious traditions from different regions of Africa. Such preservation was made possible by the formation of confreries or secret societies....Although these societies probably existed among the slaves on the plantations, they were especially predominant in the maroon communities on the remote hills in the interior of the island, where they were geographically isolated from the European cultural influences of the plantations.[20]

At first these maroon communities were small but grew larger with increased labor forces and additional ethnic groups, and formation of federated groups to the extent that Bastide referred to them as "maroon republics."[21] Each society maintained its own ancestral traditions, and through interactions with one another they modified their beliefs and practices to meet their new situations. "Although religion in these republics was shaped by a blending of African beliefs and practices, the forms that it took depended upon a number of contingent variables that left indelible marks on Vodou as it exists today in Haiti." As Desmangles concludes, their religious traditions could not remain precisely the same as those in the African homelands, as the maroons reshaped their ancestral religious traditions to include "their apocalyptic visions of freedom." Two forms of Vodou were developed: the Rada Rites, the benign form derived from the Arada area in Dahomey, and the Petro Rites, the belligerent form developed in the New World of Haiti, the lwa (loa) of which were "known to be bitter, aggressive, and forceful, inspiring revolution." Desmangles further asserts that the maroon republics were "vital to the development of Vodou," that they "fostered the maintenance of African religious traditions in Vodou" as well as "the creation of a whole assortment of creole traditions" derived from adaptations to circumstances in the Haitian setting.[22]

The Rada Rites belong to the process under which Catholicism was merged with Vodou in Haiti. One source describes a scene that reveals one way slaves were forced to accept the Catholic in Haiti as they arrived in the land.

> A hundred or so Negroes freshly arrived from Africa would be herded into a church. Whips cracked and they were ordered to kneel. A priest and his acolytes appeared before the altar and mass was said. Then the Priest followed by the acolytes carrying a basin of holy water, walked slowly down the aisle and with vigorous swings of the Aspergillum scattered the water over the heads of the crowd, chanting in Latin. The whips cracked again, the slaves rose from their knees and emerged into the sunlight, converts to Christianity.[23]

This description may be somewhat biased, but what really took place in general in introducing the slave to Christianity was not anymore effective than this in getting genuine commitment of African slaves to the Christian faith. As Barrett surmises, "Among those Africans herded into the church were several priests and priestesses who we may believe watched carefully every movement of the Catholic priest and who later incorporated every movement in his or her rituals, which were not too different from those they had learned in Africa. Between 1730 and 1790, the African rituals and those of Catholicism merged in what may be called a religious symbiosis in which Vodun copied just enough of the Catholic ritual forms to disguise the real religion of Africa."[24]

Far beyond the revolutionary function of the Petro form of Vodou that played a vital role in the Haitian Revolution of 1791–1804 and more than a mere copying of Catholic beliefs and practices, Vodou is a very complex and dignified religious system with liturgy and rituals revolving around "a pantheon of spirits known as loa or lwa who represent a fusion of African and Creole gods, the spirits of deified ancestors, and syncretized manifestations of Catholic saints."[25] Joseph Murphy describes it as "a dance of spirits: a system of movements, prayers, and songs in veneration of the invisible forces of life."[26] Performed in the elaborately adorned ounfo (temple, also spelled hounfort) and led by oungans (houngans, priests) and mambos (manbos, priestesses) who have undergone extensive initiation rites and training according to their respective spirit's requirement, Vodou ceremonies are devoted to the service of the loa/saints and the community. The poto-mitan or center post ("a vertical link between the sky, earth, and underworld") is the focus point around which ceremonies take place and from which the spirits come from Africa or Ginen to enter into the service. "Most vodou services begin the invocation of the spirits with actions de grace, Catholic prayers led by the pretsavann, the 'bush priest.' God and Catholic saints are honored in French by the recitation of the Lord's Prayer, the 'Hail Mary,' the Credo, and the Confiteor, with appropriate signs of the cross and genuflections. The invocation of the Catholic spirits provides a kind of frame around vodou, a transition from the exterior world of Haiti to the interior world of Ginen....When the Catholic prayers are over, the service moves to Creole and progressively 'heats up.'"[27] Many complex drumming, chanting, rituals, offerings, sacrifices, dances, entrance of the spirits beginning with Legba (who opens the way into the spirit world), spirit possessions, and more, take place in what Murphy says is "an orientation to a historical memory and to a living reality. The memory is of the ancestors and their lands of origin, and of the great gulf of space and time which divides Haitians from them. The memory provides the precedent for all action....Africa becomes the criterion of harmonious and moral action, and authority derives from fidelity to the traditions of Ginen." But at the same time, Ginen comes alive within the ceremony. [28]

Syncretism as an Issue in Caribbean Religion

As we have pointed out, syncretism is present in all of what we may refer to as the Neo-Caribbean religions, especially Afro-Caribbean religions or African-derived religions of the Caribbean. And all religions of the Caribbean are affected by this prevalent phenomenon, either negatively or positively. We want to look at some of the various religious responses to it, as well as some scholarly interpretations and reactions to it that have not been covered in a previous chapter. This was one of the major issues discussed at the ecumenical conference held at Lelydorp, Suriname, in May, 1994, titled Popular Religiosity and Christianity in the Caribbean, sponsored by the Caribbean Conference of Churches in conjunction with the Moravian Theological Seminary and the Roman Catholic Catechetical Centre. There were some interesting challenges to it lifted up and discussed, as well as some positive responses to it and defenses of it at that conference. Dr. Hesdie Zamuel, a Moravian minister and theologian of

Suriname, indicated that the very terms used in the theme of the conference were reflective of bias of the institutional forms of Christianity toward the non-Christian religions. Using "popular religiosity," showed a disrespect for those forms of religion that were found among the lower class people and were not held as legitimate or in high regard by the "official Church leaders." All these forms of religion were syncretistic. Zamuel sees the term "popular religion" as having become synonymous with what was in earlier times called "pagan" or "heathen."[29]

Zamuel asserts the positive view of these religions and their assimilation of other religious aspects. One suggestion he makes is the consideration of popular religions as the form of the religion which is an expression of the people's genuine engagement of the faith rather than its exposition in books and theological exposition unrelated to the life and experience of the people (similar to what has been referred to as liberation theology in Latin America and other Third World countries). In such case, "Spiritual and social life are related to one another, and give fulfillment to one each other. In that way the conception of popular religion can more or less be understood as a technical term for a phenomenon that we can find in almost every religion...[distinguished by the characteristics]: 1. a particular accommodated interpretation, 2. integration of the social and spiritual world, and 3. contextualisation.[30]

Zamuel takes into account former General Secretary of the World Council of Churches W. A. Visser't Hooft's determination of the care and distinction that must be considered in using the word syncretism. This expert Christian theologian asserts that the term must not be used to indicate the "translation of the gospel into culture," nor for the "absorption of the gospel by a culture (as is often done). And he makes a signal acknowledgment that is seldom considered by the average person trying to spread a religion to people of other cultures. It is that "the composition of a religion always takes place in the context of a specific culture."[31] Zamuel resonates with Hooft's quotation from A. Oepke as an expression of his own view that syncretism "has to do with the view, that all religions have the same origin and the same goal" (this view relates to the Hindu mystic Ramakrishna's conception of religion). The quotation from Oepeke states: "Real syncretism is always based on the presupposition that all positive religions are only reflections of a universal original religion...and show therefore only gradual differences."[32]

To support his position, Zamuel uses examples of Christianity itself in its New Testament beginning and its historical development. In his estimation, it was just such a popular religion that developed within a particular cultural setting and had its message spread by proponents from their own cultural presuppositions. As they moved into new societies they found it necessary to make use of ideas and formulation from the mental and physical world of those new societies. He uses the examples of Jesus and Paul from the New Testament and John Hus and Martin Luther from Christian Church history. Zamuel make the point that in order to get clear understanding of the faith introduced to them, converts in a different society and culture have to conceive it in a different way:

> Out of the concrete need and distress of their life, which causes a situation analogous to that of the first believers. It is as if they have a new confrontation with the message and come to an authentic interpretation, and because this interpretation proceeds from the confrontation of the godly message with concrete life, the separation between faith and life, cult and culture, dogma and ethics is abolished. Faith is then formulated anew from the context of one's own existence.[33]

Hans Ucko, who was attending the Caribbean ecumenical conference as Executive Secretary for Christian-Jewish relations, new religious movements, and Marxism in the World Council of Churches, with office in Switzerland, began his essay with an experience he had upon leaving the Seventh Assembly of the World Council of Churches meeting in Canberra, Australia, in 1991, at which I was a delegate and at which syncretism was a pervasive issue the whole 21 days due to the involvement of Aboriginal religious participants in Australia, as well as other indigenous peoples from North and South America, Africa, the South Pacific Islands, South Korea, and other places. Representatives from other world religions were also included, as well, as visitors and observers, including Hindu, Islam, Judaism, Buddhism. The theme of that Assembly was "Come Holy Spirit, Renew the Whole Creation." There had been much positive and negative reaction to the opening address and performance by Dr. Chung Hyun Kyung, a South Korean and Professor of Liberation Theology at Union Theological Seminary in New York. She had involved the Australian Aborigines and other indigenous peoples from around the world dressed in their full native regalia in a moving ceremonial ritual dance and recitation that was inclusive of different traditions. In the ceremony she carried a burning torch and, invoking the spirits of numerous persons throughout the world and in human history who had made sacrifices or been martyred in their quest for justice and liberation: Hagar, Joan of Arc, South African Steve Biko, Black Elk, the spirit of women in the Japanese prostitution army, Martin Luther King, Jr., Malcolm X, the spirit of the victims of Auschwitz; the spirit of earth, air, water, raped, tortured, and exploited, she burned the torch in their honor. Her conclusion was that,

> Without hearing the cries of these spirits we cannot hear the voice of the Holy Spirit...the image of the Holy Spirit comes from the image of **Kwan In**...venerated as the goddess of compassion and wisdom by East Asian women's popular religiosity. She is a bodhisattva, an enlightened being. She can go into nirvana any time she wants to, but refuses to (do so)...until the whole universe becomes enlightened. Perhaps this may also be a feminine image of the Christ.[34]

Hans Ucko was at the airport awaiting his return flight from Canberra when he was talking with "an indignant Greek Orthodox Bishop" regarding Dr. Chung's keynote address, when the Bishop stated, "We are in our history of mission not unfamiliar with the Christianising of Shamanism, but here we witness the shamanising of Christianity. It is perversion of inculturation. It is syncretism." This was typical of some of the negative positions of conservative Christians in regard to syncretism. It is thought of as perversion, corruption, unchristian. The World Council of Churches is considered a liberal wing or the Christian Church that maintains a sense of freedom and openness and stresses the principles of inclusiveness. Ucko asserts that the ecumenical movement has no teaching authority like the Roman Catholic Church, which states, teaches, and enforces church doctrine on its leaders at least. Ucko declares, however, that the position of the W.C.C. is confessional. "While confessing with one voice the Basis of the Council 'the Lord Jesus Christ as God and Saviour according to the Scriptures,' member Churches of the WCC interpret the Basis according to their teachings and bring their differences into the fellowship." Thus issues like syncretism are open to interpretation by each member church, and ultimately by individuals in those churches.[35]

Acknowledging the grappling with the issue from New Testament times to the present, Ucko notes the origin of the term in its negative meaning in 1938 in Tambaram, India as an "illegitimate mingling of different religious elements." But he also makes it clear that syncretism is more or less endemic in Christianity, which "once out of the Jewish context, did link itself early and eagerly to Greek philosophy and inherited the entire religious tradition of the Mediterranean world. Western Christianity is not a stranger to ancient paganism, or to be more precise, expresses the complex of Hebrew thought, Hellenistic Greek ideas, Latin and Celtic elements and modern religions, all more or less converted to Christ."[36]

Looking at the narrowness of conservative Christian viewpoints which deny the validity of any but their own concepts of Christ such as the Orthodox and the Evangelical Christians who want to divorce the Faith entirely from any culture except the ones which have been accepted and transmitted in the West, Ucko makes the case for African and Asian and South American and Caribbean and indigenous cultures who, like Western culture (infused in Christianity), cannot and will not separate religion and culture.[37]

Ucko's conclusion, after a thoroughly persuasive analysis and interpretation of Christianity as it must relate to peoples other than Western Europeans and integrated into their specific contexts and understandings, is that we should

> not remain prisoners of mystifications, that have little or nothing to do with authentic spirituality, of beginning with an assumption of some pristine, inaugural moment already given and fixed, once and for all. We are a product of an ongoing process. Faith is more than repetition or engaging in parrot-like recitation of official past formulas. Faith is a journey, where there is little use for any once-and-for-all narrowing down of the tradition to one original kernel. The existential-historical Jesus has been Jewish teacher and prophet, turning point of all history, philosopher, king of kings, embodiment of the cosmic mind, reason, word of God, perfect human, suffering servant, ascetic monk, mystical bridegroom of the soul, pattern for moral life, poet, liberator of the oppressed, iconoclast and more. This is not an example of confusion and obscurity but a demonstration of the richness of diversity, something we would all agree upon. Is there still space and openness for the manifold expressions of popular religions?[38]

Finally, other voices in objection to syncretism, especially in regard to the use of Catholic saints in African-derived religions, are heard among Africans, African American converts to Yoruba religion and Vodou in the U.S.A., and some modern-day Afro-Caribbean religious participants who no longer see the need to use the Catholic saints as a disguise of the African spirit being worshipped. U.S.African Americans in recent years who have formerly gone to places like Cuba to be initiated into the Orisa religion of Santeria/Lucumí have changed to a stance of preference for initiation into Yoruba religion from Nigeria by traveling to Nigeria for such a purpose or by inviting Yoruba priests to the U.S. to perform such initiation. And African Yoruba and other African religious leaders have embraced the trend as well. This trend appears to have been influenced by Oba Osejiman Adefunmi I (formerly Walter King), who was initiated into the Santeria priesthood in 1959, but who came back to this country and developed a great enthusiasm for the pure Yoruba traditions from the African continent. With this enthusiasm and dedication he underwent a number of changes that eventually led him to establish a Yoruba community in South Carolina, Oyotunji African Village, over which he presides as king and which has grown extensively.[39] Many other African Americans have been influenced by this trend toward the pure African religions. And in the Caribbean a number of persons in Brazilian Candomblé[40] and Trinidadian Shango[41] are expressing the same need and determination to purge their Afro-Caribbean religions of the Catholic religious elements. However, with many religious participants in these religious the connection is not easily broken.

Of course, syncretism is not simply found in Santeria and Vodou but in all the Neo-Caribbean or Afro-Caribbean religions, and in African-derived religions in other parts of the Americas, including Brazil. But these two religions are most expressive of differences in the ways in which it was achieved in the Caribbean. As to Brazilian Candomblé and Trinidadian Shango, we want to look at the manifestations or other issues as they were and are expressed in these religions in particular. And of course, they too may be present in the other religions, but we will show how these two religions best reflect the issues of ethnicity, class, race, and gender.

Candomblé and Issues of Class, Race, Gender, and Ethnicity

Candomblé is an Afro-Brazilian religion developed by slaves in Bahia, Brazil, from West African countries such as Nigeria, Benin, Togo, and Ghana in the early nineteenth century. Although it shares expressions of deity and religious practices in common with Cuban Santeria, Haitian Vodou, and Trinidadian Shango, such as the Yoruba pantheon and syncretism of Catholic beliefs and practices, Candomble has many unique features, especially in its reflection of religio-social, cultural, economic, and political manifestations. First, of course, one must take into account its colonial and post-colonial Portuguese Catholic setting. Robert A. Voeks acknowledges that the "Candomblé lexicon is derived from the Portuguese, Yoruba, Ewe, Ijesha, Kimbundu, and to a lesser extent, Tupi languages."[42] And language is very important in the religion and culture matrix. One thing we notice right away in the names of religious places and functionaries, African gods and goddesses (especially Yoruba or Nago) are the alternate uses or Portuguese, African, and Tupi (indigenous) languages. Workers of magic or witch doctors were referred to in the Portuguese language as feiticeiros, which were from a common tradition among the Portuguese transferred to African shamans and diviners. Terreiro is the Portuguese word used for the temple in Candomblé. And so is the word narcoes for nations or African ethnic groups. Similarly, the word which we used for the Orisha or Oricha become Orixa in this context. Ashe or Ache (the strong Power in the universe) becomes Axe. All the renderings of the Yoruba/Lucumí names of the pantheon of deity are different. They are as follow.

Yoruba Deities

1. Eshu
2. Obatalá
3. Shango
4. Yemoja
5. Oshun
6. Ogun
7. Olodumare
8. Ossain
9. Ochosi

Other gods and goddesses revered in Candomblé derived either from the Yoruba or the Fon are Iansa, Nana, Iroko, and Oxumare. The priests and priestesses are called pai-de-santos or mae-de-santos, respectively (Portuguese). Frequently, the Yoruba terms for these are used—babalorixa and ialorixa.[43]

The name Candomblé refers to the houses of worship and service in which the African religious practices were developed and maintained and still exist today.

Founded by three freed African women, Iya Deta, Iya Kala, and Iya Nasso, the Engenho Velho was the mother of Bahian candombles. It was clearly established by 1830, and some accounts trace its existence to the mid-1700s. To ensure the orthodoxy of this early terreiro (temple), several founding members returned to Nigeria, spent some years in the city of Ketu studying the fundamentals of Yoruba religion, and then returned to take their place at Engenho Velho. Later a fractious dispute over the leadership of the Engenho Velho resulted in the establishment of a second house of worship—the Gantois—another of Bahia's pedigreed terreiros. This was followed by another power struggle and the founding of still another house of Candomble, this by the famous mae-de-santo Aninha, at Axe Opo Afonja. These three candomblés, En-

genho Velho, Gantois, and Axe Opo Afonja, which were founded by women and
which rigidly maintained the ritual and ceremony of the Yoruba, served as models as
well as progenitors for many of the terreiros presently encountered in Bahia, the majority of which are still led by women.[44]

The origin and establishment of these first candomblés leads us to the first crucial social issues reflected in this religion, those of *gender relations* and *ethnic and
cultural continuity.* The primary role of women in establishing the religion, maintaining the cultural link with the African background, and continuing the development of the religion in Bahia is of great significance especially since it goes
against the usual practice of relegating women to lesser or subservient roles
found in African, Afro-Caribbean, and European society in general. Therefore,
taking a look at these gender relations in this Neo-African society is highly
worthwhile and can be quite revealing.

Several different ethnic groups with their respective religious tradition were
merged in the Yoruba religious pattern mainly because the Yoruba peoples were
the largest and their religious pantheon more forceful. But certain ethnic groups
reconstructed their own native traditions within the Yoruba framework. Therefore, one finds a variety of religious types, known as narcoes or nations (similar
to the naciones in Cuba and the nanchons of Haitian Vodou)[45] represented in
Candomblé. Robert Voeks identifies and six nacoes of Candomblé: Candomblé
de Ketu, Candomble de Angola, Candomblé Jeje, Candomblé de Congo, Candomblé de Ijexa, and Candomblé de Caboclo. Each of these maintains their
"lexicon, chants, deities, offerings, sacred plants and animals, and other traditional knowledge linking them" to their original sources. He describes two of
these:

> Adherents to Candomblé de Jeje, for example, which can be traced to the Fon people
> of Dahomey, invoke the *vodun,* their original pantheon—most of which correspond to
> one or another of the Yoruba *orixas.* The Candomble de Caboclo has blended the relig-
> ion of the *orixas* with Amerindian and Catholic beliefs and rituals, such as the manifes-
> tation of indigenous and even foreign entities during possession trance and the use of
> tobacco and alcohol.[46]

Joseph Murphy differs with Robert Voeks regarding the gender realities among
the Candomblés. Voeks states that the heads of the houses of Candomblé may
be a male (pai-de- santo, "father-of-saints") or female (mae-de-santo, "mother-
of-saints), and that there is a general gender division between the nation houses.
"Candomblé de Ketu is generally a matriarchy, with all of the high offices, in-

cluding the priest position, occupied by women. The hierarchies of Candomblé de Angola and Candomblé de Jeje, on the other hand, are generally dominated by men, although elevated stations may be occupied by women."[47] Murphy declares that while the male babalorixas or pai-de-santos may "preside over newer Nago and caboclo [indigenous] houses and dominate the Angolan ones, the established Nago and Jeje candomblés have been controlled by women since their founding," and he cites Landes's study, *The City of Women*, "highlighting the dominance and independence of candomblé women in every aspect of their lives."[48]

Further, Murphy cites the history of the development of Candomblé tracing it back to one woman, Iya Nasso (also mentioned by Voeks as one of three women founders) and her line of descendants, who set the patterns and standards for subsequent development of Candomblé, especially that which is faithful to the Yoruba or Nago traditions. Iya Nasso was a free woman, a priestess, from Ketu in present-day Benin (formerly Dahomey) who came to Bahia around 1830 to establish a religious community. She was influenced by her mother, who had been a slave in Bahia and after winning her freedom returned to Africa and initiated as a priestess. There she encouraged her daughter Iya Nasso and two other priestesses to take up the mission of bringing "the foundation power of the spirits (axe) to the Nago community in diaspora in Bahia. Toward the end of her life Iya Nasso sent her successor Marcelina (her daughter) back to Africa for a seven-year stay to complete her education with African religious teachers." This practice of Africans traveling back and between Africa and Brazil became fairly frequent for both commercial and religious reasons, and it made for "continual renewal of Candomblé ideas and practices." There developed a special concern for remaining faithful to "Nago theology and ritual." Murphy observes that today "every large Nago house of candomblé has sent members to Africa," and the question of purity of Bahian practices is of much concern. And he reports that "the house of Iya Nasso, most commonly called Casa Branca today, became the principal line from which most Nago houses of candomble trace their descent.[49]

The significance of the role of women and the gender relations is further revealed in Murphy's clarification of the leadership importance and transmission, maintenance of control and faithfulness to African Nago traditions. Disputes over the legitimacy of passing on leadership of the houses have led other women to branch out and found new houses. Such was the case with Maria

Julia da Conceicao in the founding of the Ile Iya Omin Axe Iyamasse (also known as Gantois); also Casa Branca priestess Aninha formed a new community called Ile Axe Opo Afonja. Each of these new houses was very successful, their leaders and founders achieving prominence in the society, but they all remained faithful to their original house of Casa Branca. Murphy states, "These three communities—Casa Branca, Gantois, and Opo Afonja—comprise what is often called the candomble elite of Bahia. They are the great houses, known for their unbroken link to Iya Nasso, their fidelity and dialogue with African ceremonial models, and the social prestige of their members." Further, Murphy maintains that "Most of the Nago candomblés of Bahia can trace their origins to one of the priestesses of Casa Branca, Gantois, or Opo Afonja," whether or not all the large numbers of houses can verify such descendency.[50]

In discussing the organization of the candomble, Murphy clarifies gender relations in leadership and participation. He found that the iyalorixa (mother of the spirit) is more common than the babalorixa (father of the spirits). He asserts that, "The closer a candomble community comes to the African standards of purity set by the elite houses, the more women are found in leadership positions." These dominant and independent women are reported by Ruth Landes to be "loath to marry and accept the legal control of men over them. Even if they were married they were always known by their affiliation with their spirits and never by that with their husbands." Bahian journalist and ethnographer Edison Carneiro is said to have told Landes: "It is almost as difficult for a man to become great in candomblé as it is for him to have a baby. And for the same reason: it is believed to be against his nature." They are thought to have "hot blood" and therefore possess neither "the patience to submit to the discipline of candomblé, nor the control of their passions necessary to incarnate the spirits." Older women who have passed beyond the youthful stage of passions are the ones who "direct candomblé and pass on the purity of the worship to new initiates." Men have roles as advisors (called ogans, meaning literally, masters), who see to the material welfare of the community. Such a board of advisors today are said to be composed of "prominent citizens of Bahia, professionals and municipal and state politicians who, for a variety of motives, wish to be associated with a candomblé. Some ogans take on "ritual roles as directors of the drummers at candomblé ceremonies or preside over the ritual slaughter of animals at feasts."[51]

The achievement of these women in Candomblé is some remarkable considering their origins in patriarchal traditions of Africa, Europe, and the Caribbean. Comparatively, although women priestesses are numerous in Cuban Santeria and Haitian Vodun, two other religions using the Yoruba pantheon and ritual patterns, women are not in controlling positions as they are found to be in Candomblé. In fact, in Cuban Santeria/Lucumí religion as well as in other Afro-Cuban religions on the island, women find themselves to be victims of gender discrimination and subjection to male dominance. Maria Margarita Castro Flores states, "The presence of factors tending to marginalize women at the core of religious beliefs in today's Cuba reflects the influence of the different religious systems that were brought together as a result of colonization." The two main religious currents that influenced the gender problems, she says, are "sui generic Catholicism professed by the European colonizers, plagued with discrimination against women…" and varieties of African religious groups that retained values that subordinated women in their religious forms developed on the island such as Regla de Ocha or Santeria, Regla Conga or Palo Monte, and the male Abakua secret societies.[52] Mercy Amba Oduyoye, a seminary professor and author, a native Ghanian married to a Nigerian and therefore has significant experiences in the cultures and religions of both countries, speaks to the gender issues in the religion and society of both, confirming what Flores says. Her experience is that in Africa, "women are rarely involved in the rituals of Traditional Religion. Among the Zulu no women are involved in magic or ritual generally, and they seldom become war doctors, rain makers, or other types of magicians, but a large majority of the possessed are women. We find the same phenomenon in West Africa: most mediums are women and spirit possession is generally found among female akomfo (mediums) in Akan traditional worship."[53] Oduyoye also asserts that colonization did not create patriarchy in Africa, it only strengthened it.[54]

Maria Flores reinforces this view as experienced in the Caribbean. She states: "The discriminatory treatment of that which is feminine in aspects of African culture was reinforced in the Caribbean by the conqueror's attitude to women—particularly African women, given the conqueror's Eurocentric racism and contempt for other peoples."[55] Flores summarizes by pointing out how the African woman received double "dehumanizing treatment from both the colonizer and the colonized. The African woman was the object of machista reaffirmation, the result of the imposition of a series of patriarchal regimes. The feminine was subordinated not only to the colonizer, but also to the colonized male. The abused woman became the carrier of racial, cultural, and religious mestizaje (mixing)."[56] Flores analyzes the comparative subjugation of women in all the Afro-Cuban religions, but one interesting phenomenon contrasts with Brazilian Candomble. That is the role of the Ifa divination priest, the babalao ("father of secrets"), the high priest of the religion who possesses the highest and deepest knowledge of the divine. Women cannot practice Ifa divination in Santeria, nor can they serve as babalao in Nigeria, with one exception, which is when the position cannot be passed on to the son of a babalao who has passed away. The eldest daughter then can succeed the father. Flores takes note of the contrasting situation of women in Candomble, "where the female mae-de-santo is the center of the religion and constitutes its maximum persona."[57] Voeks reveals that women, as well as men, priests practice the highest form of divination in Candomble, by means of the jogo de buzios, the tossing of the sixteen cowrie shells, and the use of odus or Yoruba myths suggested from shell formations to determine solutions to various problems of clients.[58] There is apparently no gender discrimination here.

Resistance to *racism* and cultural hegemony was and still is very strong among the societies in Bahia as they have struggled to maintain their culture, religion, and dignity as a people. And they possess a certain uniqueness in this area of analysis as well when compared to other Neo-Caribbean societies. **Class** is another issue that figures into the mix when we look at their assertive efforts in this capacity. The responses of Brazilian African societies in Bahia to the brutalizing and dehumanizing conditions of slavery are unique. Like African slaves in other parts of the Caribbean such as Cuba, Haiti, Trinidad, Jamaica, they strongly resisted slavery and instigated many rebellions, and as a result were restricted by laws forbidding their traditional religious and cultural practices. And in their resistance they were not able to stage a full fledge revolution as in Haiti to throw off the shackles of slavery and colonialism, but they accomplished a unique reality in their particular setting not duplicated in any other Caribbean area. Murphy rightly determines that they were able to create a "cultural homogeneity which would distinguish Bahia" as the preeminent place of "the African diaspora of the nineteenth century."[59] Their guarantee of their own human dignity and survival as a people in their own right was to create or recreate their peoplehood in this new world in contradistinction to the Portuguese Catholic world around them that was designed on destroying their humanity and recreating them in their captors' image. Their response to racism was to establish their own dignity and worth in stark denial of it and its control over their minds.

Voeks's interpretation is particularly appealing in accuracy. Acknowledging some material desires of the Africans to "reassemble African religious systems in Brazil," he says,

> They drew much of their inspiration from the specific inability of the Catholic faith to address the primary concerns of its people. Because these religious assaults challenged Catholicism—the spiritual cornerstone of Catholic civilization, underpinning the economic and social interests of the dominant class—these fronts of resistance were particularly insidious and revolutionary. Structured similarities and levels of syncretism not withstanding, the Yoruba spiritual worldview was diametrically opposed to its Catholic counterpart in ways that must have attracted both slave and free blacks during the course of Brazilian history, and that today draw adherents from all social and racial backgrounds.[60]

The contrast he surmises was between "a European folk religion that justified the earthly status quo through eventual salvation" and offered a pie-in-the-sky or future life reward, and put forward a "distant and unknowable god," and an "African religion that empowered its members, that sought to level the social and economic playing field through direct action during this life, and allowed its members to dance with deities." What was offered by Candomblé, he says, were "solutions to the problems of everyday life—health, love, jealousy, and finances," those issues "most relevant to the African population."[61]

Murphy saw their Bahian cultural and religious recreations as being motivated by a strong sense of *freedom*, another crucial issue in Afro-Caribbean religions in general. He states: "The 'memory' of freedom was and continues to be powerfully made present in candomblé, and the houses offer an alternative to the values of white society and the *racism* [my emphasis] that so frequently underlies them." American anthropologist Mikelle Omari writes: "Candomblé Nago offers Afro-Bahians a channel through which they may gain a significant measure of self-esteem, social solidarity, prestige, and social mobility in a system which celebrates African values, behavior and skin color."[62]

In contrast with Haitian Vodun, Murphy stresses the urban setting in which Candomblé was developed and a kind of class distinction existing between the two religions. He states: "Afro-Brazilian life in Bahia offered many advantages for the development of great centers of African religious learning. Compared with the Creole peasantry of mostly rural Haiti, Afro-Bahian urban life allowed for relative freedom of movement, independent patrons who could endow the centers, and sufficient wealth and mobility to sponsor teachers and students to cross the Atlantic."[63] With intellectuals attracted to the candomblé and motivated to write about them, with the establishment of a line of descent of candomblés, Murphy sees a level of institutionalization and permanence as having been achieved.

In respect to the issue of *class* distinction, Voeks describes the social hierarchy that characterized the inner structures and operations of the candomblés, as well as the rather classy and prosperous terreiros in contrast to poorer houses. Yet he says Candomblé is not a religion of celebrities but of common folk. Despite the fact that a few temples and famous priests get much media attention, the rank and file are poor and servant class people. "It is a mutually supportive environment, a parallel society where people of color give respect and expect it in return." They walk with heads high, however, confident of the levels of their positions in the candomblé, humble but not degraded. "The economic division that governs much of Brazilian society loses its meaning as you enter the terreiro. To cross the frontier of a house of Candomblé, whether small and nondescript or rich and illustrious, is to exit the European world and enter a space that is ideologically and culturally African."[64]

Trinidadian Shango and Issues of Class, Race, Gender, and Ethnicity

Pearl Eintou Springer, Director of the National Heritage Library in Trinidad, cultural activist, poet, writer, dramatist, and a Shango or Orisa priestess, elaborates on the Orisa (Shango) religion in Trinidad and Tobago.[65] In her own person and life experiences she represents the mixtures and cultural and religious interactions in Trinidad. She has strong Catholic roots and is descended from a Congolese, son of a slave on a St. Vincent plantation, her paternal grandfather. Her mother's people were a mixture of African and Black Carib and Venezuelan Amerindian heritage. However, she switched from the Roman Catholic religion during the wave of nationalism that swept the country in 1956 undermining the power of the Roman Catholic Church, and she initiated into the Orisa religion after the Black Power Movement of the 1970's. After she and many others realized that the Black Power Movement failed because it did not root itself in the spiritual needs of the African society, they turned to traditional African religion as an act of political and ideological self-expression.[66]

Dale Bisnauth parallels Trinidadian Shango (Orisa) with Haitian Vodou even though Vodou ideas are Dahomean in origin and Shango is of Yoruba derivation. He says it is due to remarkable similarities in their beliefs and their similar French influences from Catholicism. He suggests that the Obeah practices by the slaves in this once Spanish colony of Trinidad merged with religious practices brought by the slaves of French Catholic colonists who migrated to the island from St. Vincent and Grenada between 1783 and 1797, as well as from the French islands of Guadeloupe and Martinique.[67] Pearl Springer shows some of the correspondences of Orisa spirits with Catholic saints[68]:

Orisa	*Catholic Saints*
Ogun	St. Michael
Osayin	St. Francis
Erinle	St. Jonas
Erunmila	St. Anthony
Shango	St. John of the Cross
Yemoja	St. Ann
Obatala	Jesus Christ
Oshun	St. Philomen
Ibeji and Ibeja	Peter and Paul

Bisnauth includes Ogun as corresponding to St. Michael. He points out that ceremonies are held at cult centers with buildings designated as the palais, the chapelle, and the house of the priestess (the amombah). The altar is adorned similar to that of a Vodou altar. The ceremony is an annual four-day service with drumming, dancing, prayers, sacrifices, and both Catholic and African elements used.[69] Springer calls the ceremony an Ebo (commonly called feast), a four and a half to five-day ceremony beginning Sunday night and ending Friday morning. She says there are over 50 palais or Orisa yards in Trinidad and Tobago.[70]

The mixed and extensive patronage Springer describes of the religion is astonishing.

It is a religion to which every day, three hundred and sixty five (365) days of the year, people of all races, all colours, all classes, make their way; the declared devotees and initiates as well as the surreptitious needy the closet devotees. They come for exorcisms, for medication, for divination, for help in financial matters to get their cars blessed…they come, in a never ending stream; the Hindu pundits, the holder of Kali Pujas, the French Creole business men, the bank clerk wanting to trap a man into marriage. They all come. They come to make dry or blood offerings, they come to learn about the religion, they come to do research. And they come out of curiosity. Few bother to try to understand the mysteries of the religion. Few of the largely/African community of devotees try to probe its depths and harness its powers for the good of the race. Many in fact accept the social stigma attached to their religion as an extension of the social stigma attached to their Blackness.[71]

Springer decries the social stigma, ethnocentrism, racism, and other prejudices as responses to this religion as its followers. She says that the religion of Orisa remains invisible in Trinidad and Tobago despite its strong presence. There has been no mention of it in the census of the islands despite the many books, research papers, and other studies published internationally about the religion.[72]

Springer shows enthusiasm and excitement going on in Trinidad and Tobago in the context of *race* and *ethnicity*. This has to do with what is developing between Afro-Trinidadians and Indo-Trinidadians. "It is becoming more and more a question of interest for Black leaders, especially with the emergence of Hindu organisations which would naturally support East Indian bids for political power. The emergence of the Sanatan Dharma Maha Sabha as a religious organisation for Hindus has been a strong source of selfhood and for legitimisation of Indian culture, religion and language for all Indians: Hindu or non-Hindu; Christian or non-Christian.[73]

The fact that the Sanatan Dharma Maha Sabha controls more than forty primary schools and two or three high schools provides buffer both to the Eurocentric media and the excesses of creole culture, she says. She says that for "the majority of Africans the difference between creole culture and African culture is still not clearly recognised." The Indian demand for recognition is making an impression on the middle class and educated Africans to "listen to their ideologues, who have made a clear distinction between creole and African culture." The result is a swelling of the ranks of the African-derived religions. She says, "To get the mind of the diaspora negro to think African is like getting blood out of a stone." Springer is excited about incorporation of Orisa organizations by Acts of Parliament: Egbe Orisa Ile Wa (1981) and ten years later, Opa Orisa. She states, "The annual August Oshun festival of Opa Orisa draws hundreds of people." Other exciting things are happening. Rivalries between ethnic groups are being overcome. In governmental situations such as governing boards, ethnic leaders are learning to work together and cooperate for the good of all. She makes the point that sharing is taking place culturally, religiously, and politically:

> I do not think it was ever believed possible that Mr. Maharaj and myself could sit in the same place without bloodshed. These meetings [of Boards] have been happening for the past two years. The last I heard Mr. Maharaj was reading a book on the Orisa religion. I spoke recently at a Yagna at the Maha Sabha Headquarters. Ravi-Ji, High Priest, of the Kendra has come respectfully to Egbe Orisa Ile Wa. I walk with respect in the Kendra. I can count on Ravi-Ji's support in matters which affect my sovereignty as a human being. There is a growing recognition among Hindu and Orisa activists that each other is not the enemy; that we need to share this land, fertilised by the blood and sweat of our ancestors. The ancient spirits, African and Indian are willing.[74]

As to the roles of women in Orisa, Pearl Springer is a good example of the strong presence of women and their leadership capacities. The famous Iyalorisa Melvina Rodney of Trinidad and Tobago is another.[75] As to class discrimination, that is a constant battle of Orisa, Hindu, Islam and other religious groups for recognition and equal participation in the society.

Chapter Five

Crucial Issues in Obeah and Rastafari

Obeah and Rastafari are quite different in their histories, conceptions, and practices; the former being a far more ancient religious practice and the latter being a relatively recent religious phenomenon. The two have more in common, however, than is immediately apparent. For one thing, even though they are not confined to the island of Jamaica, they both have a strong association with the area. They have strong roots there, and even though Rasta is fairly recent in its origin, the enslaved African peoples from whom these two religious realities stem, wherever they may be associated in the Caribbean, Latin American, or other part of the world today, are those imported from the Gold Coast (Ghana) of West Africa. While some of the slaves that were brought to Jamaica were also from other areas such as the Congo, Madagascar, and so forth, the largest concentrations were the Ashanti, the Akan, the Twi, and the Fanti peoples who were assembled in an area called Koromantyn or Koromantee in Ghana, which is near the Cape Coast, and shipped from there to the New World.[1] Karla Gottlieb summarizes the characteristics of the Koromantyns as having been "renowned as fierce and ferocious fighters with a penchant for resistance, survival, and freedom. From 1655 to the 1830s, the Koromantees led most all slave rebellions in Jamaica."[2]

Obeah, Myalism, Shango of Trinidad, Revivalism, the Spiritual Baptists, and the Shouter Baptists have some interesting connections in Jamaica and Trinidad and other places in the Caribbean and South America. And Rastafari has certain links to some of these traditions, as will be shown later. In short, Obeah and Myal derive directly from the Koromantyns, the former belonging to the African sorcerer tradition (the obayifo) and the latter belonging to the healing tradition involving the regular Ashanti priest (the okomfo). Barrett notes that "both the medicine man and the sorcerer came to the New World on the slave ships—a blessing to the Africans and a curse to the plantation."[3] Barrett briefly distinguishes the two African survivals. "Obeah is the name for the type of witchcraft practiced in Jamaica. This type of witchcraft was found wherever the

Ashanti and the Fanti tribes became dominant and thus is mentioned in relation to many other English-speaking islands. Myalism is the type of possession which was the opposite of obeahism and it was the state of spirit possession in which obeah was discovered [through a revelation]."[4]

For reasons we will see, sources show that Obeah and Myal merged in certain areas. Trinidadian Shango developed from obeah/myal practices combining with Yoruba religious practices; and Revivalism was a result of the Africanization of Baptist or evangelical Christianity, a phenomenon that also transferred to some extent to the Spiritual Baptists and Shouter Baptists.[5] Rastafari is an African-derived religion which evolved from Revivalism and other African combinations.[6]

Crucial Issues of Freedom and Resistance to Oppression, Racisim, Ethnicity, and Gender Relations in Obeah/Myal

Elizabeth Nunez (formerly Nunez-Harrell), a Trinidadian-American professor and novelist, depicts realistically the issues of race, ethnicity, efforts for freedom and resistance to oppression, as well as class and gender relations in her literary creations as they have existed and still exist in Trinidad and other Caribbean islands. She also shows the role of Obeah as it functions and is reflected in the religious, social, and political lives of the diverse mixtures of peoples in these areas. Two of her novels in particular, *Beyond the Limbo Silence* (Seattle, Wash.: Seal Press, 1998) and *When Rocks Dance* (New York: Putnam, 1986), present very rich circumstances and incidents revealing the mixture and interactions of ethnic, racial, social class, and religious groups and their intermingling and responses to one another: the English, the East Indians, the Africans, the Creoles, the mulattoes, the poor, the rich, the middle class, the men, the women. And in both of these novels Obeah plays a key role in various aspects and stages of the plots and in the ultimate resolution to the dilemmas. The functions of Obeah and the uses of it by participants, as well as the perceptions of it by different persons, reveal much about the religious practice and its evolutionary status from its inception during the time of slavery and afterward.

Although Obeah appeals to all religious and ethnic groups, there are varying conceptions of its meaning throughout the islands of the West Indies, both negative and positive. Karla Frye gives a good summary definition drawn from

Nunez-Harrell's When Rocks Dance, which challenges widespread negative view of it and places it in the "context of resistant cultural and religious practice."

> Obeah is a belief system divided into two broad categories. The first involves the casting of spells for various purposes, both good and evil; protecting oneself, property, family, or loved ones; harming real or perceived enemies; and bringing fortune in love, employment, personal or business pursuits. The second involves healing through the application of knowledge of herbal and animal medicinal properties. Obeah, thus conceived, is not a religion as such but a system of beliefs grounded in spirituality and in acknowledgment of the supernatural and involving aspects of witchcraft, sorcery, magic, spells, and healing. In Trinidad it is strongly tied to Roman Catholicism. West Africa derived religions such a Shango and Rada [Vodou], African-influenced Protestantism, and to a lesser degree, Amerindian and East Indian spirituality. Hence…it would not be contradictory for a character to be a devout Catholic and still consult an Obeah practitioner, or for the English ruling class to uphold Protestantism and secretly seek out the Obeah-woman in dire need.[7]

In the novel *Beyond the Limbo Silence*, Elizabeth Nunez depicts the Trinidadian and other Caribbean perspectives of three young Caribbean women who are the only minority students in a Catholic college in rural Wisconsin. The main character is Sarah Edgehill from Trinidad, the other two students are Courtney from St. Lucia, and Angela from British Guiana. The focus of Obeah is brought in by way of Courtney, who secretly is a Vodou priestess who practices Obeah secretly in her room, as well. A number of crucial religious and cultural issues come out in interesting ways in the interactions of these women with one another, with the white students and the leaders at the college, and with others they meet, especially with Sam who involves Courtney and Sarah psychologically and sympathetically in the intricate and turbulent developments in the Civil Rights/Black Power Movement in the U.S.A.

It is very interesting and unique the way Elizabeth Nunez in this fictional account depicts the issues and human problems and encounters in the United States during a critical period in our history through the experiences and insights of this young Trinidadian heroine coming to self-realization amid the cultural, social, religious, and political encounters and turbulence of the times. Some of the same themes and issues emerge in Nunez's main character, Sara Edgehill's, story that we find in Marta Moreno Vega's life experiences. We are faced with the same time period of the Civil Rights Movement in the United States, a time of consciousness-raising struggle for identity. We have the similar social, cultural, racial, and religious interactions and encounters in both contexts, although the political struggle of the situation is much stronger in the novel than in the real life story of Vega. The racial conflicts and struggles are brought more directly into the story of the characters in the novel and have a direct impact on the romantic relationship between Sara and Sam, an educated, well-informed, conscientious, committed Black social activist. There are also in the novel the white liberals and conservatives, represented by Sister Agnes at the College of the Sacred Heart and the neighboring O'Briens, and the interactions with Black activists such as Sam Maxwell, and the real live issues of the time are starkly depicted and discussed at length in the characters' lives and interactions. The historical occurrences such as the assassination of John F. Kennedy, the civil rights murders in such places as Mississippi and Alabama, and other places, and the conflicts in the freedom-fighting methods and philosophies of Martin Luther King, Jr., and Malcolm X are main features of the novel's plot and intertwined with the development of the characters, both major and minor.

Also the ethnic and religious differences and conflicts between Caribbean nationals such as Sara Edgehill from Trinidad, Angela Baboolalsingh from British Guiana, and Courtney Adams from St. Lucia (all of whom are token ethnic recruits for the integration of the College), and the religio-cultural and socio-political conflicts and differences between U.S. Blacks and Blacks from the Caribbean (symbolized in Sara, Sam, and Courtney's stories) are interwoven within the plot of the story and directly affect the personal and social quests of Sara and her friend Sam, as well as the lives of all the other characters. Some of these realities figure to some extent in Vega's life story, such are her clash with U.S. Blacks in New York City, and the clashes between Puerto Rican and Cuban Santeria and other religious groups there. What motivated Marta Moreno Vega in the quest for her cultural roots and religious meaning is also similar to what motivated Sara Edgehill to do the same. They were historically right in the middle of a period of time when the search for cultural and religious identity was necessary for sensitive and conscientious individuals. And they were both raised in family circumstances where the traditional religious practices of their families were kept secret from them, camouflaged by overt adherence to the Catholic religion. And the quests of both of these women in finding their real cultural and religious identities, both of which was Yoruba, led to healing and wholeness for both themselves and others.

Sara Edgehill was raised in what was implicated as a "limbo silence" because of the many secrets withheld from her in her family situation, including
her family members' secret religious practices. When she arrived at the College
of the Sacred Heart in Oshkosh, Wisconsin, she had very little conception of
her true identity. It was in this setting in the consciousness-raising time of the
1960's that she gradually came to an awakening to complete self-awareness, personally, culturally, religious, socially, and politically. And it was through her interactions with several persons that led her to such awareness: Courtney,
Angela, Sister Agnes, and Sam, among others.

In summary of her interactions with these persons, Courtney and Angela
were the other two West Indian students brought in deliberately to integrate
this girls' college. Psychologically, they were at opposite ends of the social consciousness mentality. Courtney was a Vodou priestess, who veiled her identity
and secretly practiced her rituals in her room but strongly embraced her African
cultural heritage, as well as identified politically with the African American
struggles in the U.S. Angela was of mixed heritage, primarily East Indian, and
her social stance was assimilation in the dominant society. She appeared to rid
herself of her cultural heritage and blend in with the other girls at the school.
Both Courtney and Angela affected Sara strongly, as she tried to find her place
in this college environment. Realizing the differences between herself and Angela, both her East Indian background and her easy forgetfulness of her heritage, Sara drew closer psychologically to Courtney, with whom she shared
African ancestry who had lived the common experience of being enslaved in
the Caribbean, of being "chattel, commodities to be used and then traded or
put out to pasture. Angela's ancestors came as indentured laborers." The way
she saw it was that there was "no slight difference in countries where the people
had learned to mimic the intricacies of the British class structure. Angela's people had been treated as human beings—men and women looking for work, for a
way to feed their families."[8]

All three girls responded differently to Sister Agnes, the Dean of Students'
patronizing attitude toward them, as well as to the girlish abandon, naïvete and
racial arrogance of the white girls in the school. While Angela seemed to be able
to overlook these girls' "guileless ignorance [concerning the West Indian background and culture of the three young women], their assumption of superiority,
their patronizing generosity," Courtney and Sara could not. In fact, Sara found
herself envying Angela for the ease with which she had freed herself of the bag-

gage she herself carried: her self-consciousness, her memory burdened with histories of slavery, exploitation, colonialism, deprivation—"minor triumphs, also, to be sure, but always achieved through struggle and effort."[9]

It was Sam Maxwell and Courtney Adams who were instrumental in Sara's eventual transformation. Black Civil Rights activist and fierce freedom-fighter, Sam exposed Sara to the stark realities of racism and political unrest in the United States, filled her ears with terror of Mississippi, Georgia, Arkansas, and Alabama. At the O'Briens' she heard "Sam speak of bombs in a church in Birmingham, Alabama, hurtling bricks and slabs of concrete on four little girls. Four little girls crushed to death…. Bombs setting fire to a policeman's brains, unleashing such hatred that guns exploded and two little boys lay bleeding, dying on the street."[10] She says further, "He wrote about the bloody beatings on the streets of Selma and Birmingham. He told me about the blinding torture of tear gas that burned the insides of eyes like lye poured on a fresh wound. About the snarling dogs whipped into vicious frenzy by officers of the law, who chafed at their own bits with their hatred of black people."[11]

Sara fell in love with Sam and wanted to identify with the causes for which he fought, but their relationship was complicated by the cultural differences between African-Caribbean and African American experiences. They encountered increasing complications and thought barriers as Sara found herself trying to understand the situations in the U.S. and see the common link between the two racial/cultural realities in the face of Sam's blindness to the Caribbean situation and his romanticizing of his own people's struggles on this side of the geographical picture. He insisted that Sara could never understand the predicament and identify with the struggles. He made Sara feel guilty for being at the Northern white college in a kind of protected haven in the midst of his people's troublesome existence. Their love continued in spite of the barriers and problems, and Sara became pregnant with his child. She refused to tell Sam of her pregnancy for fear it would alienate him further or complicate their relationship even more so, as he by this time was deeply involved in the Mississippi Freedom struggles of 1964, in which three civil rights student workers were missing and presumed dead.[12] He was so engulfed by that situation and the search for these students that Sara saw no need to burden him further by her pregnancy.

Nevertheless, Courtney urged her to see that something had to be done for her situation, and she provided the solution. By her own medicinal ritual practices Courtney performed an abortion on Sara, and in this one summer Sara grew up in a hurry as she faced the realities of her predicament, culturally, politically, socially, and religiously. Here Courtney and Sam played complementary roles. Courtney informed Sara that she could now help Sam in his political struggles by use of Obeah, that praying to the spirit of her unborn child, whom Courtney saw as having returned to the realm of the ancestors and was thus able to assist humans as any other ancestor could. And Courtney interpreted positive actions in Sam's favor and in favor of the movement as the aid of the unborn child's spirit.[13] "The spirits connect me and Sam and Mississippi and all black people in America" are the words of Courtney that sent Sara into a deeper quest for her spiritual roots.

When Sam returned for a visit dressed in African garb, embracing his African heritage, Sara admitted to him her pregnancy and abortion. To her amazement, Sam was in agreement with what had taken place and her rationale for carrying out the abortion. Courtney spoke with Sam about the unborn child's spirit help, but even though he respected her religious traditions, he could not see how such an act would be useful in a political and military situation.[14] Caught in between Sam's lack of understanding of how she could relate to his and his people's world and Courtney's pressing her to submerge herself in her own self-knowledge and self-love, Sara found herself surrendering and going through the darkness and the silence to the light of self-realization.[15] Faced with Sam's distorted view of Caribbean Blacks as living in places with "blue sea and bright sunshine, green grass and happy people," Sara felt she had to show her own awakening to common links between their two worlds, to which he had been blinded. She had overcome her own distorted view of America as a "fairy tale world without troubles, a world of big cars, huge mansions, loads of money, and she didn't hesitate to inform him: "You have no monopoly on suffering or struggling. Did you think black people were always in Trinidad? We came in chains like you. Slavery was the same. There weren't two kinds." Speaking to his suggestion of the difference of Jim Crow and the experience of oppression in the Caribbean, she asserted that colonialism and Jim Crow "may be different ways of making people believe they are nobody, but they both hurt the same way....You think there is only one way to suffer and one way to fight. You think going to Mississippi is the only way for you to fight, but there are better ways if you want to win."[16]

After her final tryst with Sam, Sara resolved to welcome the dark and the silence, the spirits of her past without fear or rejection, live her whole reality, embrace her whole self, take out from its hiding place the bag of herbs blessed by the Obeah man and secretly given to her by her mother before she left Trinidad. Assisted by Courtney, she underwent the ritual in which she exposed herself to all the aspects of her past, the natural environment of Africa as she could envision it in the waters of her bathtub in her room at the college and in Courtney's room in a Vodou ritual and sacrifice, in which Yoruba claimed her. She declared:

> A blast of wind slammed into the center of my back and pitched me forward over the hen. My head crashed to the floor. The room spun around me: a million circles swallowed into a vortex at its center, faster and faster until nothing was left, no movement, no sound, no color, no light. I felt her then, My little Yoruba. I felt her when she entered my soul through my heart. My blood poured hot through every vein in my body when she came into me. My breath stayed still.[17]

Thus, Sara finds complete healing at last after a long winding journey through various encounters, religious and social, and in a context of racial and political unrest in which there is a fight for freedom and justice. And she is able to see and understand the total picture through integrating her own past, culture, and perspective within a diverse setting.

While *Beyond the Limbo Silence* does a good job of depicting the social and political situations, and many of the issues of the Trinidadian and other Caribbean places from the standpoint of the consciousness and flashbacks of the characters, it is limited in that it does this from a distance, which has its value too. *When Rocks Dance*, on the other hand, is set right in the midst of the Trinidadian world with all its complexities of personal, family, societal, religious, cultural, and political issues. And the time period is decades earlier, near the end of the 19th century and the beginning of the 20th. It is a few decades after the Emancipation of slaves in 1838. Marina Heathrow, the heroine, is a biracial character, the daughter of an African woman, Emilia, and her English lover/keeper, Hrothgar. Karla Frye sums up the socio-economic cultural complexity of the setting. Marina's quest for landownership and the power it represents "unfolds against a backdrop that seeks to connect all the island's people of color."

> Nunez-Harrell sets the plights of the Amerindians, who have been forced off the island, and of the East Indians—imported to work in place of the emancipated slaves—who form an attachment to the land as settlers, against the domination of the British, who assume a "rightful legacy" to ownership of the land and domination over its in-

habitants. As an actual symbol of material wealth and standing, landownership serves in the novel as a tangible text onto which is inscribed the meaning and value of power in the lives of the various groups, thus illuminating the complex relationships of the colonizer to the colonized and the colonized to each other.[18]

In the novel Obeah represents the African religious and cultural traditions. And it is depicted as interacting strongly in comparison and contrast to other cultural and social realities. It has strong influence on Emilia, who accepts its force and power in her life, even though she holds on to both her Catholicism and her Obeah, as is typical of most of the Africans on the island, who seem to perceive of Obeah as balancing or complementing the "power of Christianity and the role of the dominant, hierarchical church and the society it reflects in the lives of the black masses." Frye sees Nunez Harrell as illuminating through religion the "distance as well as the connections between the dominant colonial culture on the island and those who would be dominated," as well as questioning the "dominance of Catholicism and Anglicanism in the lives of their adherents" Also noted is the novel's expression of the "symbiotic relationship between Catholicism and Obeah," as it unveils the complex social relationships of the island. Emilia, for instance, uses Obeah to sustain her in her relationships with her white lovers, first Hrothgar and then Telser.[19]

Amid the racial and social prejudices and cultural clashes between the different groups: Black and White, East Indian and Black, male and female, parents and children, Obeah competed with the other religions for validity in the lives of the people. "For Alma, the village Obeah-woman, Obeah was foremost, with the Roman Catholic Church a safety net." She too mixed the practices of the two religious realities. She read the Bible, praised the Lord, and placed Obeah medicine in Marina's closet at her mother Emilia's request. "For Emilia, the pull of Obeah was strong, and even though she remained with Telser, her second lover, and professed Catholicism 'she had not deserted her African ancestors....She was faithful to Obeah.'" "For Marina's mother-in-law, Virginia, ensconced in both the Anglican Church from childhood and the Roman Catholic Church through her marriage to a Portuguese ex-priest, Obeah was frightening and enduced doubts." Of pure African ancestry, she had been adopted by an English couple and raised "white," which she embraced seriously until her "epiphany at the end of the novel." Marina had to struggle with "understanding the juxtaposition of Obeah outside and inside her life."[20]

In a final crisis, the resolution of the plot of this complex but appealing work of art comes full circle in revealing the powers of Obeah in the lives of the characters. Frye asserts: "Near the end of the novel, when Marina is fighting for her life during childbirth, she is surrounded by Virginia, Emilia, Alma, Victoria, the midwife, and the English doctor, Glentower. At one point, Virginia, sitting by Marina's bedside, realizes that a large shadow looms behind her. She 'was not afraid. She had an uncanny feeling that the person was a sort of protective shield between Marina and her and the outside world....The woman did not surprise her. She was oddly familiar (338).'"[21]

Unity and harmony, reconciliation, release from previous inhibitions, unselfishness, and personal and social realism tend to pervade the setting and affect all characters involved. It is a spiritual experience for all, steeped in the world of Obeah, reinforcing "the importance of its cultural heritage" and joining "Virginia and Marina with each other within its realm. Antonio too is both repulsed by and drawn to Marina's reputed spirits. Just as Marina entered the marriage to acquire land, Antonio, though attracted by beauty, looked to her (as his fourth wife) to 'save' him from the curse of his father, who was rumored to have killed his first three wives—all in childbirth."[22]

Each person's story or journey differs, but the journeys end pretty much in a more or less smooth transition to a sense of spiritual peace, and even healing.

> Emilia used Obeah to give Marina life and to protect her. At the same time she attempts to shield Marina from its full effects. Similarly, Virginia has Steeped Antonio in Catholicism and attempts to use it as a tool of control. Both mothers have succeeded in creating confusion in the minds of their children regarding religion and the spiritual world. In the end, both Marina and Antonio resort to a belief in Obeah to save Marina and the lives of her babies. During Marina's difficult labor, Antonio visits Alma and the Roman Catholic Church....Each of the characters' lives is marked by the type of personal, yet connected cultural journey resulting in the construction of identities affected by the experience of a particular place in time. By the end of the narrative, both Marina and Virginia have reluctantly come to accept the certainty of the power of Obeah.[23]

The extended literary portrayals of Obeah practices and involvements in the society have been portrayed prominently in the novels. And women are a strong presence in Obeah. But men and women are both practitioners in the religious tradition. They may be called Obeah-man or Obeah-woman or Myal man or woman. "Other appellations across the Caribbean region include Bush man or Bush doctor in the Bahamas, Wanga man in Trinidad, the Scientist in Grenada, Professor, Madame, Pundit, Maraj, and work-man in Guyana. Practitioners are believed to be born with special powers—to be 'born with the gift'—normally revealed to them through visions or dreams in late childhood or early adolescence."[24] Another important fact that Olmos and Paravisini point out about Obeah is that it is not communal like Vodun or Santeria or Candomble, but individual. The only time it achieves communal proportions is when it is combined with Myal or one of the other traditions like Trinidadian Orisha: "there are no group rituals, dancing, drum playing or singing connected to Obeah practice, except in the case of Myal in Jamaica."[25]

Crucial Issues in Rastafari: Religious, Social, Political, Racial, Gender Relations

The discussions of Obeah, Myal, Revival Zion, Native Baptists, are transitional links to consideration of the religious, social, and cultural issues in Rastafari. Most of these issues will be dealt with more fully in chapter 8, but it is necessary to compare and contrast some of them here with respect to how Rasta reflects issues dealt with in this part of the book, especially this chapter, as seen in the other religions. Coming into existence in the first half of the twentieth century (the 1930's), much beyond the time of the development of the other Afro-Caribbean religious systems, Rastafari has benefited from very rich religious traditions: various African ones, Amerindian, East Indian Hindu and Islam, Jewish, Christian, and possibly more. There have also been a number of religio-political movements which have passed much of their thinking from which this religion could draw energy and strength, such as the Pan-Africanist and other Black liberation struggles on the U.S.A., the Garvey movement, the Gandhi struggles in South Africa and India against apartheid and colonialism, and more. Religious, social, and political issues have abounded in the world from which Rastafari could draw for its establishment.

We should perhaps look back historically to the background of the slaves who were brought to Jamaica from Ghana, the Akan and the Ashanti, and all those who came under the name of those strong, fierce people known as the Koromantyns. Their character, cultural, and religious background are well-known. They were rebellious to the point of notoriety. They made up a large percentage of those maroon communities (composed of Africans who rejected the slave status by escaping to the mountains and setting up their own societies) in Jamaica and other West Indian areas. The Koromantyns were hard workers and played the role of leadership wherever they existed.[26] I saw evidence of their strength and leadership in my visit to Ghana in 2001. (In one case our guide for our trip to the Wili Agumath Mountain Falls was a thin man, short, but strong. When we came to rocky water paths that were not easy for me to walk through, he voluntarily carried me on his back three times, going and coming.)[27] As to the religion of the Akan people, it was and is of a highly admirable and philoso-phical nature. The name of their Supreme Being is Nyame, a name which in Ghana has become well-known and highly respected by Christians in Ghana today, who recognize in him the same qualities and traits as their Christian God. In my visit in 2001, I was confronted everywhere by images of and expressions referring to Nyame. One popular expression which appears on an emblem and is often heard on the lips of children along with everyone else is, "Gya Nyame." The meaning is "except God," in other words, nothing, no one takes God's place in our honor and respect.

The name Nyame has been translated to mean "the shining or resplendent one." Leonard Barrett elaborates further on the deity and the religious beliefs of the Akan.

> Other common names which depict his nature are Nyankopon [the word for God which appears in the translation of the Bible in Twi, Asante, *The Bible in Twi,* Accra, Ghana: The United Bible Societies, 1964), p. 5], "he who is the greatest," and Tweaduampon, "he on whom [people] lean and do not fall." Unlike that of most other West African religions…, the Akan doctrine of God is highly philosophical. There seem to be three levels of deity: first, Nyame or Onyame, who is far away; then Nyankopon or Odomankoma, who is present in the daily life of [humans] and on whom [they] call for succor and strength; and finally Asase Yaa, the god of earth, who gives life and sustenance to [people]. It is from Asase Yaa that [humans] will return.[28]

The priests and priestesses were among these people when they were brought to Jamaica as slaves, and they retained their beliefs and were able to carry on their religious practices here in this New World. We have seen that Obeah and Myal were traditions among the Akan/Ahanti, who were the dominant group in Jamaica; and though one was a form of witchcraft and the other of healing, the two merged into one, which was not the case in Africa, where the two remained separate and the sorcerer was held in check by the social mores and practices. Barrett interprets how the blending took place in the slave society. In his esti-mation, the African could see his enslavement as the work of the sorcery of the whites. Their own priests and priestesses being seemingly powerless before the magic of the whites, they faced confusion. Thus, the legitimate priests in finding their helplessness in the situation, and being 'equally knowledgeable in the techniques of sorcery, joined forces with the sorcerer against the common enemy." And though the sorcerer was also a danger to the slaves themselves, it was a risk they took. And thus the role of the sorcerer was expanded. "He became the source of authority among the slaves." In detecting thieves, providing talismans to protect their gardens, he gained status. And a more important function was his "administering the deadly oath during times of rebellion, sealing the mouth of each slave at the risk of death." Further, he was "the one who mixed the potion which was believed to make one immune to the deadly weapon of the slave master. The obeahman was the leader in the dancing and the drumming that preceded the slave rebellion."[29]

We see from this that the traits of resistance and rebellion in face of adversarial circumstances are an inherited tradition that finds expression in all the religions of Jamaica, and certainly was passed on to Rastafari. The other Afro-Jamaican or Afro-Caribbean religious forms that long-preceded Rasta were those Protestant expressions that were Africanized, so to speak, or syncretized, with Christianity (and other religions, as well). These, Barrett refers to as "Black redemption cults," the "product of a long process of incubation and result from the mixture of Christian ideas and African traditional beliefs." He asserts that the Christian "opened new avenues of thought to the slaves":

> The message of Christianity based on the Bible was, for the slaves, above all, the message of salvation and deliverance. If there were only one message that Africans welcomed, it was this message of salvation from present oppression and a future in heaven where God would wipe away all tears. Both the Old and New Testaments are full of accounts of the activity of the Judaeo-Christian God on behalf of the downtrodden. The God of the Old Testament manifested himself to the Jews as a God who stood firmly against oppression; as one who would stop at nothing to bring down the oppressors and set the oppressed free. The New Testament introduced the Africans to Jesus of Nazareth, the Messiah, the one who was sent to to earth in human form to liberate the oppressed.[30]

The slaves heard and took seriously this message of "redemption," Barrett states, and "grafted it on to their traditional beliefs, giving the millenarian flavor to the Afro-Christian movements in the new world."[31]

Developing in the 19th century, these cults such as Revival Zion, Native Baptists, etc., in Jamaica were seen as delayed reactions "to the cultural confusion brought about by the heightened expectations that had been created by the

Gospel message of the missionaries on the one hand, and the corresponding stress and frustration of colonial domination on the other." In the Great Revivals of the 1800's these hopes were aroused. One example the movements formed is the Native Baptists of Jamaica, stirred by the mission of escaped U. S. African former slave George Liele, who founded the first Baptist Church of Jamaica in 1784. Liele's naming his denomination the Ethiopian Baptist Church certainly helped get this image established in the social context that late impacted the Rastas.[32] The general characteristics of the Afro-Christian cults were: a strong belief in dreams and visions and spirit communications; the powerful role of a charismatic leader, who, whether man or woman, seldom has his or her spiritual guidance questioned; firm belief in healing, either by water or herbal medicine; cataclysmic reversal of the master/slave situation, and a latent militancy. There was not the revolutionary tendency among the Revival cults, only this implicit resistance.[33]

Rastafari is a religion that has drawn from some of the best elements found in African religions, Christianity, Judaism, and other religions to form a movement or system which is resistant to the worst that is found in these religions and the oppressive societies which they have helped to shape. The Rastas making presentations at the Caribbean Conference of Churches meeting in Suriname in 1994 were of the Order of Nyabinghi group in Jamaica, Ras Boanerges (Henry Watson) and Ras Bongo Spear. A couple of excerpts from summaries of one of the presentations and from the speech of the other reflect the sense of spirituality that reflects rejection of what is negative and embraces what is positive in the society. Ras Boanerges "affirmed the importance of perfect love, the brotherhood of all and justice over all the earth." He "pointed out the Rastafari view of African origination, that all peoples come from Africa. He acknowledged Haile Salassie as Eternal King of Kings, of the Tribe of Judah, the root of David. Haile Salassie is indeed Christ sitting on His throne in Ethiopia." He spoke of the "three evils of the world: the Dragon, the Beast and the False Prophet...politics, commerce and religion. Religion is the foundation of the Anti-Christ, that Beast which is Rome. Here is indeed the Dragon, the world-system which is termed 'Babylon.'" He spoke of the Rastafari "ethic of goodness, truth, righteousness, and fellowship," addressing concerns of "repatriation to Africa which is a Rastafari aim, and the 'herb,' 'ganja,'" which he defended as not a drug because it is natural.[34]

Ras Bongo Spear stated in his speech:

So I and I come and see that in terms of religion, that religion is nothing more than a colonial institutional framework. That is to say that in terms how people see divine culture etc., that we would call a colonial system or world powers, political, commercial and even religious, they have a way of defining or trying to define even without overstanding (understanding) the cultures and the practices and the traditions of people....From the beginning of time and even before, these cultures, these ways of life, are grouped into words, as they call it religion. Much emphasis is put on Christian religion because of its popularity, basically throughout the earth, not so much the example of the Christ man, that is to love thy neighbor as thyself. So I and I see that religion really just keeping the world within a deception. And men align themselves to religion because it is popular and because you wouldn't get ostracised, that is to say you fit into the norm and the mainstream. Judaism...all of these religions are nothing more than extensions of colonial bondage and slavery. Until people can free their minds of religion...however you worship the creative power, the Most High who I and I come and see in Salassie I, however you worshipping they try and encompass it within a religious or religion network. It is erroneous because I and I culture is not religion Look at the religions of the world. Islam just come here the other Day...six...seven hundred A.D., recent by world standards, by African standards. Christian similarly, just at Antioch, just 2000 years ago. In the name of religion these things are being professed as the unifying force throughout the face of creation and they disrupt the nation and bring the nation to shame, all nations. So I would like to think that I and I could even step up and try to deal with the principle of truth and not to use religion, not to fall for the deception of religion, as an all-encompassing or as you would say a God given right. I and I see how the instrument of Christianity as a religion has been used to subdue Black people not as the liberating force for which the Christ Man come to set the captive free and to return the captives to their homeland, their heavenly country Ithiopia.[35]

In my estimation, the best ritual expression of Rastafari that reflects the crucial issues of their religious movement as heard in these two speakers' words at the conference is their spiritual music, Reggae. Therefore, I want to take a look at excerpts from the lyrics of some of their Reggae productions that reflect these issues. Actually, Reggae, with its enchanting rhythms and mesmerizing tones and beats, along with its incisive, challenging, and penetrating words, political and religious thoughts, and social and spiritual critiques of unwholesome life, its suggestive, radical, and prophetic dreams of a truer and more wholesome way of life than the hopelessly flawed one we live in today, is modern-day Obeah of the mind and heart, the Myal of today with its spirit possession grasping the inner personhood and imparting to it new ways of thinking and acting, transforming the souls of listeners and dancers to the haunting rhythms and cadences.

Nasio Fontaine's *Reggae Power*[36] CD has songs dealing with exposing corruption in governments, love for the African heritage, pleas for justice in the society, pleas for unity among all peoples, overcoming racism, rejection of and resistance to "Babylon," prophecy of the destruction of Babylon, and repatriation. First track, "Armed and Dangerous," referring to corrupt governments and superpowers of the world as Babylon, warns of their deception.

> "Every head of government through the earth
> Is armed and dangerous
> Armed and dangerous
> Babylon armed
> So armed and dangerous
> Governments armed and dangerous
> Heads of power them armed
> So armed and dangerous
>
> Super power armed and ready
> Might and MX missiles
> Aiming deadly
> Well from the North to the South
> And the East to the West
> Them getting ready
> For a shootout contest
> They wanna see who's the best.

The song goes on to mention military demonstrations of Navy and Army: "The devil them a come with a wicked intention, well mashing up creation with them evil invention," such that the chanting over and over again these suggestive claims can have a dramatic and revealing effect on the thinking of listeners.

Another song, "Africa We Love," pleads for the preservation of Africa from the corruption and destruction of the West, Jah [God—Haile Selassie] bless Africa," it resounds repeatedly: "Yes root of creation/Mother of civilization/Yet you're a victim/Of western exploitation, deedle, deedle/deedle/Your rivers run deep/Your gold is so rich/yet there's sufferation/In your midst./So I got to sing/Jah bless Africa, Tell 'em about it." The song "Justice" expresses strongly the need for justice against racism and all other evils that are destroying people in general: "A every people need some justice/Lord Lord Justice/Down in the Ghetto we need justice..."

> Apartheid its got to go
> We got to give justice
> A chance to flow now
> Racism well that can't last
> Racial discrimination
> Is a thing of the past, so!
> We got to have
> We got to have, Justice
> Hear we cry

> Justice
> Come on and give the people justice
> Lord say we got to have
> Justice
> By any means there must be justice.

The theme is repeatedly stressed, and increasingly impressed on the psyche of the listener/dancer or reader of the lyrics.

"Unite" is another tune, this one addressed to all people urging them to unite and overthrow the evil that is threatening our lives. "Come, Come, Come, Come, /Come, Come…":

> United we stand, divided we fall
> We must unite
> To topple these walls, Lord
> Four hundred years
> Divided too long
> We must unite
> If we must be strong
> Woh! Woh! Woh! Woh! Unite Woh!
> "Everytime I look around
> I seem to feel the pain
> Why can't we unite
> Why oh! Why oh! Why oh! Why oh!
> Can't we unite Lord
> Wht can't we unite
> Black and white
> Why oh! Why oh1 Why oh1
> Can't we unite, Lord
> Come, Come, Come, Come, Come, Come
> We got to unite.

This is very forcefully chanted repeatedly until it seems its message cannot go unheeded.

"Racial Pride" urges the races to overcome their separateness and live as one. Some phrases go, "Tell you that/Be you black, be you white/Be you brown, brown, brown/We could still live as one…./Racial pride is a cancer/Prejudice is a disaster/These are ways and means/To divide the people, yeah!/Racism is a catastrophe/Reviving hate and partiality/Trodding through/The hearts and minds /Of I-Manity, yeah!" And the song, "No Babylon" is an outright rejection of "Babylon" and its attempts to hold sway over the people. It is resistance, rebellion with religious assurance: "Oh Babylon/You cyan hold Jah Jah children no more/No Babylon/You cyan hold Jah Jah children no/more now/No matter how hard you try." One other one on this album is a

Nya-Binghi tune, "Wanna Go Home." It has the theme of repatriation drummed into the listening audience.

Some lines go,

> Jah
> Ras Tafari
> Home oh home
> Oh children home
> I wanna go home
> Home oh home
> Yes children home
> I got to go home yeah!
> We've been trodding
> From Genesis
> Right on through Revelation
> We've been a subject
> To Master's whip, so bleak
> So we wanna go home, yeah!
> We are a people
> Enslaved and Sold
> Scattered through the earth
> Jacob is calling his children
> Twelve Tribes
> So we "wan" go home.

"Home" is Zion, which is Ethiopia. All the leaders of the Twelve Tribes are called and the pleas are continually repeated for return to Africa.

Two other CDs, *Black Woman & Child*[37] and *Reggae Around the World*,[38] present some different perspectives on issues, which we can see from a brief summary of their contents. The artist Sizzla (Miguel Collins) on Black Woman & Child is a popular Jamaican deejay whose lyrics are pungent and defiant. He chants out in steady rhythm and pounding beat his criticism and condemnation of the social structure for its failure of the youth and children, as well as the adults of the society. He has no hope "society's redressing so many years of injustice, and therefore, 'Babylon' is doomed for destruction."[39] The only hope from the turbulence and destruction is in gaining knowledge of what is being done to them and pursue repatriation to Ethiopia. Songs express rejection of the corrupt government and social structure in descriptive lyrics of it brainwashing, enslavement, oppression of the poor, and the deprivation of the masses for the benefit of the few. One song, "Black Woman and Child" professes love and respect for the Black woman, "For you I have so much love." The album *Reggae Around the World* is exactly what it says and shows the worldwide interest in and influence of the issues raised and pursued in the religion, especially by way of the music. It includes Lucky Dube of South Africa, Blekbala Mujik of Australia, Zeca Baleiro of Brazil, Rasha (a woman artist) of Sudan, Askia Modibo of Mali, Majek Fashek of Nigeria, Ernest Ranglin of Jamaica, Kreyol Syndikat of Martinique, Rocky Dawuni of Ghana, Burning Spear Jamaica, and Peter Rowan & Friends of the U.S.A. Although these artists are not all Rastas, but some are primarily musicians attracted to the enchanting style and substance of Reggae, all have caught the spirituality that pervades the music and promote its importance through their musical performances. Doug Wendt writes in the introduction to the album:

> It was a quarter century ago that reggae music burst forth from the Caribbean island of Jamaica, fully formed and ready to conquer the world. Through the simultaneous release of Bob Marley & The Wailers' Catch A Fire and the classic film, The Harder They Come, starring Jimmy Cliff, reggae found an enthusiastic international audience for the first time. Throughout the 70's, Jamaica's distinctive backbeat music, laced with its message of peace, love and the homegrown spirituality of Rastafarianism, continued to spread around the globe. Inspired by 60s soul and protest music as well as Jamaican independence, reggae kept the best instincts of the 60s alive with songs of love and *social revolution* (emphasis mine).

Among the songs on the album that carry the resistant revolutionary spirit are Blekbala Mujik and his Australian aboriginal band's "drangkinbala," Rasha's "Salib Fuddi" (Wendt states, Rasha employs reggae as a revolutionary marker because in Northern Africa it's considered radical to openly sing about desire. Wine, women and song—now that's a platform for pure populists. Yet religious fundamentalists may use it as grounds for a death sentence and that's why many artists must emigrate."), Majek Fashek's "Promised Land," which promotes the symbolic notion of the Promised Land as a "state of mind" rather than a place such as America or Africa or Europe; Kreyol Syndikat's "Roots Ragga" ("short for ragamuffin, a term of endearment for the regular person on the street who may be a dreadlock, but he/she's just another gentle 'sufferah' trying to get by"[40]; Burning Spear's "Jordan River"(Wendt says, "Jordan River"…takes us to the promised land. It is quintessential roots reggae soaked in blood, history and spirituality. It's painfully aware of the costs of slavery while being redeeming and cleansing at the same time").

Certainly, Rastafari is an Afro-Caribbean religion which has benefited from the many religious traditions encountered in the Caribbean context, but it reflects both continuity and change, which is also an issue in the other religions. As for Rasta, though it retains certain aspects of the other religions and reflects similar issues, it has in a great sense transformed certain aspects of other religious traditions, such as Christianity, Judaism, and Revivalism, and expanded and universalized its reflections of issues. We shall speak more of this in a later chapter.

Chapter Six

Crucial Issues in Haitian Vodou

In this chapter we are concentrating on issues that are especially characteristic of Haitian Vodou which make it especially unique and crucial to its practitioners, clients, and the societies in which it is prevalent. One major issue, for instance, is the dance of the spirit showing the unique role of the dance in this African-derived religion. A second major issue is that of community and its role in general and the role it has played in such experiences as revolt and revolution, its importance in commemoration. Also considered is the significance of African, Catholic, and Native American syncretism, as well as the significance of communities of worship. Another major issue is service and devotion, which includes the significance of discipline and service, the role of dance ritual here, and occasions for service and cultural continuity.

Dance of the Spirit

Dance is indispensable to Vodou. The film *Dance, Voodoo, Dance*[1] depicts vividly the vital importance of dance in this religion through portrayals of actual rituals of groups in Benin. Leonard Barrett illuminates this significance in his description of the dance, always connected with the drums, as a ritual form within African religious tradition in general. He states that,

> For the African in the New World, the dance became the only language that every tribe could understand. It, like the drum, was the instrument of non-verbal communication. In Africa, the dance occupied and expressed every significant emotion. There was a dance for every occasion—even death. Dance was not a separate art, but a part of the whole complex of religious and secular life. The dance was strong magic, vivifying the spirit. Through the dance the whole being entered into the rhythm of nature and the supernatural. The body, through the dance, turns to liquid steel. It is through the dance that the emotions are conveyed symbolically. And it was during the dance that, while the master looked on with great amusement, the *message of rebellion* was disseminated (emphasis mine). [2]

This description probably fits Haitian Vodou dance more perfectly than it does most other African-derived religions. For many observers and participants, such as Joseph Murphy, Katherine Dunham, Olmos and Paravisini-Gebert, Vodou in Haiti is characterized primarily by its dance.[3] Joseph Murphy opens his chapter on Vodou with the words: "Vodou is a dance of the spirit: a system of movements, gestures, prayers,and songs in veneration of the invisible forces of life."[4] Thus, his characterization of the religion in the rest of the chapter does indeed show how this is true of Vodou looked at from the standpoint of its community, its service, and its spirit. And what Murphy says resonates well with Barrett's assessment of what he sees as the cosmic achievement of the African dance per se. "The Africans, like the Asians, have a complex cosmic metaphysic which could not be expressed in verbal symbols. The dance, then, was the medium of expression. Through the dance the African is able to break the structure of physical boundaries and through rhythm be united with the cosmos. In the dance the African becomes one with the spirit world, thus uniting [the self] through vibrations with [the] ancestors and the lesser deities. In the dance [one]is immortal."[5]

We shall look at the impact of the dance in Haitian Vodou as it functions in this manner and how important it is as a crucial issue in this powerful religious expression. As Murphy expresses it, "the people and the spirits" are "the center of vodou" and are bound together as "a spiritual community." And this "shared spirituality is expressed in the communal ceremony of the dance," in which case the "system of movements...bring people and lwa together in a progressive mutual relationship of knowledge and growth."[6] We will see later what he means by this "growth" theory. But first I would like to expand further on what the "community" idea means to the Haitian practitioners of the religion.

These practitioners Leslie Desmangles refers to as Vodouisants, numbering nearly six million Haitians who practice principally both their Vodou ceremonies and the Catholic religion. And he describes their basic religious community in comparison and contrast to the Catholic Church community. This comparison is revealing and instructive. He says of the Catholics that historically they

have constituted the bulk of the elite, and they have upheld their religion's strict traditions and official order. Their churches are large, spacious, and architecturally the most elegant buildings in every town and city. Catholic priests and sisters staff many of the public schools as well as church-related schools, which provide the best available education in the country. Moreover, Catholicism is always represented by its dignitaries in all of the public and official governmental functions.[7]

By contrast, he says of the Vodouisants, they "constitute the bulk of the lower classes and the peasantry, worship in temples that, viewed from any distance, bear few distinguishing marks that would identify them as places of worship; nor do the Vodou priests or priestesses (oungans or mambos) wear distinctive garb."[8]

From this contrast one may naturally get the impression that the Catholic Church would be the more desirable and attractive religious group. But the sharp distinctions in the roles that the priests in these two religions play and resultant religious experiences achieved among the worshipers make a different impression as to the desirability of the two religions. Desmangles states:"In the Mass, the priest serves as the only conduit through which one can gain access to the sacred world; in his role as the sole dispenser of grace, he stands at the crossroads between the sacred and the profane worlds. Conversely, the oungan does not control his flock's contact with the world of the gods....In Vodou ceremonies, each believer has direct access to the spirit world through spirit possession."[9] Of this altered state of consciousness whereby the person's body is taken over by the spirit, Desmangles says the "invasion of one's person by a lwa results in the temporary displacement of one's own personality by the envisaged personality of the lwa" and is considered "a quintessential spiritual achievement" as it "represents a direct engagement with the spirit world." And this gives one religious authority and status in the *community*. Thus, the distinctive feature in such an experience is that one does not in this service merely talk about God or hear speeches about God but rather becomes God.[10]

Further characterization of the Vodouisant community Desmanles makes vis a vis the Catholic community are also very revealing. They have no formal creeds as is the case of the Roman Catholic Church, no formal theology. Concepts and practices vary from one locale to another. Their worldview allows them that freedom. There are no beliefs in abstract terms but practical ones about interacting with one another, the ancestors, the gods, and the world. In spite of their differences with Catholic religion, Vodouisants have no problems embracing and practicing both of these religions simultaneously with no attempt to resolve any paradoxes between them. Venerating both the saints of the Church and the Vodou lwa, they may spend the whole of Saturday night in ceremony in the Vodou service and leave there to attend a 4:00 a. m. Mass on Sunday. Desmangles explains that the "priest in the performance of the Mass functions as a point of contact with an impersonal Godhead who maintains the universe, including its mechanical, biological, and stellar operations," while the "oungan in his performance of the Vodou ceremony facilitates the devotees' contact with minor deities and ancestral spirits who are personifications of Bondye, the Godhead."[11] The Vodou community also reaches out and claims those 15% of the population, the Haitian elite, who know little of Vodou and disdain it but must acknowledge in and make use of it (many, at least) in times of need. All know that they have a connection to this religion and the community historically. They are "forced to recognize the historical fact that that without vodou, Haiti could not have become an independent nation as early as the nineteenth century, _for its rituals provided the spirit of kinship that fueled the slaves' revolts against their masters_" (emphasis mine). Vodouisants embrace Catholic Church connections for reasons of social acceptance. "On the one hand they have felt the need to participate in the country's official culture by claiming their unquestionable allegiance to Catholicism, and almost never to Vodou. On the other hand, because it is essential to participate in the sociocultural and religious life of their community, they have felt the need to serve the lwas as well." Desmangles notes that the suppression of the religion, that more or less forces this dual allegiance and ambivalence, helps sustain the religion rather than eradicate it by inspiring and building a stronger _sense of community_ and adherence to African traditional values.[12]

The Vodouisant community holds the two religions together (Catholic and Neo-African) in a coexistence without fusing them with each other, according to Desmangles's position, which he calls symbiosis rather than what some call syncretism.[13] This "symbiosis" uniquely grows out of Haitian history and seems firmly rooted in this society as in no other African-Caribbean religious community. It harks back to the period of slavery and has been present for one reason or another since then. For instance, as the present-day Haitian community maintain this symbiosis by holding allegiance to the church for "social recognition and stability" and participating in Vodou rituals in order to "reaffirm their African heritage," slaves did so under different circumstances and for different reasons. The slaves "needed to survive the hardships of plantation life and they found solace in their African religious traditions. Because Vodou was not allowed in the colony, they learned to conceal their practice of these traditions behind the veil of Catholicism."[14]

In order to grasp fully the "Dance of the Spirit" in the Vodou community it is necessary to review briefly how in functioned to create this community and is vital to its preservation today. *As the community dances its rituals the spirit dances in the community.* The spirit's dance may take different forms. It may be a dance of healing and whole-making, for instance, or it may be a dance of resistance and revolution, or a dance of reclamation, and so forth. In describing the Rada Vodou ceremonies and her participation in them in Haiti, Zora Neale Hurston mentions the change in the drumming and the spirited dances for each lwa, beginning with Papa Legba. After the last deity was honored, "Brave Guede," she said, "we danced for the rest of the night." "'A day of promise'—was in store for us but we danced the sun out of bed just the same."[15] Describing her witnessing of the Petro ceremonies, Hurston notes the difference between these ceremonies and the Rada ones. The Rada pantheon do only good for people, "but they are slow and lacking in power." On the other hand, she says:

> The Petro gods…are terrible and wicked, but they are more powerful and quick. They can be made to do good things, however, as well as evil. They give big doses of medicine and effect quick cures. So these Petro gods are resorted to by a vast number of people who wish to gain something but fear them at the same time. The Rada spirits demand nothing more than chickens and pigeons, and there are no consequences or hereafter to what they do for you, while the Petros demand hogs, goats, sheep, cows, dogs…. The Petros work for you only if you make a promise of service to them. You can promise a service to be fulfilled as far away as thirty years, but at the end of that time, the promise must be kept or the spirits begin to take revenge.[16]

All sources agree that the Vodou community grew and became rooted in the Haitian society through its role in numerous revolts and the Revolution of 1791–1804 that brought Haiti its independence. Here the "Dance of the Spirit" was at its most powerful with the special function of the Petro deities.[17] In a summary statement, Desmangles states, the "role of Vodou in these revolutions was one of providing a channel through which ancestral African traditions could be re-created. The emphasis on past religious traditions became vital in inspiring the slaves to revolt against their masters. Subversive activity was often preceded by religious ceremonies that included sacrifices to gods originating in diverse regions of Africa."[18] Both Bisnauth and Desmangles stress the role of the Petro rites and deities that were more indigenous to Haiti rather than being of pure African origin. Also they pinpoint the hill country and the Haitian maroons as the origin of this religious variety. Bisnauth states,

> By 1751, some 3,500 blacks had fled to the hills of St. Domingue to escape the rigours of plantation life and the brutality of slavery. The rites which developed among these blacks came to be identified as those of the Petro 'nation.' Some of the Petro deities were of New World origin. These included Dan Petro, Baron Samedi, Simbi and Azacca. Simbi was originally the local Amerindian of rain and Azacca the Indian deity associated with the maize. Samedi and zombie might well have been derived from the Arawak zemi; both were related to the spirits of the dead. Obviously, Indian ideas were assimilated into the African framework of beliefs.[19]

Among the charismatic religious figures revered in the community for their role in establishing the religion and the independence of Haiti are Macandal, Boukman, and Toussaint Louverture, Jean-Jacque Dessalines, and Henri Christophe. Macandal is said to have been originally from Guinea and was only in the colony a few years before fomented a rebellion in 1748. Somewhat like Nat Turner in the U.S., envisioned freedom for his people. Only, he dreamed of returning his people to their original homeland of Africa. He organized a large body of maroons and instilled in them a reverence for the African traditions. Asserting himself as a papalwa (high priest), he encouraged revival of African ancestral traditions. "*Ritualistic dances offered to the African deities preceded the raids on plantations—a procedure that Macandal felt was a good way to instill a sense of solidarity among his followers*" (emphasis mine).[20] He was very successful in recruiting slaves and carrying out raids from 1748 to 1758. When Macandal was captured and burned at the stake in 1758, the community believed he would be incarnated and retained their messianic hope. Not too many years hence, Boukman came on the scene, some twenty years later.

> Under his leadership the maroons conducted numerous destructive raids in the north, which were soon echoed by similar rebellions throughout the colony. Vodou was again used as a catalyst for these insurrections. After officiating at a Vodou ceremony in the forest of Bois Caiman, near Cap-Francais, on August 14, 1791, Boukman led the most devastating assaults in the history of the colony so far. His indiscriminate slaughter of whites, and the burning of nearly a thousand plantations in the northern parish alone (Geggus 1989, 29), spurred the formation of a powerful militia that combined the military, the police, and a significant number of civilian volunteers.[21]

Though he was decapitated in 1791, he had made an invaluable contribution to shaping the community. Toussaint Louverture and Jean-Jacques Dessalines led the Revolution beginning in 1797, with Henri Christophe serving as a general.

Toussaint Louverture was kidnapped and taken to France in 1802, where he died in 1803 of cold and starvation. After the success of the Revolution in 1804, the name St. Domingue was changed back to the Arawak name of Haiti.[22]

Roman Catholicism virtually disappeared during the Revolution, leaving a vacuum of decades (60 years) in which Vodou became even more rooted. Desmangles states:

> n spite of the fact that in the country's first sixty years as an independent nation the Haitian government...had attempted to suppress Vodou, Haitian culture was imbued with Vodou practices. It had disseminated everywhere and anchored itself tacitly in Haitian religious life; it had also cast itself throughout the countryside within a Roman Catholic mold, adjusting itself to the pressures that attempted to suppress it. The government officials, the elite, fearing the rebuke of the state that had attempted to suppress Vodou, adhered to the religion only clandestinely.[23]

The "Dance of the Spirit" continued in the Vodou community and was never allowed to vanish even during the periods of repression and government and church attempts to root out Vodou from the society, as well as during periods of deteriorating economic and political conditions under rapidly changing and diverse leadership trends. Murphy says, "The Haitian revolution is very much alive in vodou ceremony and symbolism, and it is this revolutionary spirit which gives vodou its critical force and fearsome image."[24]

Issues of Community, Service, and Devotion in Vodou

Murphy describes the organization of specific Vodou communities under the leadership of priests and priestesses and servitors, and the focus on development of spiritual power through stages of initiation into levels mental achievement, called konesans (connaissance). This can be seen as both spiritual insight and ritual knowledge. Murphy states: "Vodou recognizes a three-part hierarchy of involvement in konesans: ordinary devotees who are more or less active in the service of the lwa; the ounsi or 'spouses' of the lwa who have made a lifelong commitment to the spirits; and the oungan and manbo, respectively the male and female leaders of the community who have the power to make new ounsi. Thus, the oungans and manbos control the patterns of authority in their communities and can assure the proper transmission of konesans to their initiates."[25]

The community may be composed of family members related by blood or friends and neighbors attached to the temple (ounfort, hounfort). "The urban ounfo...is a family by initiation, a societe with its own traditions and very much dependent on the gifts of its presiding manbo or oungan." These officials organize and conduct the rituals, liturgies, keep discipline, and give instructions to initiates, as well as have consultations for those needing advice or counsel. This is a sort of surrogate family.[26]

When one is called to service of a lwa, the lwa will often manifest in his or her body in a type of "possession." Initially, considered "wild" until the person called (officially an ounsi bosalle) is trained and instructed "along the path of konesans in the ways of the spirit," the person is prepared for becoming a receptacle for the lwa. The head must be "washed" to remove impurities and resistance, in which case one becomes a hunsi lave tet. There may then take place years of instruction in ritual knowledge. "Finally as ounsi kanzo they take on all the privileges and responsibilities of a marriage with the spirit and become true serviteurs of the lwa and permanent members of the hierarchy of the ounfo. The most accomplished of the ounsi kanzo is selected to be the oungenikon or 'song master' of the congregation who leads the other ounsi in the invocation of the lwa."[27]

The oungan and manbo as ultimate authorities of the ounfo, having achieved the highest level of konesans, must know every "nuance of vodou ceremony, the proper drumbeats, songs, and prayers to invoke or direct the presence of the lwa." At their initiation, they are said to "take the ason," the sacred rattle "which is at once an emblem of office and a ritual tool." It is "shaken in certain rhythms to control the direction of the energy of the lwa's presence." The priests and priestesses are also experts in "the herbalist arts of physical and psychic medicines," being able to "recognize hundreds of plants" and being able to "prepare them for infusion or ingestion in proper dosages." They must know "the symbolic properties of plants and how to produce powerful statements in ouangas or 'charms.'" They must be oriented toward "insight into the invisible causes and ends of things" and develop "a second sight which allows them to understand the hidden meanings of human and divine actions." Prise des yeux is the culmination konesans ceremony of the priest or priestess where "the eyes of these leaders are fully opened to the invisible world of the spirits."[28]

Membership in the Vodou community involves service to the lwa and to other initiates, one's community of participants. Some serve the larger society as political leaders.[29] Olmos and Paravisini-Gebert state: "The oungan or manbo's first responsibility in their service to the lwa is the care and training of the ounsi. They in turn, are known for their zeal in service and devotion to the oungan and manbo. The ounsi's chief task is devotion to the lwas, which takes the form of dancing for hours during ceremonies, maintaining the peristil [sacred space for the ceremony], cooking the food to be offered to the lwa, caring and preparing the sacred objects needed for ritual, and above all, being possessed by the spirits."[30]

The tradition of service is one which stays with Haitians as they move about in other parts of the world, as presented clearly by Olmos and Paravisini-Gebert:

> For Haitians, both in the island and throughout the world, Vodou's tradition of service—and the link to the spirit world and to the past it represents—provides perhaps the clearest evidence of cultural continuity for a people whose history of struggle against poverty and oppression has known few victories since the Haitian Revolution simpered into dictatorship and chaos. The connection to the lwa, rooted as it is in traditions connected to the family and the land—to the ordinary peasant's heritage—seems at first hand threatened by migration to the United States, Canada, and beyond. If we are to judge by the proliferation of Vodou centers and the syncretization of practices in major metropolitan centers and small towns across the United States...the vitality of this life of service, the concreteness of the reciprocity of the relationship between lwa and serviteur, continues to sustain individuals, communities, and the spirits that depend on them for survival and renovation.[31]

Service also takes place when persons are in the state of possession, which benefits the whole community. Murphy describes it thus:

> It is not only the hunger for service the lwa have to communicate. They offer all the konesans of Africa for the disposal of their serviteurs. If they are satisfied with their service, they bring healing power and sage advice to those who approach them. "Tell my horse," say the lwa. Give a message to the person who is acting as the "horse" of the spirit, whose personality has been displaced and cannot be there to hear the words of the lwa. The message may be anything from medical advice to news of the departed to biting social commentary, but they have the divine advantage of always being true. Thus the dances seek the truth, and the capacity of the lwa to speak the truth and offer it to these serviteurs is a valuable, if volatile, gift.[32]

Communalism: The Expanded Community

The Traditional African sense of community is retained among the Haitians in their understanding of themselves and the world. A person is more than an individual in the African worldview. One is a part of one's immediate family, a member of a larger kinship group, an extended family, and so on and on. And so, one is obligated to think in terms of belongingness to the whole people. But the connectedness and interdependence does not end with the living relatives and neighbors. One is also connected to the unborn, to the living, and those ancestors who have passed on to the world of the spirits. All of these components serve to make up a broader, inclusive community which has strong impact on each individual life. There is a hierarchical structure to this community, and it is governed by strict religious and societal rules and rituals.

This system of thought is adapted to the lives of Haitians who hold on to their religious and cultural tradition maintained from their African past. Leslie Desmangles elaborates on how this manifestation of this system in the formation and operations of Neo-African communities in Haiti called the *lakou,* which was like the African compound. He says:

> A lakou is an area in which are gathered approximately five to six conjugal families. They live in separate dwellings, sometimes with one hut that serves as the temple (Davis, 1988, 39–40). The members of the lakou share the same courtyard around the hut of a patriarch (chef lakou) who is often the oldest member of the group. The patriarch's responsibilities vary from the settlement of domestic quarrels to social and political matters affecting the survival of each member of the group. His decisions are respected and dutifully obeyed by all. He counsels those who need economic and social advice, and his honorific title has earned him the right to participate actively in all the lakou's festivities and religious ceremonies.. Perhaps the most important function of the patriarch is that of calling the spirits of the ancestors from their abode, and he is often possessed by the lwa rasin (root lwa) recognized as the ancestral divine protector of the lakou's members.[33]

This was a practice in rural living conditions and has not survived in urban settings where it was not practical, but the spirit of community stemming from it has survived, Desmangles points out. And he observes that even in the U.S.A., especially in New York City, Haitian immigrants have in a sense revived the lakou in "house systems" that have similar arrangements and practices with the ougan or mambo serving as the controlling force.[34]

Very important to the communal inclusive community concept are the Haitians' ideas about the make-up of the human person and the nature of life beyond earthly existence, or the afterlife. As Desmangles puts it, people belong to both the visible and invisible community, which are separate in a sense and yet not entirely so. What distinguishes the two forms of existence is death, "which confers upon an individual a sacred character not to be attained in this life. The moment of death constitutes a separation from the community of the living and a transferal into the sacred abyss, the world of ancestral spirits (Ginen), where the individual takes on the divine, original, and essential bodiless form that it possessed before the creation of the world." He says Vodouisants see the human body as consisting of a spirit that derives from Bondye (the Supreme Being, God). This spirit is composed of two parts: 1) the gwo-bon-anj (big-good-angel), a life-force that is a part of Bondye (other sources use Le Bon Dieu), the immortal, cosmic spirit of Bondye manifested in the body; 2) the ti-bon-anj (little-good-angel), the personality, conscience, the moral side of one, the ego-soul. When death occurs, "the twin compartments of the self is fractured and each follows its separate destiny." The ti-bon-anj is passed from the body and believed to enter heaven, the place of which is hard to pinpoint in Vodouisant conception. It seems to correspond the the Catholic idea, that it "appears" before Bondye "to stand before the heavenly tribunal where it is arraigned for its misdeeds, and must suffer appropriate penalties."[35]

There is little need to be much concerned with the ti-bon-anj in the funeral rites. The great concern of the rituals is with the gwo-bon-anj. "Because the ti-bon-anj has transpired and the body is no longer animated, all intelligence and conscious experiences are believed to fuse with the gwo-bon-anj. The death rituals performed by oungans or mambos and the entire community send the gwo-bon-anj to Ginen to join the community of ancestral spirits, the living-dead in Ginen." Different views place Ginen under the sea, under the bed of a local river, above the sky, and so forth. From this place the gwo-bon-anj can be brought back to share in the living community through appropriate rituals. The ritual of desounen (or dessounin, as some render it) is a very formal process performed by a priest that must be done for each person who dies in order to give the proper resting place to each component of the self. The rite stems from the Fon background in Benin. In Haiti the rite is designed to "dispossess the body of its gwo-bon-anj and its met tet (master of the head, or guardian angel), the third part of the soul, the guardian lwa, which throughout the person's life has protected him or her from harm, has been the subject of constant service and spirit possession at regular intervals. Desounen sends the three compartments of the self to their respective dwelling places: the ti-bonanj to heaven, the gwo-bon-anj and met tet to Ginen, and the perished body to the navel of the earth, where it will disintegrate and await its refashioning by Bondye and the lwas."[36]

This gives us a comprehensive picture of community in Vodou so that its various practices become clearer in relation to religion, social life, cultural components, interactions with other religions and cultures, and the like. This helps to understand how Murphy can interpret the community in the way he does in relation to Ginen and the African heritage and the world of ancestors. He states: "Followers of vodou remember the different African nations of their forbearers as long lost children remember stern parents. They have been given a harsh destiny by the spirits, but the lwa have come to their aid again and again. Ginen lies over the great waters, and it is a memory of crossing waters that underlies the liturgy of vodou. It is Agwe, the lwa of the sea, who is asked to carry the lwa to the ceremony in hid boat. And Loko, the great tree that draws the lwa up from the cities beyond the seas in Ginen."[37]

Murphy goes on to expand upon the crucial issue of the spirit of Vodou in maintaining the integrity and sense of human meaning in the community. He declares: "To understand the spirit of vodou...is to see that it is an orientation ta historical memory and to a living reality. The memory is of the ancestors and their lands of origin, and of the great gulf of space and time which divides Haitians from them. This memory provides the precedent for all action....Africa becomes the criterion of harmonious and moral action, and authority derives from fidelity to the traditions of Ginen. But Ginen is not only a historical memory, a veneration of past power and precedent. It is alive and present in vodou ceremony."[38]

Murphy's description and explanation of the Vodou ceremony clearly illuminates how the two worlds of the past and present, the ancestral spirits, the lwa and the humans are brought together in living and healing reality in the sacred space of the temple. He further states, "The technique to bring about this sharing comes from the rhythms of the dance itself. By dancing together, the bodies of the serviteurs are attuned, so that their minds may be attuned, so that they may share the same konesans.[39]

Thus, Murphy can conclude, as he began, in describing Vodou as a "dance of the spirit": "Vodou means both dance and spirit, a movement of the spirit both calling for and being called by the actions of human beings. The spirit of vodou is thus a dance, and the spirits of vodou are a series of dances, brought alive by the Haitian people. In the dance the spirit is worked into presence, alive to comfort, discipline, and enable its children in their struggle."[40]

This brings to light the issue of *empowerment*, the empowerment and strength for survival under still harsh conditions of existence that the Revolution failed to remove from their lives. Hurston puts it in succinct and almost blunt terms: "Haiti has always been two places. First it was the Haiti of the masters and slaves. Now it is Haiti of the wealthy and educated mulattoes and Haiti of the blacks." She further states: "The mulattoes began their contention for equality with the whites at least a generation before freedom for the blacks was even thought of. In 1789 it was estimated that the mulattoes owned at least ten per-cent of the productive land and held among them over 50,000 black slaves. Therefore when they sent representatives to France to fight for their rights and privileges, they would have been injuring themselves to have the same thing for the blacks. So they fought only for themselves."[41]

Community has been fractured by the harsh social and political realities of the modern racially divided and economically flawed world, such that Hurston could say in 1938: "Since the struggle began, L'Ouverture died in a damp, cold prison in France, Dessalines was assassinated by people whom he helped free, Christophe was driven to suicide, three more presidents have been assassinated, there have been fourteen revolutions, three out-and-out kingdoms established, a military occupation by a foreign white power which lasted for nineteen years."[42]

Yet the spirit still dances in the Vodou community, and the spirit of the people is maintained. They are still empowered by their spirituality and religious practices, the maintenance of their heritage. They often revive the spirit by commemorations and ceremonies of restoration.

Commemoration and Revivification in the Face of Hardships

Vodou religion resists strongly any efforts to completely eradicate either it or its followers. It flowers and revivifies wherever it finds this opposition. Just as it was retained among the slaves brought from West Africa (Dahomey, Kongo, etc.), it has been retained among those who left Haiti for Santiago de Cuba, or New Orleans, Louisiana, or New York City, or Miami, or wherever its followers have gone. And it rejuvenates among its Haitian followers amidst all manner of opposition. One example of this is seen among those Vodouisants who migrated to Santiago de Cuba during and after the Haitian revolution. Three Cuban Researchers from Casa del Caribe (or The House of the Caribbean, a research institute in Santiago founded in 1982), Joel James, Jose Miller, and Alexis Alarcon, authored the study of Vodou in Cuba, El vodu en cuba (Vodun in Cuba), published in Santo Domingo, Dominican Republic, in 1992, by CEDEE. This study explores vodun as a significant belief system in eastern Cuba and examines it in the context of 200 years of immigration from Haiti. It treats of its ceremonies and beliefs, its deities and other elements.[43]

In December, 2003, Casa del Caribe announced its 24th International Colloquium with the theme "The Caribbean That Unites Us," to be held in Santiago from the 3rd to the 7th of July, 2004. This festival was to be devoted to a celebration of the 200th Anniversary of the Haitian Revolution. This had the sense of a revival and restoration of the spirit of the people, not only Haitians but all the Caribbean and the world who cherished the freedom for which this revolution was fought. The Flyer stated: "As the blaze that baptizes a Voodoo ceremony, synthesis of the Haitian spirit. As the still emigrate memory of my grandfather and the ashes of his dreams. As the beauty of the pumpkin and its seeds. As the star of their heroes and the rainbow of their writers and their artists. So is the history of Haiti: hopes of freedom, reason of living, root of the culture."[44]

Clearly, this was to be a commemorative and revivifying event for all the Caribbean, as well as for the Haitians throughout the world who still relish their history, both African and Caribbean. The importance of that Revolution for the Caribbean and the world was expressed in these words announcing the celebration: "The year of 1804 is of great relevance in the history of the Caribbean and of the world. The slave rebellion in Haiti developed into a project of defense of the ideals of sovereignty in middle of a society [built] upon racial and hegemonic basis. This emancipating action reconfigured the relations of the epoch and served as an example to future independent movements in the Caribbean region. Its legacy transcended the scenery in which it took place and maintains its influence in the world of global hegemony in which we live today."[45]

This celebration was to take place a few months after Miami Haitians and Haitians in other countries were commemorating in some fashion their victorious moment in history.[46] And such a revival of their spirits takes place in their religious ceremonies.

Desmangles says, "Just as Vodou ceremonies can be seen as the reliving of the first act of creation when Bondye fashioned the world, so the manifestation of Ogou Feray[47] in the body of his devotees represents the re-creation of the

Haitian Revolution. Such re-creation is confirmed by the mention of the names of Boukman, Dessalines, and Christophe by those who harbor Ogou's spirit within them; the ancestor spirits of these national heroes are thus manifested in the bodies of possessed devotees. A Vodou ceremony in honor of Ogou Feray is therefore an archetypal ritual, a reenactment of the beginnings of the nation. The experiences of the revolution must be relived, the sounds of battle must be heard once more, and the blood of the sacrificial pig at Bois Caiman must again seal the lips of those devotees who were present at the ceremony."[48] This ceremony in present-day Haiti revives the hopes of a constantly struggling people, and Ogou Feray is the symbolic embodiment of the struggle for a perfect Haiti. In real life, the Vodouisants call out to Ogou in extreme social situations—"in difficult and trying times—and so the strength they exhibit in themselves [the Ogou in the ceremony] and call forth in their devotees is the strength of someone pushed to the limit."[49]

Parallels between Ogou and Christ have been made by observers.[50] But such parallel is not made by the Vodouisants themselves, Desmangles says. But in the millenarian dreams spread by the priests of the Catholic Church, he says "Christ represents Haiti herself." "His sufferings and crucifixion resemble the struggles and eventual death of *the national heroes who gave their lives for the liberation of Haiti, and his resurrection suggests the political rebirth of a people whose millenarian dream is to be free from political and religious oppression, not only historically but currently* [emphasis mine]. Today, ceremonies in honor of Ogou Feray symbolize not only martyrdom and death, but the resurrection as well, for *possession symbolizes the re-vivification and the re-creation of the national heroes* [emphasis mine]."[51]

And Desmangles surmises that in the present setting, Christ's promise of heaven is rendered in practical and immediate terms: "a new order that includes their political and religious freedom as they envisage them. And Christ's promise of victory over the miseries and frustrations of their existence, and over death itself, is symbolized in the continuing struggles against political oppression."[52]

Finally, in a similar vein, Laennec Hurbon discusses the dynamic of the Catholic, Protestant, and Vodou roles and realities in the political situation in modern-day Haiti.[53] He summarizes the situation existing in the society in relation to how these religious groupings perceive their roles and functions in regard to one another. He says that a sign of political confusion "seems to be the successful charismatic movement, which reaches not only members of the up-

per middle class but also Catholics and Protestants of the popular classes."
There is a change in the way the Christians in these groups see their religious
situation, in terms of individual responsibility for their own afflictions, he says.
Thus, "Inside Protestant denominations like the Pentecostalists or the Baptists,
the popular classes" are seeking to improve social and economic life through
"an inner, spiritual change." But this is not the way the Voduisants think of social and political responsibility for change. They believe that the "Gods and the
invisible world are responsible for resolving any social and political problems."
However, a greater problem is that the charismatic, such as Haitian Protestants
are hampered by their view that Vodou is a "diabolic cult." They consider
Vodou unable to "satisfy social and economic claims" because it is "a cult of
the devil." And Hurbon believes the charismatic movement is "successful because of a crisis in Catholicism and in Vodou." In a nutshell, both Catholicism
and Vodou were fractured in previous governmental administrations: those of
Francois Duvalier (Papa Doc), Jean-Bertrand Aristide, and others, and now they
don't have the unity and social and political credibility that the charismatic
Protestant churches have.

Hurbon has a new hope for the possibility of freedom of religion
in Haiti, especially for Vodou, a religion that after centuries of being suppressed
and repressed. With the spirit of democracy being planted in the country,
"Vodou had to relinquish its clandestine nature and seek legitimacy to be practiced openly." This was granted in the Constitution of 1987, which acknowledged the right of Haitians to be Vodouists. Therefore, Hurbon urges the
continuation of this stress on religious freedom for all, including Vodou. The
only way to solve the problems between religions in the society and state is for
Catholic and Protestant Churches to acknowledge the validity of Vodou as a
religion and accept religious pluralism. He states: "To move Vodou out from
underground, we need to accept rules of democracy, which assume principles of
freedom of religion and freedom of conscience. It is not easy, however, for the
Catholic Church in Haiti to accept these freedoms, as it has been accustomed to
being the official religion of the country from the time of the Concordat, nor is
it easy to have in Haiti a regime that recognizes the neutrality of the state in
matters of religion."[54]

Hurbon raises a challenging issue which has to do with the question of the
future of Vodou in a democratic society where it is truly practiced publicly, and
with that we can conclude the chapter. "Until now, a Haitian Vodouist was

supposed to be 'possessed' by a lwa only within the context of a ceremony taking place in an ounfo [temple]. Moving that important aspect of Vodou into public view implies a transformation of Vodou's meaning. Although this may mean a loss of the sense of the sacred, it offers a way to use religion as a cultural force, as a way of affirming an identity. The status of Vodou is transformed: it becomes the place where peasantry and suburban population as well as the Haitian Diaspora, especially those who live somewhat uprooted in the United States, can affirm their personality."[55]

Chapter Seven

Crucial Issues in Cuban and Puerto Rican Santeria and Trinidadian Shango

We have dealt with issues in these three Afro-Caribbean religions from different perspectives in previous chapters. But in this chapter we consider them more in detail and compare and contrast how they reflect certain issues in their conceptions, beliefs, and practices. Major issues looked at are those concerning the conquest culture syndrome, the role of Catholicism, Lucumí ethnicity and the syncretism of African and European religions, transformations of the old religion, economic transition, uses and suppression of the cabildos, the role of Espiritismo, the ambivalence of repression and resistance, and continuity and change.

Orisa Religions in Cuba, Puerto Rico, and Trinidad: The Conquest Culture Syndrome

All three of these countries were first under the colonial domination of Spain. The Indigenous Arawaks (Tainos) and Caribs had strong presence in these lands before the coming of the Spanish and remain a part of the cultures in spite of the colonial efforts to eliminate them. The influences of West African Yoruba religion and culture were well-established in these three colonies by enslaved Africans and remain today as significant aspects of the culture and society. The Yoruba religion has come to be referred to also by the term, Orisa religion. The Roman Catholic Church was well-established by the Spanish in these colonies as the official religion. In all three of these Spanish colonies, the slaves continued to practice their Orisa religions by masking them with the characters of the saints and beliefs, and practices of the Catholic Church when they were forbidden by laws to practice them openly. While the Orisa religious practices have much in common (such as the Yoruba pantheon of deities) in all three of these countries, differences in their content and structure, as well as some of their practices do exist. We also find that the societies evolved differently in their social, cultural, political, economic, and religious character and make-up, which is very significant in terms of the crucial religious and social issues we find among them. And after the emancipation of slavery we find that laborers from China and India were brought in, and all three countries came to possess a phenomenal mixture of cultures and ethnic groups.

We will first take a look at their comparative developments under Spanish colonial domination and afterward. We have already discussed the historical development of the Cuban society under the Spanish, the tremendous mixture of peoples and cultures there, the fate of the Caribs and Arawaks under their domination, the booming sugar industry, the enslavement of the numerous mixtures of African peoples, the means of control and domination of the cultures and ethnic groups, the comparatively late emancipation of slavery in 1885, the employment of Chinese and East Indian contract laborers thereafter, and the Spaniards' continual hold on that country until the Cuban Revolution beginning in 1895 and ending in 1903 with final Independence from Spanish colonial domination. Olmos and Paravisini-Gebert sum up the struggle very well. "Black and mulatto soldiers fought side by side with the most liberal sectors of Cuban Creole society, hoping to establish a new nation on democratic principles and greater class and race representation. The victory over Spanish forces—coming in the wake of the United States joining Cuban forces in what would be known as the Spanish-American War—would disappoint the broader social aspirations of the black and mulatto sectors of the Cuban population." As they point out, the War for Independence brought on a new form of dependence, neo-colonialism. For the "American sugar corporations" took over the sugar plantations, and the United States threw its support principally behind the most "conservative military-backed dictatorships. Renewed hopes would wait until the 1959 Cuban revolution, which opened a new chapter in Afro-Cuban history."[1]

Puerto Rico had a somewhat different development under Spanish domination, although it too wound up in U.S. hands under different circumstances and conditions. The Indigenous peoples suffered at the hands of the Spanish, who tried to force them into slavery, but at their resistance the Spanish practically decimated the people. A few of them escaped into the mountains, where they intermarried with poor Spanish farmers, becoming known as jibaros (peasants, mountain dwellers). Not too many of these remain, but the Centro Ceremonial Indigena De Tibes museum and memorial grounds in Ponce, Puerto Rico, which I visited in 2004, preserves the Taino and other indigenous cultures. And the people who operate the place and officiate there are a mixture of Taino and Spanish. A summary of the historical development and immigration to the island and its great mixture of peoples states:

> Besides the slaves imported from Africa (Sudan, Kongo, Senegal, Guinea, Sierra Leona, and the Gold, Ivory, and Grain Coasts), other ethnic groups brought to work on the plantations joined the island's racial mix. Fleeing Simon Bolivar's independence movements in South America, Spanish loyalists fled to Puerto Rico—a fiercely conservative Spanish colony in the early 1800s. French families also flocked here from Louisiana and Haiti. As changing governments or violent revolutions depressed the economies of Scotland and Ireland, many farmers from those countries also journeyed to Puerto Rico in search of a better life. When the United States acquired the island in 1898, American influence was added to the culture. During the mid-19th century, labor was needed to build roads, initially, Chinese workers were imported for this task, followed by workers from such countries as Italy, France, Germany, and even Lebanon. American expatriates came to the island in 1898. Long after Spain had lost control of Puerto Rico, Spanish immigrants continued to arrive on the island. The most significant new immigrant population arrived in the 1960s, when thousands of Cubans fled from Fidel Castro's Communist state. The latest arrivals to Puerto Rico have come from the economically depressed Dominican Republic.[2]

Adding to this picture, Olmos and Paravisini-Gebert give specific facts about the economy, population, politics, and social and religious character of the land. Coffee production remained constant in Puerto Rico instead of its being destroyed by the sugar boom. Only 11% of its population was slave at any point. It was the only Spanish colony that did not fight a war for independence, despite one strong separatist movement that attempted rebellion—the "1868 Grito de Lares." Instead of a war for independence, this country obtained an Autonomous Charter from Spain, and months later was ceded to the United States in Spain's defeat in the Spanish-American War in 1898. With the great influx of European Catholic immigrants came also a new religious creation Spiritism, which became a "major ingredient in the creolized Afro-Hispanic Espiritismo."[3] This religious influence became very influential in Afro-Cuban religion, as well.

Trinidad and Tobago are twin islands in the southeast Caribbean Sea located about seven miles off the coast of Venezuela, supposedly once having been connected to the South American continent. When Columbus arrived there in 1498, he found the areas inhabited by Caribs and Arawaks. But the islands "remained a neglected corner of the Spanish empire until the 1780s, when an influx of French Catholic settlers and their African slaves marked the real beginning of the country's modern history." After the British take-over of the area in 1797, "the population began to grow steadily; during the 19th century, after slavery was abolished in the British West Indies in 1838, labourers were imported from various other parts of the world—chiefly India, but also China and the Portuguese island of Madeira."[4] The results were new mixtures of cultures and religions brought in by these laborers from the East. We have already seen discussions of how they impacted one another and were in turn impacted in their interactions with existing religious varieties such as Afro-Caribbean ones and the dominant Christian society. In 1888 the two islands were joined as one English colony, and the colony won its independence from England in 1962 and in 1976 became a part of the English Commonwealth of Nations,[5] as did other former colonies of Great Britain after independence, such as India, Australia, Ghana, and others.

As was mentioned in an earlier chapter, Trinidad underwent a significant cultural transformation during the Black Revolution that swept the country beginning in 1970. Much like the Black Revolution in the United States, as well as other countries in the Caribbean, there was rejection of racial discrimination and oppressive conditions, demands for justice and political and social equality, and assertion of rights and liberties, as well as African cultural revivals. In each country and each social setting this movement took on some differences depending on the circumstances. Pearl Eintou Springer describes some of the specific acts of that movement in Trinidad. She says that their first act of liberation and defiance was to enter the Roman Catholic Cathedral and drape the images in black. "In our youth, we did not fully understand the depth of that symbolism. All we knew was that anger and frustration had reached boiling point. The God we served, in His Whiteness seemed to mock us. He seemed represent everything that was unattainable." As in the United States and elsewhere, students played a large role in this movement. Springer says they were "prepared to destroy and be destroyed rather than continue to be unfulfilled and alienated." Once again, a comparative element to the movement in the U. S. and elsewhere is that musicians and other artists joined to give expression to the mood and meaning of the struggle. She says, "The poets and musicians blossomed and trumpeted our pain, determination and links with our history. And the political directorate was forced to listen and make concessions."[6]

George Lamming, accomplished Caribbean novelist and essayist, describes the impact this movement had on him when he arrived in Trinidad in 1970 for a speaking engagement, just after what was called the February Rebellion.

> This is when, beginning with the students…the incident with the Canadian governor-general, whom they had not allowed to come on to the campus, and then that opened up into a big sort of march and demonstration that went on then for about six or seven weeks. All sorts of forces were at work there. And also what eventually became a mutiny trial in the army. And I'd gone—I don't remember at what time the invitation came—to a conference. The Oilfield Workers Trade Union had invited me to be the guest speaker. And I go down to San Fernando, this is the part that is distressing, and there are a lot of police there, checking you. But George Weekes, the general secretary, is in prison. He is detained. He is one of the many people detained. And I spoke, but I spoke with a very heavy heart, because Weekes occupied a position of such enormous stature within that Oilfield Workers Trade Union that I didn't understand how the general secretary could be in prison and there weren't massive demonstrations.[7]

With all the gates of Woodward Square in Port of Spain, once the University of Woodward Square, locked, and other distressing occurrences, Lamming found this to be a "very weighty period."[8]

What is so important about this Black Revolution in Trinidad for our study is the opening up of the people to the importance and meaning of the African religious heritage, especially Orisa religion. Pearl Springer asserts, "Many of us came to the traditional African religion as an act of political and ideological self expression."[9] Such was the influence on Trinidadian jazz musician Andre Tanker, whose music was greatly impacted by the 1970 African cultural renaissance. He states that before 1970, "Nobody ever said anything about African music. That wasn't a pleasant word to use." He says he discovered African music, "by opening myself up, being among drummers—the music is mainly drums and voices working with them—going to Orisha ceremonies, reading," studying the Orisha faith from the music standpoint.[10] Judy Raymond says, "The Orisha faith is central to his work. But his involvement with the faith is not as crucial as, say, Bob Marley's Rastafarianism was to his music."[11] But the important thing is the self-discovery that began to happen in him and others, the re-awakening to their roots, the pride and acceptance of their heritage.

Interestingly, this re-awakening to one's roots and heritage began to take place with other ethnic and cultural groups in Trinidad, as it did for others in the United States during the Black Power/Black Liberation Movement, such as Native Americans, Asian Americans, and many other groups. In Trinidad, a Carib resurgence movement began in 1973 and continues to this day, and it has spread to Puerto Rico and the United States. Maximilian C. Forte describes the resurgence in an article titled, "The Carib Resurgence from 1973 to the Present."[12] Forte has researched the Amerindians of Arima, Trinidad and Tobago, and the modern day Carib community living there. He says the town itself emerged in colonial times as a Catholic Mission town for Amerindians, where various tribes were gathered for Catholic training and supervision for work in cultivating cocoa. His main focus is on the Santa Rosa Festival, "one of the dominant rituals to emerge in the Arima Mission," commemorating the local saint of the Carib community. He describes the content, origin, and development of this festival, and notes its decline in the 1960's, "the Carib community having seriously dwindled and apathy set in amongst the youth."[13]

Forte traces the movement to a young man by the name of Ricardo Bharath Hernandez living in Detroit, who was a native of Trinidad and who has Amerindian roots. Having a desire to return to Trinidad, he did travel back there regularly. He and others reminiscing about the Santa Rosa Festival and its treasured history developed a desire for its restoration. Hernandez moved back to Trinidad permanently in 1983. He has come to lead the revival of the Carib community, as he and others in talking to the elders of the Caribs there learned that they had Carib ancestry. Forte describes the successes of the movement in working with the Catholic Church authorities and the government. "In 1976, with the guidance and support of the Minisrty of Culture, an attorney, and a local folklorist, Bharath registered the Santa Rosa Carib Community as a limited liability company. Land they received from the Church was quickly occupied by squatters. The state, in turn, could not find land suitable for the needs of the Carib group. It was clear to Bharath that this revival and reorganization was to be a long-term affair and that he was in for 'the long haul.' This process continues a quarter of a century after."[14]

Forte recalls the socio-political context in which this resurgence is taking place in Trinidad and notes its impact on the movement. "The 1970's in Trinidad, with the country led by one of the premiere nationalist intellectuals of the Caribbean, and the society in the grips of momentous upsurges in ethnic consciousness and pride in local history, saw numerous such grass roots revival efforts." He goes on to state the demands of this Carib movement, having to do with restoration and preservation of the Carib culture, religion, language, and other traditions.

The main demands of the organization were: recognition as a "legitimate cultural sector,' research support, and institutional support, especially funding. Amongst the primary aims of the Carib Community were the preservation and maintenance of surviving traditions (even those traditions that, historically, were for the Amerindians and not by them: i.e., the Santa Rosa Festival and Parang music, a Spanish "folk" music originally developed for the catechism of illiterate Amerindians). However, a new aim also emerged: the "retrieval" and "recovery" of traditions by the Amerindians, including the island Carib language. This last aim was not only pushed forward by a new influential member in the group, one who studied about shamanic practices, but was also encouraged by Bharath as an aim that should be pursued via the vehicle of "cultural interchange" between Amerindian communities of the Caribbean. Visions of a future community also began to alter: land is being sought to not only build a "model Amerindian village," but one that could also host visiting delegations of Caribbean Amerindians on a long-term basis.[15]

This Carib restoration has been extended to establish relations with Tainos of Puerto Rico and the United States.[16] Emerging in the late 1990's, this effort is seen as one of the most important from the viewpoint of the Shaman of the Arima Carib Community, as well as from the standpoint of the public's incredulity that the two Indigenous groups are still in existence, "when both were presumed totally extinct." Their struggles are great in trying to recover their traditions, including cultivation and relearning of shamanic practices, acquiring land, and grappling with the issue of being "racially mixed." Forte describes the progress in the development of this link between the two groups from 1997 to 2000.

The private foundation, Harmony in Diversity, was responsible for bringing two Taino representatives to Trinidad in what turned out to be a mini intercontinental Indigenous gathering that included an Australian Aboriginal representative. The two representatives were Daniel Waconax and Kacique Rene Cibanakan, of the Taino Nation of the Antilles. Cibanakan has immersed himself in shamanic knowledge and traditions and shared these with his like-minded Arima counterpart, Shaman Cristo Atekosang Adonis. This relationship developed into a close one that continued well after the event terminated, with frequent correspondence and telephone calls. The second Taino delegation to Arima, on a more informal basis, came in the form of two young men from New York City, Icahuey and Waha, in June of 1998, as the guests of Ricardo Kapaupana Cruz, the second shaman of the Carib Community and founder of Kairi Tukuienyo Karinya.[17]

Cultural interchange between the two groups takes place in the Carib Shaman's Smoke Ceremony, shamans from each adopting each other's practices, such as cigar and tobacco leaves and Taino zemis, and the like. They have faced problems of being accepted as authentic indigenous persons. For one thing the issue of the "race of indigeneity" has been raised. "Both Cibanakan and Adonis have felt the derogatory scorn and suspicion that comes from feeling and claiming in

Indigenous heritage and identity while appearing in the eyes of others as 'black.' Being dismissed as charlatans, impostors, or intruders into the realm of Indigenous purity is something that individuals such as the Shaman have had to endure from Church officials, political party figures, and even representatives of other Caribbean Indigenous groups."[18] Aside from such problems, some of which they have had to overcome by rejecting the racial purity approach to indigeneity, contact has broadened to other areas in the Caribbean through contacts with the United Federation of Taino People (UCTP), members of which attended Arima's Third Indigenous Gathering "of delegates from Amerindian groups from across the Caribbean and North America"[19] in 2000. Although Forte does not mention Puerto Rico specifically in the article, I presume that the Taino community of Ponce, Puerto Rico, from Centro Ceremonial Indigena De Tibes, whose restoration site I visited in 2004, was represented at these meetings. Forte feels certain that ties between the Arima Cairbs and the Tainos will increase and deepen with time.

Notice should be taken of how Trinidad's cultural and religious groups of Afro-Caribbean, Muslim, Hindu, Spiritual Baptists, Catholic, and Carib mixture of peoples witness, and share in the various festivals or carnivals that are celebrated throughout the calendar year. In March, there is the Spiritual Baptist Shouter Liberation Day; the Hindu spring festival of Phagwa, the fun of which is spraying pink or purple dye (abeer) on other participants, and getting sprayed on. Singing and dancing competitions are a part of this celebration, as well. Also the Muslim festival of Hosay comes in March, taking up a three-night period usually. "To the beat of tassa drumming, pretty tadjahs (floats in the shape of ornate tombs) are drawn through the streets of St. James in celebration of the life and death of the two brothers Hassan and Hussein, grandsons of the prophet Mohammed."[20]

In addition to the Good Friday and Easter celebrations in April comes a festivity that brings the Catholic and Hindu communities together, known as La Divina Pastora. Indians also celebrate Arrival Day on May 30th, marking the first arrival of their ancestors in 1845. In June a sacred Hindu event takes place called the Ganga Dashara Festival, which involves visit to the Marianne River, a New World representation of the Ganges in India. Corpus Christi Day is celebrated on the 10th of June. On August 1, Afro-Trinidadians celebrate Emancipation Day, commemorating the end of slavery in 1838. Independence Day is celebrated by all on August 31, an event that took place in 1962, marking the end of the official colonial status of the island. The Santa Rosa Festival, which we have spoken of as undergoing restoration and revival as part of the Carib Community cultural revival, takes place in August, as well as focusing on a patron saint of the Carib community.[21]

November is marked by Hindu and Muslim religious festivals, including Divali, Ramleela, and Eid-ul-Fitr. Hindu Divali is a festival of lights, when "parks, temples, and private homes are illuminated by tens of thousands of small clay lamps called deyas, in honour of Lakshmi, the goddess of light, love, and prosperity. Trinidadians of all faiths love assisting with the lighting of deyas....In the weeks leading up to the festival, villages across Trinidad stage spectacular theatrical re-enactments of the Ramayana, called Ramieela." The Muslim festival of Eid-ul-Fitr is also one which attracts and welcomes the participation of members of all faiths. It comes at end of the sacred month of Ramadan (when Muslims fast from sunrise to sunset). The closing festival is celebrated with "elaborate feasts and generous almsgiving. Muslims extend the festivities to friends and neighbours of all beliefs by sharing food...." In December comes also the worldwide Christian holiday of Christmas, which has its own special character in Trinidad, as elsewhere in the world, including month-long preparations and festivities.[22]

The focus on these festivities which involve the island's multi-ethnic and multi-religious inhabitants gives a glimpse into how these peoples from diverse Western and Eastern origins are able to retain their religions and heritages in this new environment and live together in relative harmony and respect for each others' traditions and practices. How they got to this place and the adjustments they have made since their arrival has to do with something we refer to as continuity and change. Obviously, they have had to change in many ways and adapt to the new environment and social and economic situation. This is typical, of course, of all the Caribbean Islands, as well as countries in Central and South America. But each area made different demands on the inhabitants in regard to the adjustments that were necessary, and the people of each area have a certain uniqueness as to their cultural, religious, political, and economic character and make-up.

Issues of Continuity and Change, Repression and Resistance

With respect to adaptations or accommodations of beliefs and practices of traditions, George Brandon makes a very true and apt statement: "A tradition that doesn't accommodate itself to changed circumstances in ways that will allow it to persist will be unable to reproduce itself and will be extinguished."[23] Many challenging issues have faced the Afro-Caribbean religions of Cuba, Puerto Rico, and Trinidad and Tobago to which each of the religious groups have adapted in their own ways. But whatever the challenges in each case and howsoever they have managed to face them, they have all had the strength and tenacity to survive.

On a study trip to Puerto Rico in 2004, I met a young woman with whom I spent some time in visiting certain historic places, including the oldest Catholic Cathedral in Old San Juan, had what appeared to be the typical response of the average middle class Catholic in regard to questions concerning the practice of Santeria and Espiritismo. To my question as to whether or not she knew anyone who practiced these religious forms, she grimaced and expressed a strong dislike for being around such people. Getting around in San Juan and Old San Juan, I did not get glimpse of a botánica (a shop that sells books, candles, and the many paraphernalia relating to Santeria and Espiritismo). But while in Ponce, about a two-hour drive north of San Juan, I found two botánicas which I was able to visit and purchase artifacts which reveal aspects of the religious practices. The owner of one, however, whose grandson served as interpreter, anxiously asserted that she inherited the business from her father, who had passed some years ago, and she was keeping it up for his sake; yet, she herself was a staunch Catholic. This is one thing that attests to the fact that today the historical difficulties and problems facing the religions are still prevalent. And their practices are still done in not very open circumstances.

But a look at Cuba and the issues facing the development of Santeria or Regla de Ocha there and the adjustments and accommodations it has had to undergo will reveal much in terms of the development and survival of this religion. Some comparisons and contrasts with Orisa religion in Trinidad and Puerto Rico will also be revealing. Issues of race, ethnicity, religious restrictions and repressions, social and class stigma all enter into the picture in the case of all three religious communities in their struggle to survive and adjust to their situations. Race seems to have played a larger role in Cuba than in either Puerto Rico or Trinidad because of the massive number of African slaves in Cuba that the Spanish had to attempt to control. Blacks are said to have composed a majority of the population of Cuba in the first half of the nineteenth century.[24] By contrast, we have already seen that African slaves never composed more than 11% of the population of Puerto Rico. And in Trinidad are large numbers of other ethnic groups, such as East Indians and other Asians, who have been and still are stigmatized and discriminated against along with Afro-Trinidadians. We have already seen where these groups are forming organizations wherein they work together to seek to eliminate the injustices they face as being outside the dominant power group.

It has already been pointed out that Santeria in Cuba developed in the cabildos that were encouraged by the Catholic Churches in the cities as clubs where Catholicism could be taught to the various nationalities of African slaves, who also practiced their religious traditions alongside or mingled with the Catholic beliefs and practices. However, this sort of guided syncretism did not work so well, as it was not very easy for the Church to maintain control of these organizations. Tensions developed between the Church and the cabildos, and restrictions were placed on the cabildos which forced them to operate underground for long periods. And this tension operated to keep suspicion going regarding the cabildos that were dismantled and restored at times, to the extent that only two survive today, the Santa Barbara Cabildo and the San Antonio Cabildo, both of which I visited in my study trip to Cuba in 1999. In addition to restrictions on their religious practices, the Afro-Cuban faced race and color problems among the whites as well as within their own race wherein self-rejection took place on the part of free blacks who began to denigrate their African heritage and to attempt to lighten their complexions through some means, including intermarriage with whites.[25]

Racial discrimination against Afro-Cubans and Afro-Cuban religions continued to grow and exacerbate in the late 19th century and early 20th century when the Ten Years War (1868–1878) and the War for Independence (1895–1903) failed to satisfy and reward the hopes of Afro-Cubans for freedom and equality. Racism and corruption was magnified when U. S. dominance replaced Spanish colonialism after 1898, helping to spark the Negro Revolt in 1912 that caused the loss of thousands of Afro-Cuban lives. Middle class tendencies or attitudes toward African religions and cultures became mixed, showing ambivalence, vacillation, and contradiction in regard to the issue of African culture and Cuban identity. Brandon sums it up. "In the fluid political and economic context of the postindependence era, three contrasting attitudes toward the African religions emerged: an anti-Africanist tendency, a syncretist tendency promoting the blending of spiritism and the African religions, and an avant-garde tendency among Cuban intellectuals that promoted the African religions as sources of artistic inspiration and national culture."[26]

After slavery ended in 1888, a process began in Lucumí (Santeria) religious groups whereby other ethnic groups, including whites, were able to initiate into the religion. Brandon states: "In time the secret religious practices ceased to be solely the property of Afro-Cubans. They were passed on to peoples with mixed ancestry. All along the line there would have been whites who had been assisted by African healers, who sought out good luck or counsel from Yoruba diviners. These would have been the upper-class creoles raised by African house servants, the poor white peasants who worked in the fields beside former slaves in the days after emancipation, whites who inhabited the same underground into which the cabildos had been forced." Brandon notes that in the city of Regla a strong practice of Santeria was carried out solely by Hispano-Cubans.[27] In the years 1902–1920 African religions and culture were persecuted under a campaign of Europeanization "which denigrated everything revealing the African presence." The attempt was to de-Africanize Cuba, focusing from one aspect on the cabildos, which were raided and important African religious emblems and religious artifacts were confiscated and destroyed. This persecution drove the cabildos further underground. They became secret societies, losing some of their positive moral influences and in cases becoming mixed with the exploitative sorcery of the subterranean world of "the occultists and adepts of of the new religions of Espiritismo."[28]

Espiritismo in Cuba and Puerto Rico: Racial, Class, and Ethnic Issues

This religious influence stemming from France was one which spread to Cuba and Puerto Rico and affected the populace in ways that were similar but also different. It did not spread to Trinidad, which experienced its own religious mixtures, including Spiritualism more or less from the North American continent, which we shall view in a later part of the chapter. The origin of Espiritismo is the Spiritism of Allan Kardec, born Hippolyte Léon Denizaed Rivail

(1804–69) in France, a scientist and educator who wrote a number of books on the subject. Although Spiritism or Spiritualism, a movement in Christianity having to do with communication with the spirits of the dead, had developed in the the United States and other parts of Europe, Kardec's Spiritism coming out of France was unique to him. He claimed scientific and philosophical foundations for his beliefs and practices. Amalia Soler (1835–1912) is said to have popularized Spiritism in Spain through his writings, and around 1850 the literature began to spread in the Spanish and French Caribbean, and other parts of Latin America. It became highly popular among certain groups.[29]

Although these beliefs flew in the face of Catholic Church doctrines and official practices, Kardecism first became popular among the upper classes in Pureto Rico, who promoted it, adopted it, wrote of it and discussed it in published articles. But in Cuba it was the middle class who first who first took to the practice. Reason for this was seen as ideological and political. Many of the middle class in Cuba "were antagonistic toward the Catholic hierarchy they could never penetrate. Others were independistas [promoters of independence from Spain] and saw the church as an arm of the Spanish monarchy which was draining the island." Still others were disenchanted with the conservative church and promoted more scientific and liberal religious views, such as they found in Kardecism. Though their claims of scientific and orderly processes enabled them to perceive of their practices from a supposedly higher standpoint, the middle class habits of prayer, trances, and mediumship, and the like did not set them very far apart from practices of other classes in the society not on their level. Therefore, Espiritismo spread to lower levels of the urban classes and soon out into the countryside.[30]

Canizares attributes the adaptation of Espiritismo into Santeria to the decline of the egungun (African ancestral spirits) in late 19th century Santeria. "About this time, Lucumí house servants began to notice that their masters—or more often their masters' wives—were becoming possessed of the spirits of their ancestors through a practice called Espiritismo. The house servants also observed that the white people were doing this without much risk to their lives. With the wonderful adaptability that characterizes Afro-Cuban culture, santeros appropriated the technical, mechanical aspects of Kardecism—the prayers, the paraphernalia and invocations—as a replacement for the egungun." He points out further that the philosophical aspects of this belief are virtually ignored in Santeria, but the "skill of becoming possessed by the spirits of the dead has become essential to every santero." It is therefore, Kardecian Spiritism which supplies the new egungun of Santeria for the Afro-Cuban religious world.[31]

Brandon describes how Espiritismo became unique in Cuba by taking on elements in its local environment. It "grew by accumulating elements of Spanish and Cuban herbalism, Native American healing practices, and the merest scent of African magic. In Cuba Kardec's spirit guides frequently embodied the popular stereotypic images of Cuban ethnic, racial, and professional groups. Not only did Cuban espiritistas in their mediumistic trance manifest spirit guides that resembled themselves, both physically and in temperament, but black and white mediums manifested spirit guides who were Africanos de nación—Lucumi, Mandinga, Mina, and Congolese tribesmen who had suffered and died in slavery....None of this was in Kardec."[32]

Although Espiritismo became mixed with Catholicism just as Santeria did, and also had a similar occult underground, as well as the uses of saints and healing practices, there were those who held Espiritismo as more suited to the white middle class literate group. There were distinctions made, say, in their uses of the saints, which in Espiritismo were "pure and remote and not at the ready call of the medium; instead, mediums relied on a variety of lesser and more accessible spirits." Thus, spirit guides, angel guardians of Espiritismo were 'lumped together with the saints or orisha; in turn the saints or orisha assumed new roles as ptotectors, spirit guides, and guardian angels." However, practitioners of the two religions came to serve as both santeros/santeras and espiritistas, though they never actually merged the two roles together, always separating the times, locations, and symbols of the two religions.[33]

Further distinct contrasts and comparisons are seen as existing between Espiritismo in Cuba and in Puerto Rico which reveal certain important social issues in the religion in both places. Olmos and Paravisini-Gebert note the comparative aspects in the fact that in both countries, the attraction for European Spiritism was first found among the literate middle to upper class sectors of the society, who saw it as an alternative to more restrictive and oppressive Catholic traditional doctrines and an effort toward liberty and independence of thought and expression in a colonial setting. However, it did not remain among only one social class group, because "other classes began practicing their own variety of Creole Espiritismo in a culture already prepared to absorb a doctrine that reinforced existing spiritual beliefs: the spirit-oriented popular and folk Cathholicism of the rural peasant populations—the Cuban guajiro and the

Puerto Rican jíbaro who had been largely ignored by institutional Roman Catholicism—and African-based religions."[34] Furthermore, there were varieties of Espiritismo in each of these countries for various reasons having to do with issues related to social situations.

In Cuba Olmos and Paravisini-Gebert point out, for instance, that during the Ten Years' War of Insurrection fought against Spanish domination (1868–78), as the Church collaborated with the colonial government, pro-independence citizens began to consider Spiritism more liberal and progressive than Catholicism. Eastern rural Cuba, "an area harshly affected by the cruelty and bloodshed of the war," some people "turned to Espiritismo and supernatural solutions to their suffering. By the 1880s Espiritismo had spread throughout the island, provoking its condemnation by the Cuban Catholic hierarchy." The authors examine three principal forms of Cuban Espiritismo: "'Scientific' or 'Table' Espiritismo (sometimes referred to as 'White Table'), Espiritismo de Cordón or 'Cord Spiritism' (practitioners are called cordoneros), and Espiritismo Cruzao [cruzado], Crossed [Mixed] Spiritism." In the first type (Table Espiritismo) participants engage in séance sitting around a table in what they consider a more scientific and philosophical, elevated, religious practice in communicating with the spirits. This is clearly of a higher class status. Espiritismo de Cordón, however, is of a lower class status, involving the practices of standing in a circle, hand in hand, trumping, chanting, praying, other motions, and trance. It focuses on healing in which a medium is used to help solve the problem. The practice is not uniform or highly structured. "Cures are stressed over theory, and elements of possession analgous to those of African-based religions combine with ideas considered scientific, distancing the practice from the 'superstitions' and 'fetishism' of the 'blacks, and the authority and classist nature of the 'whites' represented by Catholicism." The third type, Espiritismo Cruzao (Crossed), is a combination of the first two and Afro-Cuban religions, like the Regla de Palo Monte (religion of Congo origin in Cuba), and folk Catholicism. It includes animal sacrifice and healing, private spiritual consultations, altars to ancestors, etc.[35]

Puerto Ricans of the educated class who were anticolonialists also perceived Espiritismo as impetus and inspiration to their aspirations of liberating the island from Spanish rule. And they did secretly organize a revolt but were detected and repressed by the government and the Church. While White Table Espiritismo developed in Puerto Rico as it did in Cuba, the other two Cuban varieties did not reach Puerto Rico until after 1959. The most popular form of Espiritismo to develop in Puerto Rico was a home-grown type, so to speak, which was indigenous to Puerto Rico. It emerged among the urban and rural lower classes and combines native healing systems of the Tainos (Arawaks), represented by the shaman, "called the bohique who prayed to the spirits using massage, tobacco, herbs, and magic to effect cures—and the herbal medicine and folk healing practices of both the Spaniards and the enslaved Africans. All these were syncretized to create an indigenous, healing-oriented, popular Espiritismo which incorporated traditions that had been around in the country for centuries.[36]

Impact of Afro-Cubanism on Cuban Santeria

Afro-Cubanism was the movement in Cuba that paralleled the Harlem Renaissance in the United States that focused on a revival of Afro arts and culture, the general dynamism of the socalled primitive. It was part of an international movement including Europe and North America. "The primitive became the advanced. Peoples without culture suddenly possessed it in extreme modernist forms. Black heads, formerly seen as the abode of a dull and empty void, became filled with magic, an irrational, intuitive élan vital with which avant-garde artists and intellectuals hoped to vivify or destroy the decaying structure of Europe." Seen as a response to the political, social, and cultural problems of the Cuban Republic, the Afro-Cuban movement was concerned with questions of race, social inequality, economics, and Cuban national identity, as well as a critique of Western civilization.[37]

The works of renowned Cuban anthropologist and author Fernando Ortiz (1881–1969) were quite influential on this movement. Jean Stubbs notes Ortiz's being "most attributed with lifting the veil on 'the other side' of Cuba's history: that of the Cuban population of African origin."[38] Both Stubbs and George Brandon take note of the motivation for Ortiz's earliest research and writing in the area of Afro-Cuban religion and culture as being his work with the Cuban prison system, admitting that it his approach was from the criminalistic approach dealing with and exposing the "most feared and reviled element: sorcery" in *Hampa Afrocubana: Los Negros Brujos* (Afro-Cuban Underworld: The Black Obeah, Havana 1906).[39] Brandon regrets the negative racial aspect of the earlier work of Ortiz and adds that its value to Afro-Cubanism "was that it provided a first systematic account of Afro-Cuban culture, especially Afro-Cuban religious beliefs, myths, and rites."[40] Brandon points out the "strong biological determinist underpinning" of Ortiz's earlier work, *Los Negros Brujos*, stating that his "solutions to one aspect of Cuba's social and cultural problem were ethnic selection of the superior (white) over the inferior (black) race and the civilizing of the primitive mentalities of the blacks through cultural assimilation."[41] However, Brandon asserts that Ortiz's works helped fuel the Afro-Cuban movement rather than spearheading it, and he was converted to it as it got going. Also, he gained enormous respect in it, though Ortiz's "basic ideology remained that of a liberal bourgeois reformist: positivistic, rationalistic, seeing the inevitable, gradual progress of Cuban history and society leading to the obliteration of African culture on the island.[42]

It must be noted that there are other scholars who would disagree with this critique of the later views of Ortiz. Stubbs, for instance, notes that from the 1920's on Ortiz's views changed. "Painstaking and thorough in his knowledge, positivist in his outlook and methodology, he developed an encompassing humanist view of humankind and pioneered modern sociology and anthropology in Latin America." She likes especially Ortiz's rejection of "acculturation" and preference of "transculturation" in regard to cultural interactions: "He rejected 'acculturation' as a one-way process whereby a newcomer culture adapts to the already existing, in favor of a two-way process of transculturation whereby each culture becomes influenced by the other, thereby creating a dynamic new culture."[43]

Canizares's assessment of the Afro-Cubanism movement, which he calls negrismo in Cuba, was this: "Unfortunately, the success of negrismo did not filter down to the colored masses, and it remained an elitist movement."[44] Brandon agrees with this and further clarifies and elaborates on its effects and impacts. He declares:

> Although Afro-Cubanism extended a degree of legitimacy to Santeria and other Afro-Cuban religions, the profound reevaluation of African culture this group of white and mulatto intellectuals brought about was by no means the dominant current in Cuban thought in the 1920s and 1930s. Afro-Cubanist ideas competed with anti-African and liberal reform tendencies throughout the period. Furthermore, the majority of Cubans did not derive their image of Santeria from state officials, social reformers, or intellectuals but from the mass media and stereotypes embedded in popular culture.[45]

Africa's Oshun in Cuba, Puerto Rico, and Trinidad and the Multifarious Image of *La Virgen de la Caridad del Cobre* (The Virgin of Charity of Cobre): Symbols of Continuity and Change in Caribbean Religions

Cultural historian Maria Elena Diaz does a revealing and an interesting analysis and interpretation of what is generally recognized as Cuba's most important religious tradition in her essay, "Rethinking Tradition and Identity: The Virgin of Charity of El Cobre."[46] She begins by stating that "El Cobre is a small and deceptively plain village of legendary character for the Cuban people. Black or white, resident or exile, religious or secular, Cubans still identify it as the abode of Our Lady of Charity, patroness of the Cuban nation and often Cuban version of the Yoruba deity Oshun. The story of the Virgin of Charity has been linked in the island's cultural imagination throughout most of this last century to ideas of the nation, creolization, race, syncretism, and to all sorts of miraculous and historical interventions in the world."[47]

Migene González-Wippler recalls the Nigerian background of Oshun and gives an explanation of why she became syncretized with Cuba's Virgin of Charity. As she states, Oshun is the goddess of the river by that name "that crosses the regions of Ijesha and Ijebu in Nigeria." She has a title of honor, *Ya-lodde*, the highest that can be bestowed on a woman of the land. She points out further that, being the symbol of river waters without which life on earth would be impossible, Oshun thus "controls all that makes life worth living, such as love and marriage, children, money, pleasures." The author further asserts that the main reason she is syncretized with "Our Lady of La Caridad del Cobre, the patron saint of Cuba," is that "in Nigeria cobre (copper) was the most precious metal in ancient times. Oshun is said to have been passionately fond of copper jewelry and part of her ache is deposited on this metal. Now that copper is no longer a valuable metal, her tastes have changed and now she is partial to gold, which is one of her attributes."[48] This is a plausible explanation that comes out of the lore surrounding the goddess and the saint, but it does contain certain verities.

Canizares cites another story with a different twist to it to explain the journey of Oshun from Africa to Cuba. It is not of African origin but is derived from the inventiveness of Cubans of relatively recent times.

Oshún, goddess of love and of the rivers, watched sadly as great numbers of her children were forcibly taken away to a far-away land called Cuba. Confused about the situation and her inability to stop strange white men from abducting her followers, Oshún went to see her older sister, Mother Yemayá, to ask her advice. "Wise sister, what is happening? Why can't I stop this tragedy from occurring?"

"It had to happen this way, Oshún," answered Yemayá sadly. "Our children will tell the entire world of our wonders, and millions who have forgotten us will worship us again."

Moved by an intense desire to be with her suffering children, Oshún decided on an impulse to move to Cuba. But she had never before left her kingdom, the Oshún River, and was afraid. "Tell me, Yemayá, you whose seven seas caress all of the lands of the world, what is Cuba like?"

Thinking pensively for a moment, the stately queen answered, "It is much like here: hot days, long nights, lush vegetation, tranquil rivers."

"Is there anything about Cuba and its people I should know before I move there?"

"Yes," answered Yemayá, "Not everyone is black like us; there are also many whites."

Impulsive as she is, Oshún asked Yemayá to grant her two wishes. "Make my hair straighter and my skin lighter so that all Cubans can see a bit of themselves in me."

With a majestic sweep of her hand, Yemayá granted her sister's wishes. That is why Oshún in Cuba has long, wavy hair and light skin; this is why all Cubans worship "Cachita" (the pet name for Oshún), regardless of the color of their skin.[49]

This is a very rational myth that aligns well with the historical/cultural situation that exists in the Santeria/Catholic, secular, social, racial, and political milieu of Cuban society as well in the Cuban/Puerto Rican diaspora. And it adds richness to the oral version of the story describing the finding of the image of the Virgin and subsequent actions which contributed to the development of the tradition regarding it.

Maria Diaz states, "According to oral legend and popular viaual iconography, long ago the virgin appeared to three (racially identified) fishermen in the Bay of Nipe: a black mulatto, and Indian, and a white. These fishermen have come to represent the trinity of races or ethnicities constituting the Cuban nation (excluding the usually excluded Chinese). The virgin herself has become in the last century not so much an icon of lo cubano, but to many, of cubanía itself.[50] Everyone tells the story of the appearance of the virgin differently. C. Peter Ripley describes his encounter with the virgin on one of his Cuban journeys in the 1990's and recounts the story and later events regarding the tradition, as well as its impact in Cuba today.

Describing the location and the event, he says, "The church of El Cobre stands high in the foothills of Sierra Maestra overlooking the town, a town as needy as any in Cuba, a town surrounded by a landscape ruined and depleted by open-pit copper mining....In 1608, at a time when the town prospered, two Indian brothers [other stories say a slave and two Indians[51]] collecting salt at the Bay of Nipe spotted something floating in the sea. They pulled into their boat a foot-tall wooden statue of Mary carrying the Christ Child on one arm and a gold cross on the other. The image was supported in the water by a plank that bore the inscription Yo soy la Virgen de la Caridad: I am the Virgin of Charity." Ripley then cites the legend of the statue's being brought back to Cobre and placed in a hut. The virgin being dissatisfied with that location would disappear three nights in a row and be found each morning at the top of the hill. Convinced of her miraculous power, the people built a second church in the next century and placed her high on the main altar. "Over the years she was credited with all manner of miracles, including siding with the local slaves in their rebellion of 1731, which gained them freedom. In 1916, at the request of the veterans of the Cuban War of Independence, the Pope declared her the patron saint of Cuba. In 1926 she was moved into a new church, a beige and red basilica that backs up to the mountains and looks down upon the destitute community and ruined land." Ripley's Cuban host told him that most people in Cuba believe in the Virgen of Charity, in her miraculous powers, and in the story of her rising out of the water.[52]

Maria Diaz finds little memory among Cubans today, however, of an "earlier colonial historical context in which the Virgin of Charity's story and cult grew. Most people today seem unaware that the modern national tradition itself flourished from another locally reinvented tradition in the past." Therefore, she recounts setting, political, social, and economic circumstances in which the incidents took place and in which the tradition was established. She brings to life the original characters in the drama of the story and interprets its significance. Her analysis and interpretation sheds much light on the Virgin of Charity as a plurivocal symbol. First she brings to light the historical situation of the Spanish crown's confiscating from its private contractor the copper mines and slaves of El Cobre in 1607. The 271 slaves became the king's slaves. Several historical developments followed that significantly affected the status of the slaves and Indians and other persons in the area. The royal slaves were reconstituted a pueblo, which was a community with special political status, with certain privileges, including a opportunities of rooting themselves.[53]

Diaz states, "By 1730, El Cobre was one in only fourteen duly constituted settlements—cities, towns, and villages—on the island, at least two of which were Indian corporate pueblos in Oriente [province]. By 1773, El Cobre had grown into a sizable village of 1,320 inhabitants, of whom 64 percent were royal slaves, 2 percent personal slaves, and 34 percent free people of color, mostly manumitted descendants or relatives of royal slaves." With this kind of established power base, they were able to solidify their status and negotiate their place in society. In this context, Diaz is able to examine what the appearance of Our Lady of Charity must have meant to the people of El Cobre, mostly a community of royal slaves in the 17th century. Therefore, she brings into the picture the real names in the story and the official recount of the story of the virgin to a real audience. It was in 1687 that "the elderly royal slave Juan Moreno recounted to an official audience of ecclesiastics the history (or his story) of a small effigy of the Virgin of Charity. He spoke as a Creole slave, as a privileged witness, a protagonist in a portentous story about the past, as a chosen instrument of divine will, and as oral historian of his community." She states further that "Moreno's story about the finding of a miraculous statue was based on a Marian master code whereby the mother of God appeared to the wretched, lowest, and most disempowered all over the world: to children and women, to shepherds and peasants, to Indians and (more rarely in the colonial world) to blacks and slaves. This genre of stories and legends codifies an important ideological tenet of Christianity—namely, the value of all men and women in the eyes of God, where, in fact, the underprivileged can become overprivileged through divine favor."[54]

Diaz gives the details of the notarized account which Moreno gave to the church officials. The incident happened when he was about ten years old as he and the two Joyos brothers were on their way to the salt mines in the Nipe Bay. They caught sight of the image of the virgin engraved with the words, "I am the Virgin of Charity." Miraculously, the clothes were dry. They took her to their overseer of the cattle ranch of Barajagua, "who in turn informed Captain Don Francisco Sanchez de Moya, administrator of the mines at the time, about the vent." It was Sanchez de Moya who gave orders to build an altar to the virgin in the pasture lands, which of course was not satisfactory to her. And we know from Ripley's account what happened as she made her wishes known as to where she wanted to be placed. Ultimately, it was realized that she wanted her "sanctuary built right next to the mines, in the Cerro de la Mina….She became, at least in Moreno's implicit text, the protector of the mines and its slaves. Indeed, she became their representative in the supernatural sphere."[55]

Diaz looks at the story of the virgin as having radical implication for the social order of the time in Cobre. For one thing she says, "the introduction of the virgin into the mines represented a new imagined order brought about by the slaves and the Indians. The new local order symbolized by the virgin protectress of the cobrero [dwellers in Cobre] miners—represented the cobreros' own appropriation of the space of El Cobre to found a community of their own—one, moreover, where her cult could become the focus of religious worship." The author goes on to read the symbolism of empowerment in the story in that the virgin appeared to the slave and the Indians in the natural environment outside the realm of colonial structure. "For it was in this natural sphere, away from the fetters of the colonial system, including the institutionalized church, where Creole slaves and Indians alike shared a common destiny by establishing an unmediated connection to a supernatural order represented by the virgin. It was in this supposedly natural uncolonized space of the sea that Indians and Creole slaves—or later cobreros—were empowered by the miracle of the apparition, and it is there where the vision of an imagined order in which they were the sole actors unfolded."[56]

Finally, Diaz notes the radical significance of this story of the virgin for the slave community as such. She states:

> The ritual of notarization may have been unusual itself insofar as the voices of slaves were juxtaposed against that of a white clergyman. Indeed, it is also extraordinary insofar as the memory and testimony of a Creole slave became the main narrative to accredit the miraculous "authenticity" of the effigy. The inclusion of slaves in this Christian narrative, the role of a royal slave (Juan Moreno) as main witness and living repository of this memory, and the development of the island's major eighteenth-century shrine in an Afro-Cuban pueblo all constitute remarkable (yet all too often unremarked) historical aspects in the making of this "Cuban" Marian tradition. It is as if in the case of the Virgin of El Cobre, slaves wrote themselves—and were allowed to write themselves—into a popular kind of mainstream story, one that would eventually be rewritten and remembered as a foundational story of the Cuban nation.[57]

In Puerto Rico the Virgin of Charity of El Cobre though she is acknowledged as the patron saint of Cuba syncretized with Oshun, is revered and worshipped along with the numerous other saints and orisha of Santeria. So although she does not have that centrality to the nation that exists in Cuba, in the ceremonies of Santeria and the celebrations of the santos and feast days, the Oshun/El Cobre link is honored along with other syncretisms of Catholicism and African beliefs and practices. One book I picked up in the Botánica San Lanzaro in Ponce, Puerto Rico, *La Fe en Oración* (Faith in Prayer), which contains 132 prayers, opens with the tribute, "Viva La Virgen De La Caridad Del Cobre," p. 1.

In Trinidadian Shango, Oshún is a vital part of the orisha pantheon and religious practices, but the Virgin of Charity is not a popular figure. Oshún is the goddess of the sea there more so than of the river. Since she and Yemayá are associated with bodies of water, the name Oshún Yemayá is sometimes used.[58] All the gods and goddesses are honored and manifested in the annual Ebo: Eshu, Ogun, Shango, Osanyin, Oyá, Yemayá, Oshún. Yoruba religion in Trinidad experienced a fusion of a different character than found in Cuba and Puerto Rico. There was the Catholic syncretism, certainly, but other blending as well took place, of which we should take special note.

Linguistic scholar and author Maureen Warner-Lewis speaks of growing up in Trinidad in the 1950's and being "primarily aware of ethnocultural diversity. The more subtle interconnections between cultural behaviors and class differentiation were to unfold themselves as teenage progressed into early adulthood." In spite of the restrictions placed on her overt associations as she grew older, she was still silently aware and appreciative of her mixed cultural environment. She was fascinated with the French Creole she heard on buses, in the market and in her neighbors' yard, "just ast the ornate descant of Indian music borne on the air from El Dorado, and the periodic night drumming which" her "persistence led her to discover was Shango's." She pursued and researched early her interests in the diverse elements: Caribbean proverbs, folk music records from Trinidad, Carriacou, India; "read stories set in Mandarin China, and sought enlightenment through paths as diverse as Christianity, Vodun, Buddhism and Hinduism." But her formal education instilled pride in European culture and overlooked or denigrated her African roots that still very much existed in Trinidad, the appreciation and understanding of which she and other Afro-Trinidadians had to pursue outside the formal educational structure. This led her to research and studies which correct this cultural imbalance in the educational system and the society.[59]

Warner-Lewis's studies bring out not only the submerged and overlooked aspects of Yoruba and other African cultural realities, but reveal also their influences on and fusion with other cultures and religions. Her essays point to synthesis "between African and other ethnocultural concepts and practices which have proved mutually compatible": processes of fusion "not only between African and European cultures, or among those of Africa, India and China, but also among African national cultures as well. Igbo and Congo and Yoruba have met in the New World and amalgamated their analogous worldviews and practices."

She notes the distinct imprint of Yoruba, which played the more dominant African cultural role in the society, "on the African/French/English synthesis which constituted Creole culture." She further states that, "The similarity between certain Yoruba and Asian institutions served to make Creole culture a more favorable avenue for inter-racial cultural synthesis"[60]

In the area of religion, Warner-Lewis points to "overt Yoruba influence in the persistence and spread of *orisha* ritual and its fusion with the Afro-Protestant Spiritual Baptist religion; and the inheritance in the early *kaiso* (calypso) of the rhythmic intricacy, melodic line, tonal key, and call/response structure of specific *shango* chants." Also notable is her observation of the overlapping of the African "mutual self-help financial" institution called "susu" with similar ones among the Chinese and Indians. Note is made also of the significance of the Yoruba contribution to making religion central to popular imagination. "Just as, among the Africans, it was the Yoruba for whom Catholicism had a special appeal, in the same way we see in Trinidad society how religious ritual and insignia have a tremendous impact on popular imagination, regardless of personal religious affiliation."[61]

The issues of continuity and change in the African Yoruba or Orisha (Shango) religion of Trinidad (as well as Grenada and St. Vincent) are exemplified in the narrated experiences of two Spiritual Baptist practitioners who participated in the Caribbean Religions Congress held at York University in Canada in 1996, sponsored by the Caribbean Religions Project at the Centre for Research on Latin America and the Caribbean (CERLAC) at York University and the Canadian Association of Latin America and Caribbean Studies (CALACS). The two women are Queen Mother Bishop Yvonne B. Drakes and Archbishop Doctor DeLores Seiveright, both of whom are from or have roots and associations in the West Indian countries of Grenada and Trinidad. Both also hold high offices in the Spiritual Baptist religion, which is a syncretism of Orisha and other African-derived religions and Protestant Christianity. They are both a part of the West Indian Caribbean communities and the Caribbean diaspora in Toronto, Canada. Their experiences demonstrate the great versatility and adaptability as well as the strong influence of the African religions.[62] It should be noted that in comparison with the Espiritismo (derived from European Spiritism) that spread to Cuba and Puerto Rico and impacted Yoruba religious practices in these Latin American countries, it was Spiritualism (or the North American brand of Spiritism more or less) that spread in the British West Indies and impacted African religious practices there. We see this revealed in the personal narratives of Drakes and Seiveright.

Yvonne B. Drakes unites within her the two faiths: Orisha and Spiritual Baptists. She summarizes her initiation and ordination in both the Orisha and the Spiritual Baptist religions and her functions in each. She states:

> I experienced an advanced period of training when I journeyed to Trinidad in August 1985, to officially take over the work of the Orisha Queen. This ceremony was performed at my aunt's property in Trinidad, where everything was set up for the transfer of stewardship of the Orisha ancestral work, handed down in my family for three generations. After the "acceptance" ceremony, I returned to Canada to continue my work there. Since my initiation and "crowning" as Queen of the Seven Orisha Tribes, I have continued my journey by fasting, praying, and "mourning," receiving along the way first the nine tribes and now the twelve tribes of the orisha. I have also grown within the Spiritual Baptist faith, and two years ago I became eligible to be ordained as a Minister of the gospel. I was ordained as the first woman Bishop in the Spiritual Baptist Faith in Canada.[63]

Drakes holds her Orisha "feasts" under the banner of her Spiritual Baptist Church and hosts the three-day Ebo or "African Prayers" to the orisha once a year as is done in the Orisha religion in Trinidad and elsewhere in the West Indies where Orisha is practiced. In her "African Prayers" ceremony, she feeds hundreds of homeless people in Toronto shelters.[64]

Drakes recalls how she inherited the Orisha religious practice through her great-grandmother who was brought from Africa to Grenada as a slave and continued to practice Orisha, healing and caring for those who needed spiritual guidance. The practice was passed on to her grandmother, who after her death passed it down to Drakes's aunt. The aunt refused at first to continue the work, disdaining it as not being a part of the "civilized world." But after difficult trials, serious illnesses and near-death experience, the aunt accepted the work which honored the ancestors and kept them "alive" through her manifestations until her death. Drakes herself first encountered the Orisha powers and was chosen to carry on the work at age 13 at the annual Ebo, African Prayers." But she delayed taking on the Orisha work until she prepared herself through traveling to Canada and being baptized in the Spiritual Baptist Faith. She says she felt the need for the knowledge of this religious practice in order to learn the work of the ancestors. Fasting, praying, and mourning, she received spiritual visions of her grandmother instructing and teaching her the fundamentals of Orisha work.[65]

Delores Seiveright describes more fully the practices and beliefs of the Spiritual Baptist Faith and its origin and African religious components. But her spiritual journey appears to have begun in the Caribbean diaspora in Toronto, among those from Guyana, Jamaica, Barbados, St. Vincent, Trinidad, and others. She was originally in the Pentecostal but encountered and began to embrace the Spiritual Baptists in Toronto in 1974. What influenced her in this direction was her odd spiritual experiences of shaking in her limbs and glossalalia, and the like which caused people to think she was a madwoman. But a Guyanese woman sensed that she was not crazy but spiritually gifted and helped her make contact with those who could assist her in developing her spiritual gifts.

Seiveright says:

> We went searching for the "Tie-head" woman or man, as the Spiritualists within the Spiritual Baptist Church are called. Most of the churches we visited were connected to a form of spiritualism that sought to communicate with our dead ancestors. Their practice was very quiet….Finally, in 1971, I met a Jamaican woman named Mother Brickley, who told me about the churches of African-Caribbean people who worshipped in their basements. I visited these churches and met one Leader from St. Vincent, one from Barbados, and another from Jamaica. Their followers were mostly Trinidadian by birth, with some worshippers from other Caribbean countries. They knew about the Faith, but spoke very little of the Faith. The same gifts and talents were hidden because they could not find a church or other Caribbean people who understood the cultural basis of the religion.[66]

Seiveright went in search of the Spiritual Baptist Churches on her own and found two Revivalist churches in one part of town and two Spiritual Baptist Churches in another section. She established another Spiritual Baptist Church in 1976. And she was instrumental in helping the churches increase. She doesn't say so precisely, but apparently she did travel to Trinidad, as advised by a Trinidadian visitor, to consult with Elton George Griffifth of the Spiritual Baptist Archdiocese.[67]

She begins her essay by saying that she describes the Faith as "awesome" and referring to the late Elton George Griffith as her Spiritual Father, who described is as "a diamond." She defines the Faith as "Christianity with African traditions. The Faith originated in Trinidad through a vision received by a Grenadian, Elton George Griffith. The call was that he should lead the people to spiritual freedom with the Shouter Baptist concept of the Divine." Seiveright recalls the obstacles the African people had to overcome in being permitted to worshp in the Faith, with their hand clapping, chanting, beating of drums, bell ringing, pouring of sweet oils, etc., which were outlawed by the state.[68]

She was among the ministers who established the Faith officially in Toronto in 1984. She says, "A group of Toronto Spiritual Baptist Ministers and business leaders helped me to set up a structured organization and present it to the solicitor general of the Province of Ontario. There are now approximately fifteen to twenty churches in Ontario, with approximately five to ten thousand people living and practicing the Faith." She is proud that they have overcome periods of struggle in Canada and have been able to unify the Faith by keeping the name and customs intact. She declares, "This has been done with the help of God and the Trinidad and Tobago Archdiocase, as well as members of the Caribbean community."[69]

Seiveright gives an interesting overview of the beliefs and practices, rituals and ordinations, services, community outreach, etc., which are both Christian and African, with the Bible as chief authority in all doctrinal and religious matters. She states, "The church is set up as the four corners, helped by archangels. The center of the church is the pole, which represents the heart of the human and is surrounded by all of the emblems of a garden as well as African symbols and seals. Different-colored flags represent the twelve tribes and nations." One of the ritual practices is very much like an African religious initiation rite. She says,

> After the "baptism" is the "mourning" ritual, which is conducted by a "pointer," that is, one who is qualified to do such a ritual. This ritual consists of self-sacrifice, a process that lasts for several days, during which time the candidate is given no food or water and is placed in a secluded, consecrated room. Nurses are in charge of the candidate during this period. This ritual enables the candidate to be cleansed and reach a higher calling in the Faith. This is the unique part of the Spiritual Baptist Faith, which cannot be explained, but must be experienced. Such a journey is called "A Pilgrimage Road," where the candidate meditates and meets teachers and guides from the spiritual realm, including angels and archangels.[70]

Seiveright's strong endorsement and firm commitment to this Faith is reflective of the commitment to African-based religions in general among those who follow them, especially their practical grounding in the African heritage and the spiritual power they impart to their daily living. She declares: "These rituals and practices all have significance in our worship as they do in our daily lives. This faith can be discussed, debated on, placed in books, preached to all, but having the personal experience of such a rich and cultural faith brings mystery and powerful knowledge."[71]

Chapter Eight

Crucial Issues in Jamaican Religions

The issues in Jamaican religions are many and varied and make for richness in cultural study and understanding. The religions include Obeah and Myal, of which we have had some discussion; Revivalism, Rastafari, and Native Baptists, which we have also touched upon. But there is much more that has to be more fully presented regarding the crucial issues of these religions. One of the major issues is native religious identity and problems between Revivalism and Rastafari beliefs and practices. Other major issues include religion as resistance in this context, the significance of land, syncretism, resistance and appropriation, and political, economic, and gender issues.

A few facts about the country of Jamaica and its history will serve to set this discussion of the religious issues in perspective. Next to Cuba and Haiti, Jamaica is third largest in size. With a population of right at two million, 90% are of African origin. The other 10% are distributed between Caucasians (1%), East Indians (3%), Chinese (2%), and Jews and Lebanese constitute the greater portion of the remaining four percent. The Spanish destroyed the Arawak population found there between their take-over of the Island from 1502 to 1655, at which time the British took control of the island.[1] The economy of the island was maintained by the labor of African slaves shipped mainly from the Koromantyn slave castle on the Cape Coast of Ghana, which I visited in 2001. These Africans were largely of the Ashanti and the Fanti ethnic groups, well-trained in guerrilla warfare. Being highly resistant to the grueling conditions of slavery, numerous slaves escaped into the mountains of Jamaica and formed their own maroon communities, attracting other runaways and waging continual wars with the British until treaties were established in 1738, 1739. A number of slave rebellions still took place, notable of which was the Sam Sharpe Rebellion of 1831 –32. The British abolished slavery in 1834, but the British colonial rule did not end until 1962, when independence was established and Jamaica joined the British Commonwealth of Nations.[2] Numerous struggles had taken place, religious, political, social, economic, and cultural, and continue today, in the Jamaican society. Crucial religious issues form an integral part of these struggles.

Issues in Native Baptist Religion and Revival Cults of Pukkumina and Revival Zion

Native Baptists in Jamaica and three types of what are referred to as Afro-Christian sects or cults: Pukkumina, Revival, and Revival Zion reflect significant religious, social, cultural, and gender issues in their history, development, beliefs, and practices. As Jean Besson in her essay, "Religion as Resistance in Jamaican Peasant Life," well clarifies, the Baptist religion spread in Jamaica in the second half of the 18th century by ex-slaves George Liele and Moses Baker from the United States became a formal symbol of resistance. This religion was more appealing to the slaves in Jamaica than the earlier missionary religions of the Moravians and Methodists that had come to the colony in the first half of the 18th century.[3] Leonard Barrett characterizes the Native Baptists as a redemptive sect which, developing from the Baptist teaching of ideas of hope, and salvation, blended them with their own dreams and hopes of freedom and liberation from slavery and repression.[4] More specifically, the slaves took eagerly to the Baptist teachings because they were readily able to absorb them into their traditional African religious framework, such as myalism and obeah. And the Native Baptist Movement was formed from this syncretism. However, the members maintained a dual membership in the two groups, the Baptist Church and their traditional religious associations. Sam Sharpe, who led the Great Jamaican Slave Rebellion of 1831–32 involving over a thousand slaves, was a part of the Native Baptists. Chevannes sees this rebellion as being instrumental in speeding up the process by which Emancipation was granted in 1834.[5]

Pukkumina is described as being mostly African in its rituals and beliefs, Revival as partly African and partly Christian, and Revival Zion as mostly Christian and the least African.[6] These cults grew in the wake of the Great Revival of 1861 in Jamaica. Edward Seaga summarizes and explains the crucial religious issues involved in the syncretism of these groups with Protestant Christianity. He says, "the means of achieving salvation implicit in the Great '61 Revival were far more African than European. These stemmed from…the basic African religious belief that the spirit world was not separate and apart from the temporal world but formed one unified whole; and this belief in the unity of the spirit world has persisted to the present day among those sections of the population whose cultural formation remains Afro-Christian." He goes on to state that the "Great Revival died and was succeeded by other Movements," of which Revivalism has persisted as the "main heir of the Great Revival in so far as Afro-Christian religious sects are concerned, and two major groups exist, Pukkumina and Zion."[7] Pukkumina is said to have derived from Kumina, a traditional African religious practice brought to Jamaica by indentured laborers from the Kongo region of Central Africa after Emancipation and syncretized with Myalism.[8]

Seaga explains why orthodox Christian Churches in Jamaica have great difficulty coming to terms with revivalist cults, bringing into focus major religious issues significant to these cultic groups. He says that the "Revivalists have found the cold formality of Christian orthodoxy unsatisfactory." He goes on to explain the root of the problem.

> At the root of the whole problem lies the basic difference of religious thinking: on the one side, stands Christian Monotheism, exclusive, guarded by a jealous God who condemns the worshippers of the Golden Calf and other idols. On the other side there is African Polytheism, all embracing and able to accommodate the Christian Trinity, the Angels and Saints, the Prophets and the Apostles, combining these, however, with the spirits including the Ancestral dead, and even with the diabolical host. Christianity, in particular Protestant Christianity, because of its exclusiveness and reliance on the truth of doctrine based usually on the Bible alone, has given rise to a multitude of Christian denominations, none of which have really learnt in the final analysis to co-exist in doctrine. The Revivalist has no such problem. His Gods permit him free intercourse with the available pantheon of spirits.[9]

Seaga pinpoints other problems between Revivalism and the orthodox Christian groups, having to do with worship practices, spirituality, and social class distinction. The more ecstatic, physically exertive, and emotional manifestations of the spirit so central to the cultive varieties are frowned upon by those in the orthodox Church. As he declares, "a cultist would get little satisfaction in a service where his [her] participation is restricted to hymn singing and responses from a prayer book." A key issue here is the acceptance of the practice of spirit possession. "From this dividing line Christian groups are classified as [either] 'temporal' or 'spiritual.' It is true to say that sects or cult groups which accept the doctrine of personal possession by spirit forces, classify themselves as 'spiritual' and correspondingly categorize those which do not as 'temporal.'" The orthodox Church groups obviously fall within the temporal category, while "spiritual groups include many Church of God and Native Baptist sects such as Pentecostal, Four Square and others in addition to Revivalism."[10]

For reasons that are probably obvious, social class distinction attaches to the differences in membership participation in the more orthodox Christian Church and the cultic varieties. The reality of a mutually upbuilding and sustaining social and spiritual community that offers its members cultural rootedness, healing, as well as internal social status, a solid sense of place and human dignity makes these Afro-Christian cults meaningful to their adherents. But the negative stigma to which they are subjected or their "low prestige value within the dominant Christian code of values" causes status-conscious Jamaicans to "disguise their true religious allegiance by claiming to be members one of the orthodox and accepted churches, e. g. Baptist or Anglican in order to enhance their status" while in fact they "secretly" belong to a Revivalist group. Seaga asserts that "Revivalists are mostly outside the socio-economic framework of the middle-class; membership is drawn primarily from the working class." In Kingston, the capital city and largest urban center, they are often "not employed on a full time basis" and when they are they usually work as "laborers, hagglers, household helps, fishermen and tradesmen's assistants, port-workers; rarely do they own land or property." And their earnings are less than 5 pounds per week. Furthermore, the Christian middle-class has denigrating views of them as "pagan, superstitious, comical in ritual behaviour, tolerant of dishonesty...." Seaga observes rightly, as is true in the case of the attitude of the African American middle-class toward such African-expressive religions in other places, "The ambivalent attitude of the middle-class groups toward their African heritage contributes to the contempt."[11]

Olmos and Paravisini-Gebert summarize the crucial significance of the African-derived practices in "Zion Revivalism" as being similar to those in Vodou and Santeria—the insertion of "familiar elements of the Christian faith—God, the angels, saints, apostles and prophets—into the worship patterns characteristic of African religiosity. Spirits demand that they be fed regularly...with each spirit having specific preferences for food, colors, and music, all of which are incorporated in the fundamentals of worship." In turn, the spirits assist the worshipers in their personal lives through guidance and protection, healing, and the like. The authors' concluding assessment of this religious expression is that it is "a profoundly Afro-Caribbean religious manifestation of Christianity, the hybrid product of a process of transculturation that allowed the remnants of practice believed lost during the devastation of slavery to be reconstructed through the incorporation of new theological content."[12]

In looking at the practice of Pukkumina/Kumina, Olmos and Paravisini-Gebert stress the similarities and difference in reflection of important issues relating to culture and survival. They see Kunina as differentiated from Zion in its "shunning of the Bible as the central textual authority behind faith and worship" and its more dynamic and conspicuously African-derived practice. "Practitioners of Kumina share a deep African identity consciousness based on a constant awareness of a legacy of African persecution and suffering." They see this, for instance, in their focus on healing, their "deep knowledge of bush medicine and the complex rituals involved in the gathering of plants, leaves, and flowers for use in curing rituals," and the like. In summation, the authors note the significance of all of these religions in their value and meaning for the practitioners. "The dynamic syncretism displayed by practices such as Myal, Zion, and Kumina showcases the enduring potential of African-derived religions in helping Caribbean peoples heal from the uprootedness and impoverishment imposed upon them by a history of dispossession—of land, culture, environment, language, and gods."[13]

Gender issues are also expressed in these religious varieties in Jamaica in different ways, both between the groups within the urban areas and between the expressions of these religions in the urban and rural areas. Seaga points out in his focus on the Kingston area: "Revival Bands of both Pukkumina and the Zion cult have a preponderance of female membership. Women can become leaders in either cult, and Zionists appear to have more female than male leaders; in Pukkumina however, female leaders are rare. Approximately one tenth of the Zion membership is male as compared with one quarter to one third in Pukkumina."[14] These facts and statistics are highly suggestive of the thinking and associations in the groups, especially since Pukkumina adheres more closely to the African traditional religious practices. By contrast to both cults, however, it should be noted that orthodox Christian groups of Baptists, Moravians, Anglicans, and others are in general not as open to female leadership.

In her comparative examination, "Religion as Resistance in Jamaican Peasant Life: The Baptist Church, Revival Worldview and Rastafari," Jean Besson has much to share regarding the issue of women's roles in the peasant or rural culture of Jamaica. She concentates her discussion especially on the "free villages of Trelawny, a parish that was the centre of the Myal movement in Ja-

maica and an important area of Baptist proselytizing and Native Baptist development and where the Baptist Church, Revival worldview and Rastafari movement co-exist today." At various junctures throughout her discussion, she
pinpoints the roles of women in the religious groups and the society in capacities of resistance to slavery, cultural denigration, and economic oppression. In
showing the linkages of the three religious groups in the peasant resistance culture, she makes the point that while the Rastafari movement has only made
"impact in Trelawny since the 1950s, Revival and its precursors—Myalism, Native Baptism and the Great Revival—have been central themes of African-
Caribbean cultural resistance in Trelawny, at the heart of Caribbean plantation
society, for three centuries of African-Caribbean life." Besson sums up the roles
of women as she has presented them in the chapter, which reflects an alternative perspective of Revival, highlighting

> the role of women in African-Caribbean cultural resistance, from the days of slavery to
> the present time. During slavery this included the creation of proto-peasant adaptations
> and the embedding of African-Caribbean culture in plantation slave communities. It
> was at the heart of these communities that Myalism evolved, a movement which has
> culminated in the Revival worldview of today; and in Revival, so integral to the peasant
> culture of resistance, women play a centrol role as in other aspects of the peasant econ-
> omy and community. African-Caribbean peasant women are therefore not, [as argued
> by some male observers], perpetrators of Eurocentric values in either their daily or reli-
> gious life; nor are men the sole creators of African-Caribbean cultural resistance.[15]

This is a good transitional point leading to our next section, which centers
on the crucial issues in the Rastafari Movement, of which resistance is a vital
component, among other concerns.

Crucial Issues of Resistance, Religious and Cultural Identity, Land, Syncretism, Political and Social Radicalism in Rastafari

Barry Chevannes asserts that Jamaica has a long tradition of resistance,
"nurtured in the deep isolated recesses of its rugged interior, where after emancipation a new class of peasant freeholders fashioned their life and culture."
Further, Chevannes states that religion is the most central institution to the tradition of resistance in Jamaica. "Whether resistance through the use of force, or
resistance through symbolic forms such as language, folk-tales and proverbs, or
resiatance through the creation of alternative institutions, religion was the main

driving force among Jamaican peasants."[16] All of these means of resistance may be seen to exist in the varied forms of the Rastafari movement.

The most succinct yet inclusive definition I have encountered regarding Rastafarianism is the one offered by Olmos and Paravisini-Gebert, which describes it as "an Afro-Jamaican religious movement that blends the Revivalist nature of Jamaican folk Christianity with the Pan-Africanist perspective promulgated by Marcus Garvey, and Ethiopianist readings of the Old Testament."[17] Rastarianism was born in and is constantly nurtured in resistance. At the heart of the resistance is the Christian Church and the imperialist/capitalist society (Babylon). Rex Nettleford summarizes the Rastas' religious challenge to Christianity. He says, "Theirs has been a deep response to the power of the master's religion (orthodox Christianity) over the 'oppressed.' Here the paradox of human existence played its accustomed trick. The orthodoxy of the Christian faith was to be fought by weapons out of its own armoury—the Old Testament, particularly those parts of the Old Testament which satisfied the needs of a people deprived and degraded for too long. The books of Daniel, Isaiah, Deuteronomy, Leviticus, and Numbers figure greatly in the sources of Rastafarian doctrine."[18]

Joseph Owens points to the basis of this religious rebellion. He considers the story of Rasta as that of the black man, the "castaway black man of the New World, in its fullest philosophical breadth and depth." He tries to communicate clearly "why the Rastaman must be a truly contradictory figure. At one and the same time a symbol of rebellion and of reaction, of progressive forces and of archaic impulses, of praise and of contempt, of freedom and of negation, of hope and of despair." What he asserts must not be forgotten is the "historical time, place and space during which Rastafarianism took shape." He calls our attention forcefully to the reality of the context and the religious response of resistance and creative spiritual challenge.

> We must not forget the backward colonial society that Jamaica was in the 20's and 30's of this century [20th]. The Rastaman appeared, peasant without land, a proletarian who never worked in a factory and who could not sell his labour if he wanted to. Nevertheless he appeared, with a bible in one hand, and in the other an indignant, imprudent black pride and consciousness. He was literate only in the scriptures but a philosopher nonetheless; he reminisced on the words of the prophet Marcus, he reveled in the grand pageantry of the Garveyite marches through Harlem, Kingston, Bog Walk, May Pen.[19]

Interwoven in this response are religious, social, racial, and political elements and forces.

The religious, racial, and political creativity and inventiveness is also seen in the central spiritual reality of the faith of the movement. Joseph Owens states further: "At the center of it all a grand, authentic coronation. A king crowned in Africa. A world event for the black man. No lie, the world turned its eyes, all the world of 1930. A king like any other king—King, Emperor, Ruler of the longest reigning monarchy. No, not just a king—black for one thing, but look closer, a King of kings, a Lord of lords, Elect of God, Conquering Lion of the tribe of Judah. No mere king, a God, a Messiah."[20] This of course has reference to Emperor Haile Selassie of Ethiopia, who is worshiped and celebrated as God.

Owens goes on to depict the individual figure of the Rastaman in a Jamaican slum mostly of the 1970's proudly asserting the radically opposing religious and cultural/social positions to traditional Christianity.

We foresee all the budding contradictions, and yet we encounter sharper irony still, as we meet the Rastaman proud and grand as a prince in front of his pathetic hovel in the appalling slums of the city of Kingston. More ironic still when the first words he speaks are from the Bible. He knows the back alleys of his shanty town. The Bible—Christianity—the most insidious instrument of ideological and cultural imperialism, in the hands of a Rastaman! He sleeps, eats and does everything by it and never stops reading it and meditating on it. But as we have come to expect, Rastafarian theology diverges significantly, radically in fact, from traditional Christianity. It reinterprets the Bible in terms of the black man's experience and needs and in so doing—here is the profundity of the whole dialectical movement—it renders it somehow universal. Because what is involved most basically is a critique, a profound and thoroughgoing critique of the ethic of Western civilisation and its manifestation of Western religion.[21]

Crucial Issues Reflected in the Beliefs and Practices and Religious Forms of Rasta

Above and beyond its philosophical, religious, political, and social critique, Rastafarianism is a religion, like any other religion: with beliefs in God and human and divine relations, Holy Scripture, worship practices and rituals, ethical teachings, and afterlife. Though not a centrally organized religion with established institutions of worship, but principally acephalous, Rasta has two organized bodies: the Twelve Tribes of Israel and the Bobos. The Twelve Tribes is a middle-class group headed by Prophet Gad. Members are organized into the biblical tribes of Israel. The Bobos are led by Prince Emmanuel Edwards and "are the only Rasta group living a truly communal life, on the outskirts of the city of Kingston."[22] Significant religious issues, social, racial, social class distinction, gender realities can be seen through looking at the beliefs, rituals, and organized forms of the religion. We shall first examine how the beliefs and rituals and other practices reflect crucial issues. And then we shall look closely at the organized forms and the issues reflected in them.

Olmos and Paravisini-Gebert in their summary of the basic Rasta beliefs show how significant religious, social, and political issues are reflected in them. They point out that the earliest theology of the movement was fairly simple. "Haile Selassie was the embodiment of Christian divinity (the Black Christ or Black Messiah) and the entire African race shared in his divinity; and there would be a mystic return to the African homeland (known as Repatriation) as a path to redemption. This Repatriation was not a call for massive migration to Africa…but was linked to notions of cultural recovery through spiritual connection to the African homeland." This African homeland was mystically interpreted as Ethiopia, "considered to be heaven on earth, gleaned from Protestant sects with millenarian approaches to the bodily transportation to the New Zion."[23] Focusing on black people as the new Israel who were subjected to slavery as punishment for sins and were now to be delivered from the new Babylon ("the white Euro-American society, its social and political structures, responsible for centuries of black oppression and exploitation), this religion had enormous appeal to the poor and oppressed of Jamaican society, who were quite numerous during the time, which was the period of the Great Depression.[24]

Barry Chevannes summarizes the rituals of Rasta for the majority of the members as being of two kinds, reasoning and the "binghi," "both sometimes referred to as a 'grounding' or 'grounation.'" In the Reasoning sessions there are small informal gatherings of brothers who share in smoking of ganja, the holy weed, and engage in lofty discussion. All partake of the ganja from the same water pipe, called a chalice, passed around in a circle in ritual fashion accompanied by an initial prayer by the one who is honored to be chosen to light the pipe. This ceremony is compared to the holy communion of Christians. Leonard Barrett says of the ganja usage that it, like peyote among North American Navajo, "produces psycho-spiritual effects and has socio-religious functions especially for people under stress. It produces visions, heightens unity and communal feelings, dispels gloom and fear, and brings tranquility to the mind of the dispossessed."[25] The reasoning dialogue involved religious and social issues derived from reading and meditation on Bible readings, thoughts and beliefs regarding religious understanding and human relationships. As Olmos and Paravisini state, there being no single authoritative voice regarding the Rasta beliefs, the reasoning sessions allow for individual interpretation as a basis for coming at acceptable doctrine.[26] It might be noted that the gender problem, of which we will treat later, is an issue in the reasoning sessions. For women are excluded in the "Reasoning" ritual.

The second ritual practice, according to Chevannes, is the "nyabinghi" ("binghi" for short), which is a dance held on special occasions throughout the year. It may mark the "coronation of His Imperial Majesty (2 November), His Majesty's ceremonial birthday (6 January), His Majesty's visit to Jamaica (25 April), His Majesty's personal birthday (23 July), Emancipation from slavery (1 August), and Marcus Garvey's birthday (17 August)." This ritual definitely reflects strong political and social loyalties that are important to maintaining heritage and social memory. Chevannes says that the word is "thought to be of colonial origin, originally referring to a secret order vowed to bring 'death to White oppressors.' During the Dreadlocks era [the 2nd phase of Rasta development, 1940's to 1980, See Chevannes, pp. 12–15], Rastafari would on occasion 'dance nyabinghi' to bring 'death to Black and White oppressors.' Today these dances are purely ceremonial celebrations, lasting for several days, depending on the resources of the House [loose organizations or assemblies, led by Elders, to which each Rasta considers having membership, see Chevannes, p. 16]." These celebrations are held in different parishes on a rotating basis, bringing in numerous Dreads from all over Jamaica who lodge in camps and makeshift dwellings.[27]

Leonard Barrett identifies prayer as a ritual act done in many ways among Rastas. He cites a particular prayer used at Rasta meetings dating from a very early period. And this prayer is very reflective of religious and social issues, as well as divine-human relatedness. It opens with the words: "Princes shall come out of Egypt, Ethiopia shall stretch forth her hand unto God. Oh thou God of Ethiopia, thou God of divine majesty, thy spirit come within our hearts to dwell in the parts of righteousness. That the hungry may be fed, the sick nourished, the aged protected, and the infant cared for. Teach us love and loyalty as it is in Zion." It goes on to plea for deliverance from the enemy (who should be defeated in the end and "decayed in the depth of the sea or in the belly of a beast"), for faithfulness, for a place in the kingdom of God. Appeal is made to "Our God Selassie I, Jehovah God, Ras Tafari," "Great and terrible God Ras Tafari," "Who sitteth in Zion and reigneth in the hearts of men, and women."[28]

Chevannes identifies food restrictions in Rasta as personal rituals relating to nature, spirituality, the environment, and to the African connection. There are taboos and practices regarding foods such as pork and crustaceans (avoided by all), all meat and fish products (avoided by some). Salt is avoided, and food cooked without it is referred to as ital, natural. They reject, if possible, things artificial and celebrate the use of the natural. For instance, manure is preferred to artificial fertilizer and sprays; herbs and barks to pharmaceuticals. And symbols of Africa adorn their homes, such as pictures of Haile Selassie, of his wife ("Queen Omega"), of other African leaders, and maps and posters with African themes.[29]

The two organized groups of Rastas, the Twelve Tribes of Israel and the Bobos in their beliefs, structures, rituals, and practices reflect crucial religious, social, cultural, and gender issues. Barrett gives a summary characterization of the Twelve Tribes as residing in the prestigious suburb of Saint Andrews and catering to middle and upper class youth, and even recruiting white members. Modifying Rastafarianism somewhat and reinterpreting some of its doctrines to fit into the mores of its highly intelligent followers, they still maintain a strong repatriation program and have sponsored members who desired to move to Ethiopia. They have an evangelical trait and claim to have branches in the United States, England, and elsewhere.[30] When they began in the 1970's the Twelve Tribes were referred to negatively as "the uptown Rastas whe believed they were better than anybody else."[31] And one can see why, of course, because a lot of issues of social class distinction do separate them from what may be referred to as vintage Rasta.

The founder of the Twelve Tribes was Vernon Carrington, born in a classy neighborhood in Kingston, thus setting him apart according to the thinking of the class-conscious citizens. "A man of superior native intelligence and some leadership ability, he became head of the Ethiopian World Federation (EWF), Chapter 15," which is an organization founded in New York City in 1937 "by the authority of Emperor Haile Selassie." The constitution of EWF "granted the Ethiopian World Federation 500 acres of land in Ethiopia's Goba Valley, known as Shasemani," which was a grant to Western Blacks that had the intent of rewarding those who supported Ethiopia in its war against Mussolini. Chapter 15 of this organization in Trench Town was among several splinter groups of it in Jamaica. As head of Chapter 15, Vernon Carrington combined other aspects of his association. He was both a Revivalist and a Rastafarian, a psychological mixture, according to Barrett, that produces dreams and visions. Therefore, he combined also studies of the Bible, books on Judaism, Egyptian religion, and Ethiopian religion, and developed a "new synthesis of Christianity, cabalistic numerology, genealogy, astrology, and Rastafarianism," which became the Twelve Tribes of Israel.[32]

Their beliefs and practices reveal a number of important issues including, spirituality, gender, and religious unity. They have a Bible reading regimen which requires each member to complete the whole Bible in three and a half years. They hold to religious and spiritual significance of the number twelve, such as seen in the twelve tribes of the Bible, the twelve signs of the zodiac, etc. Each member is named according to his/her place in one of the tribes, determined by the phase of the moon at the time of that person's birth. In regard to divinity, they believe that "Jesus Christ was manifested in his second coming in the person of Jah Rastafari, Haile Selassie I," and they use the names interchangeably, that is, Jesus Christ and Jah Rastafari. Their other beliefs and practices may be summarized. Repatriation is a central goal, the "holy weed" is central to the practice. They revere their founder Carrington, whose name became Gad, after his tribe in the Bible, as the Prophet. Bob Marley was a prominent member of this group, and they have a monthly dance to reggae music as a ritual of a sort. Marley is known as Joseph, according to his tribe and revered and sort of enshrined among them. Their liberal policy toward women is highly remarkable. Barrett states, "Unlike vintage Rastafarians, men and women have equal roles, as a matter of fact, they have been among the trend setters in women's equality." Barrett also lauds this group as having probably "provided the most convenient interchange between society at large and the Rastafarian movement to date. Because the sect is built around reggae—the music of the King—they have had great success in recruiting members. It is also the only Rastafarian sect with a significant number of white members in executive positions."[33]

The Bobos are in a number of ways with regard to religious and social issues quite the reverse of the Twelve Tribes of Israel. They have an interesting
history as a part of what Chevannes calls the second phase of Rastafarian development, the 1940's to 1980. This was a period of a new type of resistance
and innovations in character, beliefs, and practices of the Rastas, such as dreadlocks, ganja-smoking, Rasta talk "(sometimes called 'I-talk' because of the piv-
otal concept of I, the personal pronoun)." Haile Selassie, previously referred to
as the King, "was now praised as Jah or Jah-Jah." Resistance activities included
anti-colonialist illicit street marches, disruption of courts, defiance of police, and
stress on repatriation. Chevannes describes the emergence of the Bobo movement in 1958, founded by Prince Emmanuel Edwards, in this context.

> Against the background of migration to the United Kingdom, Repatriation marches
> and other forms of agitation started. In 1958 one young leader, Prince Emmanuel Ed-
> wards, issued a successful call for an all Rasta convention. For two weeks Rastafari
> from all over Jamaica converged on Back-o-Wall, a notorious slum adjacent to King-
> ston's largest market, which hosted many a migrant fresh from the country. At the end
> of two weeks they marched to the central square of the city, planted a flag and symboli-
> cally "captured" the city. It was alleged that many had sold off their belongings in the
> confident expectation that at the end of the convention they would be transported to
> Africa.[34]

The convention did not have the desired effect, and rather diminished Edwards's credibility among the Rastas; thus, he "retreated with his group into a
sect known as Bobos."[35]

Leonard Barrett refers to Prince Emmanuel Edwards as a   charismatic
leader who, "after moving from Back-O-Wall, with the 1969 bulldozing of of
the Rastafarian communes by the government," established Mt. Zion at St.
Thomas and "has held his followers together for over a decade."[36] Located in
Bull Bay, St. Thomas, about an hour's drive east of Kingston, the community is
a very strictly organized one based on patriarchal Black Jewish-Christian Biblical
principles. We visited this community in 1996 when we (the Society for the
Study of Black Religion, SSBR,) were hosted in our Annual Meeting by The
University of the West Indies in Kingston, (I was then the President of the Society).[37] The hill on which it is built seemingly replicates the Zion Hill in Jerusalem, and the open air temple structure is a sort of a rough idea of a replica of
the Jerusalem temple. It is certainly intended to reflect such. We were told that
the group had "captured" the land from the government, having become squatters on it. It is reported that the group has been recognized by the United Na-

tions as an independent flag-bearing country. Olmos and Paravisini-Gebert describe them as black supremacists, "known for their radical adherence to the principles of black nationalism," living "in ascetic contemplation of Rastafarian principles, closely observing a series of taboos...that they believe will lead to pure and selfless community."[38]

Leonard Barrett has quite a positive and descriptive view of the Bobos' place of existence, character, lifestyle, and practices, from his field trip there.

> The camp sits on the edge of the mountain two thousand feet above sea level, about two miles in from the main road, with a view of the sea almost indescribable. It occupies seven or eight acres of "captured lands," on which sit a large tabernacle, a small school for Rastafarian youths, a shed for broom making, another for the making of sandals, the living quarters of the prince, and about eight houses for the followers and many others in various stages of completion. The camp is surrounded by a wire fence with entrance through a large gate under the protection of the guard, but in my case, these rules were waived.[39]

Barrett's description is very accurate and pictorial; it squares with our own experiences in 1996. We visited all of the places and structures he mentions and some he does not, such as the shop where they sell their wares of brooms, shoes, and artifacts, as well as the Reasoning Hall, where the brothers assemble for that ritual.

In Barrett's thinking, this Prince Edwards group represents "the religious wing of the Rastafarian movement." Perhaps he means that they exhibit more spiritualized and ritualized biblical religious structure and behavior than the Twelve Tribes of Israel, who also are very "religious." Indeed, as he says, they verge on the monastic, except for the fact that a few women are found among them. Ethiopianism is strong among them in dress and manners, and the like. "The members wear an unusual outfit consisting of a turban, a modified form of the Ethiopian Orthodox religion, with flowing robes mixed with the colors red, black, and green, and the Rastafarian sandals round this off." The hierarchial structure has the Prince (Edwards) as the more or less divine head (Priest of the order of Melchizedek—the mysterious priest of Genesis and the Book of Hebrews who ministered to Abraham and who is equated with Jesus) "to whom worship is given as one of the triumvirate of the movement over which he rules." The other two are Haile Selassie and Marcus Garvey. Others in the hierarchy are the Prince's wife, known as the empress, and who controls the women; the priests, apostles, and prophets.[40]

When I visited the camp in 1996, Prince Edwards had died and was now being revered as God and kept alive through various artifacts, letters, writings and short publications. One of the books is titled *Black Supremacy in Righteousness of Salvation,* with authorship given as Jesus Negus Christ Emmanuel "I" Selassie "I" Jah Rastafari in Royal Majesty Selassie "I" Jahovah Jah Rastafar "I." These phrases all referred to Prince Edwards, whose picture as inside the front cover with the caption: "The Father Who Send I Jesus Is Greater Than All." Among other pictures in the book are ones of Marcus Garvey and Haile Selassie. The book has 73 pages, with several documents of front matter and 4 chapters. The front matter includes: "Ethiopian Royal International Cree," "Spiritual Documents of Salvation To World Heads of Governments," "Selassie: What Life Has Taught Me," "I Wish You All God Speed," and "The Black Christ Salvation." The four chapters are titled respectively: "Black Supremacy & His Commandments," "One God For Us All," "The Lion of Judah Hath Prevailed," and "There Is A City Upon A Hill." The Rasta Prayer quoted earlier is found on page 11 in this book, which contains teachings and preaching from Prince Edwards. One section beginning on page 52 is titled: "Man of Right Is God In Flesh: Men of Wrong Is Satan In Flesh." A few quotations from this section will reveal some of the essential beliefs.

> Give thanks for being Black: Give thanks for a Black Christmas (Jan. 7th – 20th 1988). Two full weeks of joy and happiness. Peace and love and prosperity to all Black sons and daughters.

> Come one, come all to this Black fullness of life: Come and see the Black fullness of God. In flesh: Give thanks to the Black Father who live in the hearts and reign in the flesh.

> Prophesy and History spoken to anyone is good to the soul. The voice of the people will bring forth seven miles of Black Star Line coming through the head of the United Nations to settle peace on earth and send every man to His own Vine and Fig tree.

> Calling upon my people in all walks of life for unity and love. As one Black blood brothers and sisters of African descent. Africa the Black man's heaven from creation. The Black Christ is righteousness in His government bring forth equality, justice to all. Let us make a union with Negus our Lord, the Black Christ who shed His blood for a ransom, for redemption for His people.[41]

One may see clearly the religious, ethical, political, and social class issues reflected in these statements of belief and hope. There is not anger or bitterness but beliefs and principles that are meant to encourage and uplift a people who are being oppressed and denied their rights and heritage.

There remain some rituals and practices which Barrett and Chevannes bring to our attention which reflect the religious and social meanings of the Bobos. Barrett points up "sacrifice..., the washing of the saint's feet, and prayer by prostration. The daily services resemble Pukumina, but with Rastafarian chants, drumming, and dancing. Services are continuous from 7:00 A. M. until late at night."[42] The beliefs are reflected in the rituals, of which Chevannes (also visiting with the group while Edwards still lived) give further details. He says that, "At sunrise, noon, and sunset, each Bobo prostrates himself [seemingly like the Muslims] and prays with his head turned toward the east." Chevannes describes the evening services "conducted in in the open yard before an altar facing east. They begin with the drumming and singing under the leadership of three priests." Those in attendance must wear black robes. "The songs are, many of them, familiar sankeys. At the end of the singing comes a series of ovations or tributes, first always to Emmanuel, the High Priest, then to Marcus Garvey, the Prophet and next to Selassie the King." When Emmanuel arrived on the occasion when Chevannes visited, Chevannes says he began his message by saying, "man is God and God is man." Chevannes states," The man who was talking here [43]now represented Jesus Christ here on earth. God could not be spirit; he must be flesh."[43] Intertwined in these rituals and beliefs and reflected in them is the mystical union of the sacred and the secular, the divine and the human, the oneness of all things. This is a part of African cosmology.

On my visit with the Bobos in March, 1996, with some members of the Society for the Study of Black Religion, of which I was then the President, we witnessed some religious practices and rituals, which I will relate from my own perspective. Some changes had apparently taken place.[44] Prince Edwards was no longer living,[45] and there were many more women in attendance than other sources have reported. Our visit took place on the Sabbath, Saturday, and we arrived right in middle of the worship service, which was being held in the temple or tabernacle. There were about 25 persons in our group, approximately 10 women and 15 men scholars. As we proceeded to leave the van and head toward the temple, the men were allowed to enter as they were, dressed in their suits or more casual men wear. But a few sisters hurried up to us women and ushered us to a place where we could be more properly dressed for the service. They covered our heads and placed some sort of wraps around our bodies.

Then they led us into the temple to the left side where all the women were seated. All the men were situated on the right side. The service proceeded with music and singing and drumming, readings, and the like.

We used a hymn book with a colorful hard back and front cover (with the face of a lion with mane on the front cover, a regal picture of Haile Selassie on the back cover) and various Jewish-Christian hymns xeroxed and pasted within the covers under various themes relating to the issues reflected in the religion of the Bobo group. The hymn book was titled *The Black Christ Salvation, Jerusalem School Hymn Book* (Formerly at 54b Spanish Town Road, Now Headquartered at 10 Miles, Bull Bay P. O., St. Andrews, Jamaica). Inside the front cover is a faith statement, "Conquering Lion Shall Break Every Chain," from Prince Edwards. The hymns on pages 7–12 are ones of praise and glorification to God such as "Lord of the Sabbath! Hear our vows," "Holy, Holy, Holy, Lord God Almighty," "Guide Me, O Thou Great Jehovah," Ride on! Ride on in majesty!" The theme beginning on page 12 is "Freedom, Redemption, Repatriation" with such hymns as "Amazin Grace," "The God of Abraham praise," "Peace! Perfect Peace! In this dark world of sin," and "Ring the bells of Zion! There is joy to-day." Page 16 begins a group of hymns under the theme, "Black Supremacy," including "Behold, what love, what boundless love the Father hath bestowed," "Jerusalem the golden, with milk and honey blest," "On Christ the Solid Rock." Page 19 has the theme, "The Black Star Line," with hymns that could relate to repatriation and return home to Ethiopia (Africa), such as "Jerusalem, my happy home, Name ever dear to me, When shall my labours have an end, Thy joys when shall I see," and "In the land of strangers, Whither thou art gone, Hear a far voice calling 'My son! My son! Welcome, wanderer! Welcome! Welcome back home.'" This song goes on to mention coming back from the land of hunger, fainting, "come to love and gladness." Another section has the theme, "I Being Black," one of the interesting songs of which is "O Come, O Come Emmanuel," which seems very appropriate. This page has pictures of Prince Edward standing with a staff like that of Moses, a picture which also is found on other pages. In fact there are symbolic and suggestive pictures throughout the booklet relating to various ideas of the religion, such as a man conquering a lion.[46]

After the sermon, we were allowed to leave the service and were given a tour of all the grounds, the various residences for men and those for women and other persons. The traditional social and cultural practices adhering to Bib-

lical Jewish patriarchal ways were explained to us. We discovered in our tour
what once source says of the group, "Their lifestyle closely emulates those of
the Old Testament Jewish Mosaic Law, which includes the observation of the
Sabbath from sundown on Friday to sundown on Saturday, hygiene laws for
menstruating women and special greetings amongst themselves. No work is allowed during the Sabbath and the consumption of salt and oil is avoided."[47] We
were told that the women do not do the cooking for reasons of cleanliness, the
men did that chore. All of these practices seemed very interesting, as well as
odd, to our group. But we understood and accepted them as a part of the religious context. After our tour, our group was allowed in a "Reasoning" session
with the men where we would be able to ask questions and discuss aspects of
the religion we had observed. At first the leaders would not allow our women to
participate in this session, as it was restricted to men alone. But an exception
was made for us when the men of our group explained that we were all scholars
seeking an understanding of the faith to be used in our studies. So we felt privileged to share in the discussion, which was truly enriching.

Finally, we were able to visit the gift and souvenir shop and make pur-
chases, as well as take some of the literature of the movement. Before we left,
we had quite a friendly and communal relationship established between us and
the brothers and sisters of the movement. In fact, I found the group to be
friendly and sociable, kind and considerate so long as there was no deliberate
disruption of their rules. Though they are very strong in their social and political
viewpoints on the faith, this group is not offensive and socially disruptive. As
one source puts it, "The Bobo strike a compromise with the existing society by
accentuating respect for certain values....All the aggressiveness characteristic of
the Dreadlocks is alien to the Bobo, who go out of their way to cultivate excel-
lent relations with their surrounding community."[48] Another source says of
them, "The socalled kings and queens of this commune consider themselves
freedom fighters. Their fight is not only for survival but repatriation. In their
eyes, the Back-to-Africa Movement is very alive, so much so that they have sent
petitions to the Queen of England and Prime Minister Patterson to speed up
the process."[49]

More should be said regarding the issues of land possession and roles of
and regard for men and women in Rastafarianism. These are regarded differently by different segments of Rastas and by the society. The relationship of
land possession, religion, and family ties[50] is basic to the African and to the an-

cient Jewish traditions as seen in the Bible. Descendants of African slaves in the United States maintained their strong attachment to the land, as has been the case of Africans in the Diaspora in the Caribbean, Central, and South America, and elsewhere. The land is sacred, a divine gift. The feel for the land is an integral part of the African heritage, as well as a part of the Judaeo-Christian heritage they encountered principally in the Diaspora. Having been dispossessed of their homelands and taken to foreign places where they worked the land, another land, for the benefit of a strange race of people must have been a traumatic experience for peoples who came out of cultures where views of land possession were almost entirely different from the views of those whom they were forced to serve as slaves.[51]

The Black Nationalist/Black Power/Pan-Africanist Movements of the 19th and 20th centuries which swept the New World and Africa had the repossession of and recovery of land as a key issue in the thrust for power on the part of the dispossessed and oppressed descendants of African everywhere. Rastafarianism was very much a part of this movement, as were Black Nationalists and Pan-African groups in the U.S.A., such as the Nation of Islam under the leadership of Elijah Mohammed, Malcolm X, and others; and the Republic of New Africa under Milton Henry and others. And of course, Marcus Garvey, with prominence in both the U.S. and his home of Jamaica, was the major influence of this movement in the 20th century.

In our consideration of Rastafarianism, this issue of land is very significant, howsoever it was regarded by any particular segment of the different groups. It naturally comes up to be dealt with. Scholars point out that land is central to the Rastafarian movement in general, and has been since its inception. For instance, the symbol of Ethiopia (Africa) as the homeland, was very strong in the early founding of the religion. The freedom and economic empowerment of the dispossessed African descendants everywhere, according to Garvey's prophetic leadership positions, was dependent upon the return of all the sons and daughters of Africa to their own land and heritage. As Barry Chevannes points out, Leonard Howell, Archibald Dunkley, Joseph Hibbert, and Robert Hinds "were the main architects of the Rastafari movement for the first twenty years. Stretching Garvey's Back-to-Africa programme, they all saw redemption as 'Repatriation,' the return of all Africans to Africa."[52]

How the issue of land was and is handled in later developments of the religion and different branches is of crucial significance. Chevannes discusses the transition from the literal concept of "Repatriation" in Rastafari of the earlier period to a more symbolic or theological concept in Rastafari of later periods. At first the concept was basic to the belief that the Emperor Selassie was God. "Underlying the belief in the Emperor's divinity is the conclusion that Black people were destined to return to their native Africa." They sang about it in numerous songs with lines such as, "Our forefathers were taken away, O, Jah Rastafari O, Selah! Open up da gate mek I repatriate." They likened themselves to the "ancient children of Israel who were rescued from captivity by the intervention of God. Here, the image is used not as metaphor, but as reality itself." They were the new Israelites, and the Bible prophecies referred to them. "Babylon of old is none other than the White colonial and neo-colonial world."[53]

In his first study among the Rastas in the 1970's, Leonard Barrett saw them as not thinking of themselves as Jamaicans,

> but as Ethiopians awaiting repatriation. For this reason a Rastafarian owns no property. He may rent land for farming or business, but he does not buy property. Wherever a group of Rastafarians needs a place to stay, they 'capture' a piece of land, which, once captured, is difficult for the owner to regain. Sometimes police action and even occasional loss of life are required to get the land back in the hands of the rightful owner. The Rastafarian concept of property is summed up in the biblical assertion that 'the earth is the Lord's and the fullness thereof.' As children of Jah Rastafari, the brethren feel that they are free to take whatever land they need.[54]

Changes came about in the concept of repatriation, however, among later expressions and beliefs of Rastas in Jamaica.

After failures of prophecies and attempts at repatriation such as those of Prince Edwards Emmanuel (1958), Claudius Henry (1959) and occasional individual acts, the literal belief in the concept began to wane and various theological and symbolic concepts began to be expressed, such that Chevannes can conclude that, "Rastafari is essentially not a Repatriation movement." He describes Repatriation as a "theological, not a political, concept." He sees three aspects to it. It is, first of all, "a divine not a human act. It is different from migration, Rastafari insist. Many Rastafari even dissociated themselves from activities like the 1961 Mission, holding that while governments could bring about migration, only Jah could bring about Repatriation." Second, it means "the return of Africans not to [just] any country of Africa [or West Africa], but specifically to Ethiopia," to "Zion," which is Ethiopia, where God, Jah Ras Tafari, dwells. And third, Repatriation implies justice, in which case Europeans would give up the lands seized from the Amerindians and return to Europe.⁵⁵

Jean Besson clarifies a practice in the peasant culture of Trelawny province in Jamaica called the family land system, which smacks of the African past, involving male and female slaves and their descendants. She says that it "drew on the symbolic as well as economic significance of land in Caribbean plantation slave society, and transformed the principles of colonial legal freehold within the formal framework of the plantation." When slavery ended, she says, "This proto-peasant kin-based tenurial system mushroomed into the customary institution of family land in those Caribbean peasant communities, including Jamaica's Baptist land settlements, established by ex-slaves purchasing small landholdings." This family land is considered "the inalienable corporate estate of a family line," the rights to which are "generally validated through oral tradition, rather than legal documents, and transmitted through intestacy." All "children and their descendants in perpetuity are regarded as co-heirs of the land, regardless of sex, birth order, residence or legitimacy, with marriage not being regarded as a basis for inheritance." In having the "unrestricted cognatic descent principle," the family land system contrasts with the "unilineal systems predominant in Africa, and was created in resistance to the Caribbean plantation system."⁵⁶

Furthermore, around this family land system in Trelawny's Baptist villages complex African-Caribbean cultural traditions were built in resistance to imposed colonial culture.

> These include Creole language and oral tradition, transforming the standard English of colonial society and its Eurocentric history; the house-yard complex, providing the nucleus of the peasant culture and community; provision grounds and peasant market, transforming the export-oriented monocrop plantation economy; a multiple tenurial complex for yard and ground, maximizing land resources within the constraints of land scarcity, bilateral kinship networks, maximizing ego-focused kinship ties and bases of mutual support and exchange; complex marriage systems of multiple conjugal forms and serial monogamy, transforming colonial legal marriage and maximizing ties of alliance and affinity; and occupational multiplicity, migration and mutual aid, expanding and reinforcing the peasant economy.⁵⁷

Besson points out that both men and women are central to this peasant culture of resistance, "as transmitters and trustees of family land, and as crucial agents in socialization, cultivation, marketing, kinship networks, marriage systems and mutual aid." And she notes women's central role in the Revival cult, an important dimension of this peasant culture of resistance. "Like family land and other aspects of the peasant economy and community, the Revival worldview—which co-exists with the Baptist Church in Trelawny villages—is rooted in African-Caribbean proto-peasant cultural resistance." She comments on Revival's emerging from Myal traditions and reflecting African continuities within "a dynamic process of Caribbean culture-building."[58]

Having pinpointed the central role of women in the peasant culture of resistance, Besson goes on to point to the fact that Rastafari has its roots in part in the 18th century Jamaican slave religion, in which the ideology of Ethiopianism emerged. And the "link between the ideology of Ethiopianism and the Baptist Church during slavery can be clearly seen for the parish of Trelawny." And her studies showed a complex of interrelated religious forms in villages of Trelawny, including the Baptist Church, Revival, and the Rastafari movement, "which co-exist in their contemporary peasant cultures of resistance; and which are rooted in the interweaving of Myalism, Baptist Christianity, Ethiopianism and Native Baptist faith that were variants of religious resistance among the Trelawny slaves."[59] Besson goes on to point out the intermingling of family members living together in Trelawny villages who are of these different religious groups. "For example, in Granville the male Revival leader has a Rastafari son who shares his household; while in Martha Brae a woman who is committed to both the Baptist Church and Revival cult has a Rastafari 'son-in-law' living in her yard. The central figure of contemporary Alps, Mr. B., a stalwart of the Baptist Church and member of several of the village's overlapping Old Families including the central family...also has a Rastafari son living in his yard. This 'Dread' is well versed in Rastafari faith and has links with Prince Edward Emmanuel."[60]

This is a very good juncture at which to enter the specific discussion of the issue of women's and men's roles in Rastafari, and the perception of women. We have already seen that men and women play equal roles and are regarded as equal in the Rasta House of the Twelve Tribes of Israel, which is of great significance since this appears to be the only group where this happens to be the case. Other groups tend to be fairly satisfied with relegating women to submissive roles and inferior status. But Besson has shown that in the peasant culture of resistance, especially in Trelawny, which includes African-derived religions co-existing with Rastafari, women play roles of equality.

Barry Chevannes points to the downgrading and downplaying of women in the movement after the earliest period of the development of the religion, when women were involved, and the status of women and attitudes toward them from around the 1960's up to the present time. He first examines the views of women in Jamaican folk consciousness, which is mixed. In one respect, they are not complimentary, for they tend to blame women for men's troubles in the society by singling out negative traits such as deceitfulness, stressing only negative, temptress, images of women in the Bible such as Eve, Jezebal, Delilah. Positive women characters in the Bible such as Naomi, Ruth, Esther, and Miriam were not were not stressed. Concepts of the woman in contrast to the man are that woman is a receptacle, a vessel, the bearer of the male seed, rather than a person in her own right. However, in the family structure, more positive images and roles of women exist, such as being the dominant one in managing the domestic unit, even in male-headed households; and there is the role of mother. "Motherhood is also conceived metaphorically by the peasant, and Mada is a term reserved only for the most respected women in the community." The author says that the women leaders in the Revival cult are given this honorific title Mother. Other negative attitudes toward women in the folk consciousness that seem to influence or parallel those in Rastafarian development include notions of menstruating women as dangerous to certain crops.[61]

Chevannes summarizes his findings regarding the views of women in the folk consciousness as being both negative and positive, and shows how Dreadlocks (later Rastas) drew upon the negative impressions for their own ideas about women. Symbols used to promote male dominance or hegemony include the dreadlocks as associated with the mane of the lion (suggestive of Haile Selassie, "Lion of Judah") and a male symbol of power (as the female lion has no mane, God thus divinely ordained the symbol to suggest dominance of the male over the female); and the "Black man sees himself as Anansi, the spider-hero of Jamaican folklore, who uses the wiliness of his intellect to deceive his way into dominance over other animals of the forest." Women were required to cover their dreadlocks at all times. Seeing women as a strong source of distraction from focus on divine things, some Dreads chose a celibate lifestyle. The negative concepts and attitudes toward women are fully exhibited in the Bobo group, where menstruating women are "secluded in a hostel for the entire period of their showing, plus twelve purifying days. Non-menstruating women attend to them." And all cooking at all times is done by males. In the formal ceremonies and sacred rituals such as the reasoning, women take no part. "Only males may exercise the privilege of beating the drums." Further, Chevannes declares that, "One of the tenets of the Dreadlocks is that only through the enlightenment of her spouse may a woman declare Jah,' that is, achieve [religious] conviction." Finally, Chevannes asserts that the term of address for a woman of any age reduces her to the status of a child: she is referred to as Daata (Daughter). Practices such as these, Chevannes says, suggest some of the ways the "Dreadlocks movement established its total hegemony over womanhood and in so doing reinforced its separation from the world of Babylon."[62]

As would probably be expected, changes are taking place as women themselves enter into the picture to bring them about. Chevannes states in his conclusion that, "With the increased numbers of women among the Dreadlocks, to a large extent the result of growth among the middle classes, many of the...tenets and practices [he discussed] are undergoing change. The Rastafari movement is not unaffected by the wider struggle by women for equal status. Rastafari women are taking issue with the taboos, such as those against contraceptives and menstruation, and public display of locks, even within male presence...,and the right to speak in public and to participate on official delegations...."("The Symbolism of the Dreadlocks," p. 124)

The influence of women in this changing of the negative views of women is reflected in a literary work by Barbara Blake Hannah (Makeda Levi), obviously of the Twelve Tribes branch of Rasta, titled *Joseph: A Rasta Reggae Fable.*[63] Obviously, this is a fictional version of the experience of Bob Marley, who in his membership in the Twelve Tribes is known as Joseph. The cover description reveals this connection: "Joseph is the story of a legendary Rasta-Reggae singer and his spiritual journey to find his cultural roots in Africa and assist the journey for his fellow Brothers and Sisters. He is helped by Ashanti, a Rasta sister; Mikey, the 'firebingi' whonis his best friend; Zuelika, a beautiful singer who loves Joseph; Peter, Ashanti's King-man; Sam, the American journalist who follows Joseph's journey; and Busha, the white-Jamaican record producer who makes Joseph a millionaire superstar."[64]

The travels of Joseph include areas in Jamaica, Ethiopia, England, Miami, and Cuba. The experiences, insights, and revelations brought out in these travels are many, all of great interest and understanding among peoples. One of the scenes that reveal striking insight into the more liberal views of women, which we have seen to be typical of the Twelve Tribes group anyway, is the one set at

Bull Bay, at the commune of the Bobos. Sam, the American, is interviewing Joseph on all sorts of issues in Rastafari. At this point, he inquires of Joseph: "how it was that he did not obey Rasta rule that woman was inferior and unclean, but instead had many women and allowed them into his inner circle." "Joseph threw back his head and laughed, long. 'That a-no Rasta rule—that is rascal rule. Me LOVE woman. And so I should, for woman is I, and I am woman.'" When Sam asks what he means, Joseph replies:

> Well, the Father is Creator and He made mankind in His image. Well, for Him to create man and woman, he has to be Man and Woman too. For example, when He was to make Christ, He went with a woman, Mary. So to make Adam, He was both Man and Woman. And Woman is also in His image, like he says. Woman is the other half of me that makes a complete copy of God – Jah. So woman couldn't be inferior, she had to be equal, else she and I could not unite in equality and produce a child like Jah.[65]

It is significant that the author set this scene at the location where the issue of women's inferiority is most evidenced in the beliefs and practices: the Bobo communue on the hill at Bull Bay. As a literary artist, journalist, broadcaster, film maker, and former Independent Senator in the Jamaica Parliament (1984–1987), she is certainly one of the women of today who are becoming effective in influencing change in Rasta attitudes toward women.

Chapter Nine

The Moving of Spirit: A Comparative Vision

Of what is one to make of so much religious vision and insight as seen in the various expressions and manifestations of what can be called Spirit in the multiverse Caribbean world? As our overall venture in the book has been issue-oriented, the issues in this concluding chapter are the very diversities and differences we encounter in exploring the rich religious conceptions found in these Caribbean contexts, and what common vision possibly unites them. Without a doubt there are common threads of spiritual reality that run through all the religions, of whatever dimension and practice. There are the universal religious perspectives that are found in all religions if we but open our minds and spirits to them. Many open-minded religious figures have seen and expressed this understanding, especially regarding the socalled great world religions (the developed religions, as such) which we know as Hinduism, Buddhism, Confucianism, Judaism, Christianity, Islam, and perhaps others. But not so many have glimpsed the universalist perspective as found in the indigenous religious traditions that have manifested in various forms in the New World, stemming from African Traditional Religions and socalled Amerindian Religions, and have survived legal restrictions and efforts at elimination and remain intact today as strong spiritual challenges to the socalled official religions especially of the Western hemisphere.

In *The Sermon on the Mount According to Vedanta*, Swami Prabhavananda states that his religion of Vedanta, derived from the Hindu scriptures called the Vedas, teaches that "all religions are true inasmuch as they lead to one and the same goal—God realization." Thus Vedanta "accepts and reveres all the great prophets, spiritual teachers, and aspects of the Godhead worshipped in different faiths, considering them to be manifestation of one underlying truth." He further asserts the character and beliefs of the founder of his religious order, Sri Ramakrishna, as one of the illumined saints who expressed in his lifetime "to a greater degree than any other teacher the idea of religious universality and harmony. Not only did he undergo the disciplines of divergent sects within Hinduism but those of Mohammedanism and Christianity as well. Through each religious path he achieved the supreme realization of God, and thus was able to proclaim with the authority of direct experience: 'So many religions, so many paths to reach one and the same goal.'"[1]

Universal religious perspectives have been embraced and experienced by other religious practitioners, functionaries, leaders, scholars, thinkers such as Mohandas Gandhi, Thomas Merton, Howard Thurman, and others of various religious backgrounds. Howard Thurman, for instance, who engaged in a lifelong quest for religious understanding, for God-reality, was able to determine from his experiences of every religious expression from the socalled developed religions to the indigenous religions of Africa, Asia, Australia, and the Americas that "truth is found in every religion, and it is not true because it is found in those religions, but it is found in those religions because it is true."[2] It is significant that Thurman's religious quest as an African American involved many struggles against the odds of religious, social, and economic oppression which he was able to transcend. His understanding of God was drawn from his unique religious struggles, from which "he was able to envision not a universal religion but a universal religious and human perspective that lends crucial meaning to the whole of human life."[3] He states in summary: "God bottoms existence; therefore, the deeper down I go, the more into Him I find myself. None of the categories of classifications—of faith, belief, etc.—have any standing in the presence of this transcendent experience, because I think that whether I'm Black, White, Presbyterian, Baptist, Buddhist, Hindu, Muslim, that in the presence of God, all these categories by which we relate to each other fade away and have no significance whatsoever. For in his presence I am a part of Him being revealed to Him."[4]

Howard Thurman was speaking out of the wisdom and insight of a vision he had received from long years of experience and spiritual searching as a lifelong practicing mystic. Probably the average person never arrives at this point or height in her or his religious understanding. But we all in our genuine religious experience do begin at the same place Thurman and other great spiritual giants begin—and that is the point of personal religious encounter with Spirit. And the most vital and gratifying spiritual encounter is had by the person when he or she is able to bring to the encounter all that she or he is, including one's familial, racial, cultural, ethnic, religious, social class traits or identity. Consequently, experience has shown that where people are stripped of much of their identities and attempts are made to introduce to them elements of identities foreign to them, as was done in colonial societies in places such as Africa and the Americas, human and social abrasions or damages occur that must be fixed at some point in the historical process. We have seen that in the New World including the Caribbean, South, and Central America (other places, as well, of course), processes have occurred whereby conquered peoples have resisted dehumanization and destruction of their identities by holding on to them, even in disguised ways, as well as by recovering or restoring them in cases where they were for the most part divested of them.

The religious groups we have explored in this book reflect these processes, showing that being human, being oneself in every aspect is essential to genuine spiritual reality. In their quest for freedom from domination, and in their freedom of self-expression, they find it necessary to recover and restore their selves, their heritage, before they are willing to or can relate meaningfully to the foreign cultures and religions that have become officially dominant in the societies in which they live in this New World situation of so much religious and cultural diversity. Therefore, the importance of being rooted becomes primary. As Thurman points out about his quest for self-understanding in his religious journey, "I must be at home somewhere before I can feel at home everywhere."[5] Two aspects of the Caribbean experience, as well as other New World and even to some extent continental African experience, are crucial to this conclusion. One is the maintenance of and the recovery and restoration of the self and the genuine religious experience, and the second is the experience of self-transcendence or the universal religious vision and how the two are related.

The Maintenance of and the Recovery and Restoration and the Self and the Genuine Religious Experience

I don't believe it can be denied that all the religious expressions we have discussed reflect these tendencies of self-identity and self-possession. In their book devoted to introducing the "creolized, African-based religions that developed in the Caribbean in the wake of European colonization," Olmos and Paravisini-Gebert assert that the religious systems such as Vodou, Santeria, Obeah, Espiritismo, etc., developing in secrecy and posing a challenge to official Christian practices, "allowed the most oppressed sectors of colonial Caribbean societies to manifest their spirituality, express cultural and political practices suppressed by colonial force, and protect the health of the community."[6] Dale Bisnauth characterizes this spiritual self-maintenance and self-assertion of these Caribbean religions as the "Africanization of Christianity,"[7] wherein the African spirituality and identity is retained within the veneer of Christian elements and traditions.

George Brandon points to the opposite reality, the unhealthy and unwholesome trend of self-denigration, rampant among middle and upper sectors of the free black population of Cuba in the early nineteenth century due to exposure to Cuban racism. "Denial of the African past, efforts by light-skinned members to pass as white, the breaking of kinship ties with darker-skinned relatives; opposition of white parents to their children marrying people of color, opposition of mulatto parents to their children marrying people darker then themselves, legalistic machinations by which one could buy white status or overcome the imposed burden of color through a fee and a piece of paper—all articulate a dizzying merry-go-round of imposed inferiority and self-hatred."[8] Such an experience of escape from one's self and racial and ethnic identity and roots is common among many, if not most, New World Africans who have been exposed to racial discrimination in the Western hemisphere. And where such self-denigration exists, genuine religious experience is hard to find.

Personally, I found among leading Afro-Trinidadians of the Orisha Tradition or Religion with whom I visited, worshiped, and interviewed, the expression of a quest, to one degree or another, for what I choose to call **self-totalization**, that is, the total realization of the self, a rootedness in total self-knowledge and self-acceptance. This I see as deeply connected with honoring and accepting their Yoruba Orisha religious and ancestral traditions. An atmosphere and sense of pride, wholeness, peace tends to pervade their attitudes, and relations, in spite of the fact that tensions and frictions exist within their communities over syncretism with Christianity and other religions and maintaining the purity of African Yoruba traditions.[9] I refer in particular to Baba Erin Folami, Baba Sam Phills, Iya Patricia McCleod, Mr. Eddie LeCointe, Dr. Althea Jones-Lecointe, and Iya Pearl Eintou Springer, whom I interviewed.[10] I must say that I have not much observed this phenomenon among worshipers in many other places and religious groups. Some Orisha priests refer to the rootedness in the African heritage and traditions or worldview as afrocentricism, such as Erin Folami[11] and Pearl Springer[12] point out.

Rastafarianism has unique insight into the self-rootedness of religion and spirituality. Joseph Owens pinpoints and summarizes this vision in the Movement. He states that, "A presupposition underlying all Rastafarians' assertions about God is the conviction that every [person] must seek his [her] own God, for the brethren comprehend the truth that cultural differences are integral to one's conception of God. God is seen as the possession of a people, not of an individual alone, and the brethren hold it unreasonable for one people to be asked to submit to the foreign conception of another people." Owen quotes one informant of his research who asserts that his people cannot see God through the spectacle of Rome, but they must see God through the "spectacles of the Asiatic," through the black person's eyes. Owens states further, "The God of the Rastafarians is fully incarnate and is no longer to be sought in ethereal realms. Either [one] will seek and find God in this most humble human flesh, or else [one] will not find [God] at all."[13]

Owens's critical assessment of this view is a positive affirmation. He states: "By announcing that God is fully a man living among men, the brethren have not debased divinity, but have enhanced a whole people's awareness of their own humanity. By claiming that God is not experienced in books, however sacred, or in rituals, however elaborate, the Rastas have made their people aware of the need to explore personal history and communal experience in order to find the Lord."[14] Interestingly, Howard Thurman in his long search for truth followed a path that led him first through his own cultural experiences as a Black man in America. He stated in a little book that records essential aspects of that search, *Jesus and the Disinherited*,[15]

> Many and varied are the interpretations dealing with the teachings and life of Jesus of Nazareth. But few of these interpretations deal with what the teachings and the life of Jesus have to say to those who stand, at a moment in human history, with their backs against the wall. To those who need profound succor and strength to enable them to live in the present with dignity and creativity, Christianity often has been sterile and of little avail. The conventional Christian word is muffled, confused, and vague. Too often the price exacted by society for security and respectability is that the Christian movement in its formal expression must be on the side of the strong against the weak.[16]

Thurman is quick to point out that this being "on the side of the strong against the weak" is a reversal of Christ's early church focus. So his answer to the central probe of his search, what is the meaning of the religion of Jesus for the person with his/her back against the wall, is that Jesus "announced the good news that fear, hypocrisy, and hatred, the three hounds of hell that track the trail of the disinherited, need have no dominion over them." For his search had led him to a great discovery: that "Christianity as it was born in the mind of this Jewish teacher and thinker [Jesus of Nazareth] appears as a technique of survival for the oppressed. That it became, through the intervening years, a religion of the powerful and the dominant, used sometimes as an instrument of oppression, must not tempt us into believing that it was thus in the mind and life of Jesus."[17]

In my estimation the Rastafarians and Thurman are on essentially the same track in that they insist on rejection of the religion of Christ transmitted by a culture and a system not only foreign to themselves and their own peoplehood and experience, but one which has also turned the religion of Christ as scripturally presented on its head so that it upholds their people's dispossession and dehumanization. So what they do, both the Rastas and Thurman, is to search the Scripture and their own experiences for the truth of that religion as it is expressed and played out in their own experiences today. We will see in the next section that the Rastas' views are not confined to exclusivity, as Thurman's were not, but move on to inclusiveness and transcendence.

We should note that the quest for self-expression, understanding and affirmation in religion and rejection of religion transmitted by foreign, enslaving, colonizing cultures is a major issue in continental African religions today and in African-derived religions, notably in Orisa religion in the United States and in Trinidad and Tobago. For instance, it is what is behind the authenticity debate and the focus on afrocentricity among Orisa worshipers which I encountered in my visit with them in the fall of 2004 and which is treated at length in Frances Henry's book *Reclaiming African Religions in Trinidad*, cited earlier in this chapter. I want to first take a look at that debate and expressions of it and then examine the issues in certain representative West African situations.

According to Frances Henry, the dispute in Trinidad is between the older Orisa worshipers who retain the syncretisms with Christianity developed during the period of enslavement as a means of disguising their actual African Yoruba religious beliefs and practices, legally forbidden during the time; and the younger group of worshipers, who subscribe to ridding the Orisa religion of the syncretisms and a return to a pure form of the African Yoruba religion. The dispute is over what is authentic and what is inauthentic in African religion in Trinidad. One group claims that syncretisms "taken from Christianity, Hinduism and other religious forms merged naturally with the African forms of worship" and what resulted is presently a hybrid or merged, somewhat New World religious form. Another group believes strongly that "syncretisms are examples of Eurocentric slave and colonial oppressive hegemonies that must be removed from the religion."[18]

Henry notes that this rejection of the syncretism in Trinidad is reinforced by developments taking place in the United States,

> where the Orisha religion is one of the fastest growing religious movements among African Americans. As a result of increased contact between African American and migrant Caribbean Orisha worshippers, new arenas of debate are opening. For example, it is now claimed that the truly authentic Orisha worship is one in which worshippers have learned the religion straight from African sources without the need for Christian intervention, as occurred in the colonized Caribbean. This movement towards the authentic source took issue with the Cuban practice of Santeria, in which Christianity is given equal pride of place with the Yoruba faith.[19]

One of the promoters of this position whom I interviewed and who was one of my hosts in my visits among the people of the Orisa Tradition in November-December, 2004, was Babalorisha Erin Folami. He expressed views adamantly in favor of abandoning any syncretic elements in the African-derived religion and engaging in what may be considered total immersion in African Yoruba traditions and religious worldview. In fact, Baba Folami is more of the Afrocentric persuasion,[20] well-described by Henry as growing out of the Black Power movement that embraced many areas of the Caribbean, the United States, and other parts of the world in the 1970's. Trinidad was tremendously impacted, as has been previously discussed in an earlier chapter of this book, and numerous persons were involved in the leadership of this movement, from the Prime Minister Dr. Eric Williams on down. Henry accurately pinpoints the political aspect of this Afrocentrism as a focus in Orisa religious tradition in Trinidad and Tobago. She finds that underlying the objectives to rediscover original Yoruba ritual and remove the Christian elements is "the need to reassert African ethnic identity as an African-derived people, even while living in multi-ethnic Trinidad. At the heart of their dedication to Orisha is a political commitment to the philosophy of Afrocentricity and its valorization of African identity."[21] Henry's assessment, I believe, is fairly accurate on this point, for it is close to what I perceived in my interaction with Folami and others of this persuasion. But this is not a negative thing if it is properly engaged in an ongoing or growing religious perspective with open-mindedness. I would say that it can serve as a necessary phase of the self-totalization process I mentioned earlier.

I would call what Henry describes as the "Africanization" or the "re-Yorubanizing" the Orisa religion a part of the self-totalization process that is significant for genuine religiosity. Henry gives an overview of such efforts on the part of the Orisa leaders and the communities in Trinidad such as the language changes to be more in tune with Yoruba language and terminology, changes in cosmology to greater sophistication and development of ancestral traditions (e. g., the incorporation of the Yoruba Egungun festival), and the development of the Orisha Family Day Celebrations (designed to introduce elders of the faith to the community and especially to the youth). The author cites the leaders of these Africanization efforts such as Iyalorisha Patricia McCleod, Iyalorisha Amoye (Valerie Stephensen Lee Chee), Professor Rawle Gibbons, Iyalorisha Pearl Eintou Springer, Iyalorisha Melvina Rodney, Babalorisha Sam Phills, Babalorisha Clarence Forde, and others,[22] many of whom I met and interviewed during my stay in Trinidad in 2004. Henry concludes that "Being able to worship traditional Yoruba deities, following ritual practices that originated in Nigeria and are centuries old, and defining aspects of their world through the prism of such 'original' religious traditions are far stronger stimuli to African identity than are the wearing of a style of clothes or even the assumption of an African name."[23]

We know that Islam and Christianity invaded West Africa, the lands from which predominantly the descendants of Africans in the New World came. And the indigenous Africans had to contend with similar encroachment on their traditions and ways of life, including Traditional African religions such as Yoruba, Ibo, Hausa-Fulani, Ewe, Akan, Fon, and many others. At the same time that the Europeans were forcing their cultures, religions, and social and political domination on the indigenous peoples of the New World and the enslaved Africans, they were also doing a similar job of dominating the African homelands of the captives they had brought as slaves to this New World. Both Christianity and Islam attempted to displace African culture and religion and replace them with their own. But where they had a measure of success in doing so, they were never able to wipe out entirely the people's cultures and religions. At best there was a mixture of these so-called world religions and the Traditional religious traditions, and the Traditional worldview and ancestral and spiritual traditions always remained as a threat to the encroaching religions from without.

For comparison with what took place in the Caribbean, especially Trinidad and Tobago, we will look more closely at what took place in terms of Christianity and European dominance in West African societies, and particularly Ghana and Nigeria. Quoting and referencing Lamin Sanneh, Robert B. Fisher describes the Africanization of Christianity in Africa, similar to the way Dale Bisnauth does regarding Christianity among enslaved Africans in the Caribbean. He states that the Christian missions came to West Africa under the false notion that the peoples there did not know about God. But they found the opposite to be true. They found among the Africans well-defined concepts of almighty God, the Creator and sustainer of all life, called by names such as Nyame in Ghana, Olorun or Olodumare in Nigeria, and sophisticated philosophy and cosmology. Fisher states:

> The God of Abraham, Isaac, and Jacob, and the God and Father of Jesus Christ, was assimilated with the God of the ancestors. Only there was a difference: The God preached by the foreigners was a jealous God, who did not tolerate lesser gods, a God who promoted intolerance and wars. On the other hand, the God of the Africans was a hospitable God, who was mediated through lesser deities…. The process of the Africanization of Christianity commenced almost immediately with the replacement of the exclusive notion of Western Christianity with the inclusive rule of African Religious Traditions.[24]

However, Europeans did succeed in dehumanizing Africans and denigrating their culture and society under domination of colonial powers. While in many cases of domination Africans mixed their religious elements and practices with Catholicism and its feasts and saints, etc., as was done in the Caribbean Catholic areas, they faced discrimination and laws restricting their cultural practices. Fisher cites the Portuguese as an example. He states, "The Portuguese method of padreado, which required that the Africans in their territories accept both Catholicism and the rule of the king of Portugal, met with strong opposition everywhere. Moreover, the policy of requerimento meant that Christianity in its totality required obedience to church authorities. Nothing of traditional practices was to remain. Nothing of traditional value was permitted to continue." Referring to the 19th century evangelization process on the part of European missionaries, Fisher notes the collusion of the missionaries with the colonial powers and their cooperation with them in allowing themselves to be used by them to exploit the vast wealth of Africa. And any efforts missionaries made to try to counteract colonial policies were not of much consequence.[25]

Fisher cites the more or less involuntary efforts of Christians to rectify encroachments on African cultures and religions by translating the Bible into African languages and the Africans' efforts at restoring their African roots in the Indigenous African Christian Churches (IACC). What was seen as a necessity for the success of their Christian missions was turned into a benefit for restoration of power and identity for Africans. Fisher quotes Lamin Sanneh, who states that the Protestant missionaries had to rely on indigenous languages to get their gospel messages across, which created a distinction between European culture and the indigenous traditions. "Consequently, however much mission tried to suppress local populations, the issue of the vernacular helped to undermine its foreign character. By the same token, the new interests in creating vernacular Scriptures for societies that had no Scriptures of their own ushered in a fundamental religious revolution, with new religious structures coming into being to preside over the changes." And a most notable change was "the mass participation of Africans in this process." Thus, African populations began to see that this "missionary adoption of vernacular categories for Scripture was in effect a written sanction for the indigenous vocation."[26]

Fisher summarizes the impact of this event of translating the Bible in African vernacular languages as resulting in the beginning of African self-recovery and self-restoration, or what I am calling self-totalization that is essential for genuine religious experience and expression. He states:

> As Sanneh and other Africans have noted, the translation of the Christian scriptures into the languages of Africans resulted in an affirmation of their ancient languages and cultures in a revolutionary form, the written medium of grammar and alphabet. It provided not only a continuity between the ancestral religions and Christianity but a new lever in the brave new world which required the peoples of clan, ethnic group, and nation to stand proudly in the face of foreign cultures. No longer needing to express themselves in a foreign language, Africans have through Christian efforts been able to write about themselves, keeping in mind their own ancestral origins. Thus the Christian translation project resulted in the emergence of African literature and in the African independence movement.[27]

The way was now paved for the formation of the Independent African Christian Churches (IACCs), as Fisher notes, which was an indigenization movement whereby African prophets and ministers withdrew from the mainline European Protestant Churches such as Methodists and Presbyterians and formed truly African Churches in their thinking. Fisher's sources showed that there were more than five thousand independent Christian denominations in Africa, "all bearing the marks of pentecostal spirituality [stemming from the Los Angeles Azusa Street revival in 1906], but also with truly African qualities of their own."[28] In Appiah-Kubi's description of the IACCs, one sees comparisons with the Spiritual Baptist Churches of Trinidad and Tobago and other West Indian countries in the Caribbean. He says that while they maintain Jesus Christ as the supreme object of devotion, they manifest the emotionalism of African religions and preserve traditional values, emphasizing healing, reverence of the ancestors, and helping members cope with the stresses and problems of everyday life.[29] The names of some of these churches are long and descriptive such as in Zaire the famous Church of the Lord Jesus Christ on Earth of the Prophet Simon Kimbangu, with more than eight million members; and the United Native African Church in Lagos, Nigeria.[30]

Fisher describes in more detail the Independent Church movement in Nigeria led by the Prophet Josiah Olunowo Oshirelu, who founded the Church of the Lord Aladura (Yoruba word for prayer, for its emphasis is on healing through prayer). Fisher states:

> At first it was a gathering of Yoruba people, who drew from Africanized Islam and the Bible, to emphasize healing and prayer with a millennialist condemnation of the colonial system. His followers split several times. Among the splinter groups were the Precious Stone Church, and the Cherubim and Seraphim Church, founded by Moses Orimulade Tunolashe, who became known as Baba Aladura, the "Praying Father," along with a young lady, Christiana Abiodun Akinsowon, both of whom led a "Praying Band," the Egbe Aladura. This latter movement retained many elements of Yoruba Traditional Religion, including belief in the orisha and the use of Ifa divination to determine the will of Oludumare.[31]

Of course, Oludumare is conceived of as the same God in Christianity (the Father, the Creator), Judaism (Yahweh, Jehovah), and Islam (Allah). The restoration here is the Yoruba language for God. This then represents an important stage in the self-totalization process I am stressing.

Spirituality Beyond Religion: Transcendence and Universal Religious Vision in Caribbean Religions

The other issue before us is how to determine the common spiritual vision running through the religious conceptions, practices, and encounters in the Caribbean context, including Western, Eastern, Indigenous, African-Derived Traditional, Creole, and other religions. We will consider these religions that have been discussed from the perspectives of the issues reflected in them and how we may determine the religious vision significant to all religions. For though there are clear distinctions among the religious varieties, there are issues common to all, and the visions of hope for human understanding and genuine meaning running through them can also be seen.

In my experiences and encounters with key persons of the Orisa Religion in Trinidad and Tobago in November and December, 2004, I gained some significant insights into the possibilities for seeing the common spiritual vision running through Caribbean religious expressions. One of the chief religious figures I interviewed and conversed with considerably is Baba Sam Phills, the Chairman of the Council of Orisa Elders of Trinidad and Tobago, Incorporated. Baba Sam Phills is a unique individual among religious leaders. It is understandable that Frances Henry found him to be a mediator who manages to negotiate between the various groupings of the Orisa faith in the country.[32] I will share the insights here that I gained from that formal interview.

Baba Phills talked first about the philosophy and spiritual concepts of Orisa and its efficacy for expressing and sustaining human meaning and understanding. He spoke of four aspects of the divine: Oludumare, Olorun, Obatala, and Orunmila,[33] as Creative Force. These four aspects give divine light; they are "Almighty God (as in Christianity and other religions)." He further refers to the creative forces as relating to earth, sun, rivers, wind, sea, all creative forces of life. One must acknowledge them and gain understanding of Oludumare, the Great God. The "divine graces, the creative forces" produced humans. Interestingly, Phills referred to the woman as Oddudua, a creative force, the caring hand. Each Orisha in the pantheon, with different functions, go together to form a divine whole. Oya, for instance, goddess of the wind, guardian of the cemeteries, etc., blows from mountain to mountain carrying pollination and forming and spreading creation work. Emi is the first element to enter the human body and the first to leave at death. (I took the emi to be close to what we call the soul in some contexts.) The primordial waters in the high mountains form the source from which creation stems. The Almighty gave Orunmila the power to plant trees, and he secured Oya to assist him. For her assistance she was given Ochenma, the rainbow.[34]

Phills went on to speak about the meaning of life as brought out in the thousands of odus found in the Ifá corpus, the vast source of stories and poems used by diviners and prophets in the Orisha tradition, a sacred book really which provides divine guidance for worshipers. Many odus in the tradition, he stated, "teach what life is all about." He described the odu as being like "a prayer, really"; it "enlightens the thinking aspect of humans." He spoke of the life of a person as being "like a tree" in its structure and symmetry. "The ori— the wisdom [the head, mind, reason]" must be in harmony with the emi. If these are not "perfectly synchronized, the body becomes sick." At the age of eighty years now he said he felt in his own experience the gift of such symmetry of mind and body. He had come to know that the Almighty exists, not simply to believe, but to know. He stated, "There is no mysticism about the reality of life." One must strive to become what he referred to as "iwa pele [a Yoruba expression], the greatest one can be. You strive to be that to share with others," this harmony and symmetry and divine knowledge.[35]

The Baba continued, moving to the stage I have referred to as the self-recovery, the restoration of self and identity necessary for a people who have been oppressed and denied their true self-expression and forced to assume the culture and religion of another people. He stated, "Orisha people whose rights were taken away are now restoring their place and human meaning, once degraded. Reclaiming this equalization [emi-ori], we are looking for our space in the world now, looking for understanding and love of ourselves, our families, and our people." He spoke of 51 shrines in palaises in Trinidad and Tobago [other sources say 75 or more][36] where the people can come together and keep in touch with their religious reality. After much struggle and petitioning under the leadership of the Council of Orisha Elders, they have obtained from the government a designated plot of land consisting of ten acres on which to build a temple and a place for the "Orisha people to become united and develop their culture." He stated that, "Orisha is also universal [having spread in the diaspora to most areas of the world], as are the other socalled major religions of the world." He spoke of his vision to build a big temple where people from all the shrines may come together in worship, such as other major religions have (temples, mosques, etc.). He spoke of the beautiful litanies and songs their choirs could sing that are in their literature and oral traditions.[37]

At this point in the interview, Baba Phills had come to the universalist, inclusive, mystical perspective I sensed in him and that is possible in Orisha as in any true religion. He gave his response to the statement by Thurman quoted earlier, that one "can't feel at home everywhere until one is at home somewhere." He declared, "I understand that very well. For you see, a house is not a home until that house makes itself a home." He gave his views on mysticism. He saw it as a sixth sense within oneself, a deeper insight into things underneath. One achieves this mysticism "by concentration, not by studying some paraphernalia. Some people abuse this by claiming themselves mystics and going out for making money. But true mysticism is a divine gift, and one develops this sixth sense, the inner self, the spiritual aspect by sincerity of purpose and through vibrations coming to one not from the outside but from the inside.

In responding to my suggestion of his being, like Thurman, rooted in his own religious tradition and yet being able to transcend, to reach out beyond to embrace the truth as found in all religions, he recounted an interesting experience in which this became evident in his life. It was when he by invitation went on a journey to Mombay (Bombay), India, to visit a huge university built on fifty acres of land. Children were often invited here to study every aspect of the culture and religion. While on this trip, they were taken up into the Himalayas for three or four days' meditation, a flight or spiritual journey. This was a tremendous experience for him, for as one came back down from the mountain one pondered one's own life and its meaning. They then visited the Ganges River, and up a hill stand two temples within which Hindu Gods are represented. And he was told that Jesus is believed to have spent times in these temples, and especially after the Resurrection, the last time he went there, after which he never came down. It was a two-mile walk up the hill to these temples, which he did not visit, and he said somewhat humorously: "If all the philosophies are true, when you go up there, you're not supposed to come down."[38]

He went on to describe what he called that "inner peace of mind," of "going way beyond religion," of "spirituality beyond religion." This he felt should be guarded and protected, for it "can be corrupted by money and greed." He spoke of this in relation to Howard Thurman, of whom he said, "Thurman was well ahead of his time, the world was not ready for him then, but now the world is ready for him; his theories can be put in motion." But he felt that guard must be kept against charlatans who may be out for materialistic exploitation.[39]

In response to the question of doing his spiritual biography, he declared, "My spiritual biography is going to be very dangerous [referring to the radical nature of his religious journey]." In brief, he stated that his spiritual journey began in his birth. His mother was Anglican and used to sing in the choir at the Anglican Cathedral in downtown Port of Spain (Trinity Cathedral), and he declared that she "could have been the Mahalia Jackson of Trinidad" had she pursued her singing capabilities.[40] Picking up the short overview of his life, Baba stated that his grandfather was Ibo (a cultural group in Nigeria) and his grandmother was Congo (from Central African people). He stated, "My spirituality was meant to be. I never felt anything against the church." But he simply decided he wanted to pursue his own spirituality, and his mother supported him. His journey was set when his great-grandfather, whom he had never known, came to him in a dream one night and strengthened him and gave him something that determined the direction his life should take. And that course is reflected in the role he plays in realizing the dream he has had for many years: in being "able to get the Orisha people respected and not ostracized any longer but fully accepted."[41]

Baba recounted his earlier life in this direction in which he spent many years in the United States as a part of a performing group playing Orisha drums and doing Orisha dances in cities all across America in places such a Chicago, New York, Orangeburg, South Carolina; Memphis, Tennessee; Tallahassee, Miami, and others. He referred to his life's journey by the word "madness," by which he seems to have meant something like enrapture. He played quite a bit of drums, even performing on Broadway with such famous persons as Joyce Cary and others. He was a member of the Federated Brotherhood of Musicians, and he still carries his Actors' Equity card. This is part of another story he will enlarge upon in another work to be produced.[42] Enough is said to note that his has been a long spiritual journey that has led to deeper perceptions and ever-broadening avenues of spiritual development and understanding.

Other religious leaders of the Orisha tradition in Trinidad and Tobago who are of similar persuasion or are on a similar spiritual track, as I would call it, are Rawle Gibbons, one of the architects of the Council of Orisha Elders and the Director of the Festival Center for Creative Arts and Professor at the University of the West Indies; and Mrs. Pearl Eintou Springer, activist, poet (Poet Laureate of Trinidad), dramatist, librarian. My interviews with both of these persons show them to be of similar thinking to that of Baba Sam Phills, although each is unique in his or her own way. I will cite briefly representative perceptions taken from each interview.

Gibbons is well-focused in the Orisha tradition of Trinidad and Tobago, and at the same time open to and quite comfortable with the changes that have been created in the New World involving syncretism with other religions, Christian, Hindu, Amerindian, Islamic, Buddhist, and otherwise. He is much in favor of inclusiveness in all religions, as he stated, for instance that, "Hinduism in its best sense is universalist." He says it's a part of the "richness" of Orisha religion to be "entirely open." The belief that there is only one way that the religion can be practiced is a kind of "fundamentalism" that can be found in many other religions which has a political implication. He stressed the need for Orisha religion to become more organized to deal with the "realities of the present situations," such as the steps made in forming the Council of Orisha Elders and the Orisha religion becoming a part of the Inter-religious Organization of Trinidad and Tobago, which includes Hindu, Islam, Christian, Orisha, and many other religions of the country. He also is much involved in exposing students and others in the community, especially young people, to the varieties of cultures expressed in the community festivals of Hosay (Islamic), Rameela (Hindu), and others in order to encourage wider acceptance and understanding.[43]

Mrs. Pearl Springer has a religious perspective coming out of her life experiences as a social activist, poet, dramatist, and librarian (founder of the National Heritage Library of Trinidad and Tobago), mother, and priestess of the Orisha religion. Her religious experience growing up in Santa Cruz (Trinidad and Tobago), a heavily Catholic town, was of a strong Catholic nature; but her mother was from mixed African and Black Carib Indian stock, and her maternal grandfather was a Congolese African, son of a slave on a plantation on the Island of St. Vincent. Her story from its origin to the present time reveals much about how she arrived at her unique spirituality. Her grandfather was well-versed in medicines of healing. She says that he taught her slave songs of the plantation, and though he died at the age of 108 years, he "still walks with" her. Her Catholic religious background was challenged when she as a young woman spent time in England in the Black Panthers movement of the 1960's and came back to Trinidad and Tobago and was intensely involved in the Black Power

Movement of 1969 and 1970. Afro-centricity led her to the realization, "You cannot be liberated at all if you serve the God of another."[44]

At this point in her life, her spiritual mother, Iyalorisha Melvina Rodney, the Head of the Iyalorishas of Trinidad and Tobago, came to her aid. Through divination it was determined that Ogun, the Orisha of iron, war, strength, etc., had claimed her, and she was advised to go to Nigeria to be initiated. She did and later questioning of the validity of her initiation and receiving assurance only made her realize the depth to which Christianity had misguided her. She was also claimed by Shango, the deity of fire and lightning, war, etc., and Oya, the mother deity of the sea, guardian of cemeteries, etc., and she was also initiated there, becoming even stronger in her religious commitments. She says that hers was "a fascinating journey of self-discovery." She was led toward the realization of Iya Rodney's and the Ooni's[45] dream of bringing all the numerous shrines together in one and achieving legitimacy for the religion in the society. They went to work on this and accomplished it. For up to two or three years ago, "You had to apply for a permit to beat the drums in the palais." Drums were still legally banned. They petitioned for many months and demonstrated at Parliament until they were successful in getting the restrictions removed. She stated, "The history of the religion was a fragmented one, and bringing the different shrines together was a monumental task." Achieving this through formation of the Council of Orisha Elders, they were able to celebrate a public mass of Orisha religion. But they did not stop here. Achieving greater acceptance in the society meant becoming a part of the IRO (Inter-religious Organization) of Trinidad and Tobago. This meant branching out and recognizing other religions and being recognized by them. They had assistance in achieving this goal. "Three years ago we were at a Hindu celebration of the God Ganesh, and we walked together and made joint petitions to the Prime Minister, that if the Orisha people were not admitted, the Hindus would come out of the IRO. So Orisha is now a part of the IRO and can officiate at the opening of Parliament." This was quite a feat. She continued, "Now the people wear their Orisha clothing openly and openly practice their religion."[46]

It was clear from the interview that Mrs. Springer is deeply-rooted in her own religion of Orisha, and she is quite comfortable in relating to other religions on an equal basis and working with people of those faiths in the society. Her life story shows that she has successfully achieved spiritual and cultural self-recovery and restoration of the culture of her people and is able to transcend to what Baba Sam Phills, one of her mentors, called "spirituality beyond religion." She is still very much the activist and does much travel, writing, and speaking on social and cultural issues. She says that the Orisha powers are working in and through her, and she obeys and does as they direct, as well as respecting and obeying her elders such as Iya Rodney and Baba Phills. She had at the time of the interview just come from a trip to New York City at the Shomberg where she had been invited along with other top women literary artists including Toni Morrison and Alice Walker for a conference on Black women's issues, and the like. And she was preparing to deliver the featured address for a cultural celebration at the Prime Minister's Residence in Barbados.

Like other persons and groups discussed in Africa and Trinidad, Mrs. Springer has achieved what I have referred to as self-totalization. And once one achieves self-totalization or recovery of the true self from an oppressed and dehumanized state, one is a ripe candidate for transcendence or the deeper and more universalist perspective, the experience of oneness, as expressed by Howard Thurman and Babalorisha Sam Phills, as well as Mr. Rawle Gibbons. This is not to diminish the importance of the self-totalization process, which is vitally significant. In fact, several persons I talked with and interviewed were vitally involved in this process of recovering the original Yoruba or Orisha tradition among the people. They have training centers and schools, for adults in general, women and children in particular. Among these persons are Babalorisha Erin Folami, Dr. Althea LeCointe, Mr. Eddie LeCointe, Iyalorisha Patricia McCleod, and Kambiri Osunreyeke.[47]

The self-totalization and self-recovery process is taking place throughout the African-Caribbean communities in the Caribbean and in Central and South America as the African-derived religions are being practiced and expanded. The struggle for self-expression and recovery goes on as other groups like the Orisha people of Trinidad and Tobago are seeking to maintain and legitimize their own religious realities in the midst of restrictions and prejudices. But the more they face restrictions and prejudices the stronger they hold to their religions. And these religions are spreading to other parts of the Western World and Africa and Asia. They are gaining converts or new initiates to their religions. Rastafarianism is a good example of this. And this phenomenon of spreading to other parts of the world manifests a universalizing trend in these religions, which are coming to compete with the other world religions in terms of attracting converts and gaining exposure, acceptance, and legitimacy of spiritual significance. People practicing these religions are beginning to see the deeper and more universal spirituality of their religions and the link with the spirituality of other religions.

Many scholars and interpreters are recognizing and exploring this character of these religions. Clyde W. Ford interprets the African spiritual journey as an inward one, for instance, and sees the divinities and experiences of spirit possession in an interesting symbolic light which gets at the universalist perspective. He looks at the African spiritual journey in the context of the hero's quest and concludes that, "Symbolically... we, as the hero, have awakened to our life's adventure; we have encountered and surpassed the hindrances on our way; and we have gone into the dim recesses of our own unconscious for the rebirth of courage from fear, hope from despair, and faith from misgivings...African mythology reminds us that while we have thus valiantly conquered the kingdoms of the earth and the underworlds, we have still neglected the celestial sphere. This home of the gods is the apex of the hero's journey, a metaphor for the province of human spirituality—the site of the soul's highest adventure."[48] Ford pinpoints that adventure as an inward one and notes its universality.

> The ultimate journey of the African hero, like the heroes of all times, is a spiritual quest. Myth, of course, represents this quest as an outward journey to a far-off heavenly realm, populated by a single great god or by a constellation of gods and goddesses amidst whom the spiritual hero seeks his fate. But in truth, there is no heaven "out there:" the kingdom of heaven is "in here," within each human being, and the task of the true spiritual hero is to find it by traveling deep within. Nor are there any larger-than-life men and women stepping lightly above the clouds, keeping track of every human move; the many gods and goddesses of myth are "in here," too, as different aspects of our own divine nature. The task of the spiritual hero is to meet these gods and goddesses and realize that divinity within.[49]

This line of thinking leads Ford to an understanding of the phenomenon of spirit possession in a similar way to that of the divinities. Seen as "personifications of those archetypal energies that manifest in nature and within human life," the "orishas are beheld not outside the individual but deep within; and the individual, through ritual address, possesses the gods and goddesses as a way of repossessing those essential, divine aspects of one's self." For support of this view he cites Yoruba literary celebrity Wole Soyinka as taking "just such an approach to understanding African mythology" in his *Myth, Literature, and the African World*.[50] He states that Soyinka calls these archetypal energies "essence-ideals."[51]

The inner divine reality of the person is incorporated in Rastafarian beliefs, as well as the universality of spirituality. Rastas see God (Jah) as being within all peoples, the Europeans as well as Africans and others. Joseph Owens states, "The Rastafarians claim that their knowledge of God is 'inborn': it does not come from outside, but is already within man by virtue of his God-likeness and his direct union with the divine."[52] Owens cites the Rastas' idea of universality but also of the natural disposition of the poor for divine knowledge. "Although every man is called to know God, the poor people have a decided advantage in the Rastas' view, since they are forced to look into themselves and confront the basic reality of human existence—and only there can God be found."[53]

In his introduction to Owens's book, Rex Nettleford clarifies this spirituality and universality in Rastafarianism.

> At the heart of his religious system is the notion of his own divinity and the first-person image of self. As if for emphasis the terms "I-n-I" and "I-man" are used as a constant reminder of the final transformation of a non-person (as the old slave society and the new Babylon would have it) into a person, as is defined by "Jah RastafarI" and asserted by the Rastaman himself....For the Rastafarians each member of the "masses" or the "proletariat" has a personality, and individual and finite identity, a divine dimension with direct routing to the Creator, Jah, himself. Father Owens sees in this very individuality the "unity of mankind" and the source of the Rastafarian universality expressed in the brethren's call to universal brotherhood and their injunction of "peace and love." The net result is a level of consciousness that eschews racism and exalts the dignity of man, the offspring of God, whoever he may be.[54]

To conclude, enough has been said to indicate that the religions of the Caribbean, whatever their origins and constitutions, are religions just like any religions anywhere in the world. They are essential efforts of peoples to find their own way to the divine and to self-knowledge and understanding. Human dignity and meaning are vital to these religions as they are to any others. But here among these many peoples who have been oppressed, and still are so, and denied the basic character of humanness, religion is of utmost significance in the journey of life. The numerous issues in Caribbean religions we have discussed are reflective of the pervasiveness of religion in the Caribbean and how important it will be in working out and resolving the problems faced in the region.

Appendix I

Santeria Ceremony in Tampa, Florida, at Home of Max Griffin-Maya

Picture Illustrations of Feeding the Warrior Deities: Eleggua, Ochosi, Osun, and Ogun

Max Griffin-Maya Greeting the Babalao, Who Conducts the Ceremony

Griffin-Maya Prostrate in Continuation of Greeting

Babalao Greets Other Family Members

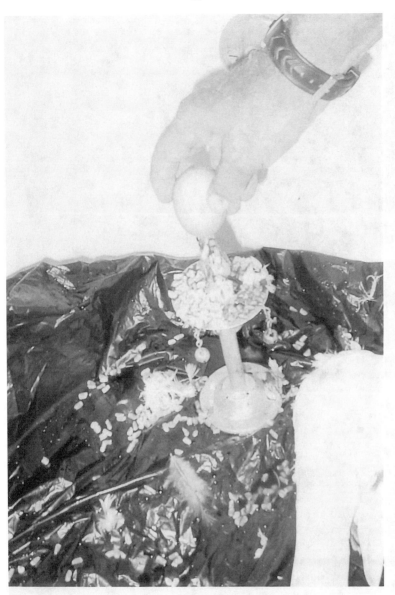

Aspects of the Ebo or Sacrifice Preparation

Preparing the Sacrifice

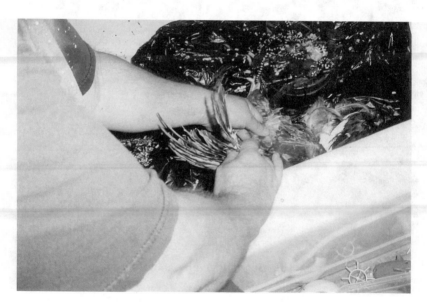

Making the Sacrifice

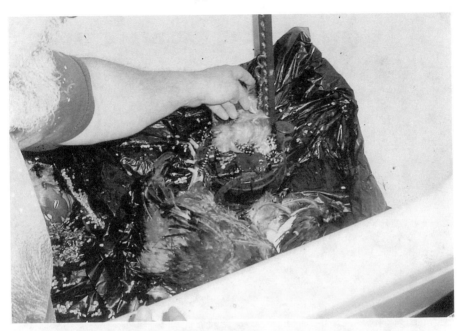

Feeding the Warrior Deities

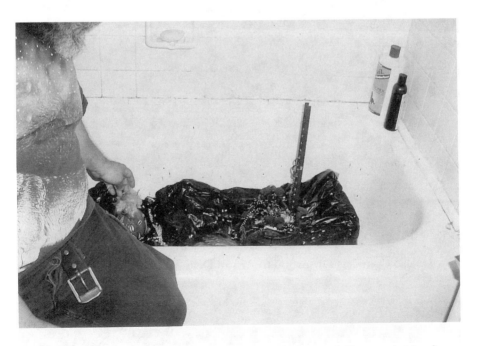

Continuing the Feeding (Image of Eleggua Underneath Devotee's Hand)

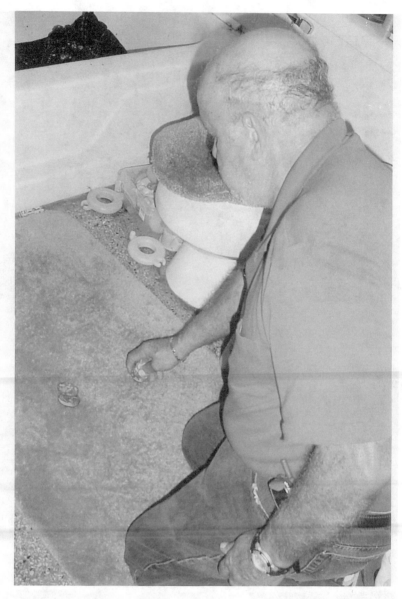

Babalao Conducts Divination to Affirm Deities' Acceptance of Sacrifice

Appendix II

Orisha Practitioners and Interactions with Other Religions in Trinidad and Tobago

Picture Illustrations

Mountain View of Port of Spain, Trinidad and Tobago

Detail View of Ibo Village Outside Port of Spain

Babalorisha Erin Folami, A Leader of the Orisha Community

Iyalorisha Patricia McCleod, Priestess of the Oshun-Shango Shrine
of San Juan, Trinidad and Tobago

Statue of Shango at Entrance to Shrine

Altar at Oshun-Shango Shrine

Batá Drums at Shrine (*iyà, itótele, okónkolò*)

Mr. Eddie LeCointe, Ogun Devotee of Oshun-Shango, Preparing
Ceremony Room

Mr. Eddie LeCointe and Wife Dr. Althea LeCointe, Oya Devotee

Babalorisha Sam Phills, Chairman of the Council of Orisha Elders
Trinidad and Tobago, making Presentation at the Interreoigious
Organization (IRO) World AIDS Day Program at Trinity Cathedral
Port of Spain

Brother Noble Khan, Muslim Leader, Saying Prayers at Program

Rev. Cyril Paul and Babalorisha Sam Phills

Brother Noble Khan and Rev. Cyril Paul

The Very Rev. Colin Sampson, Dean of Trinity Cathedral, Port of Spain

The Author Flanked by Religious Leaders at Program

Professor Rawle Gibbons, Orisha Elder and Prof. at University
of The West Indies, St. Augustine, Trinidad and Tobago

Mrs. Pearl Eintou Springer, Iyalorisha, Poet, Playwright, Activist

Chief Ricardo Bharath Hernandez, Santa Rosa Carib Community Center
Arima, Trinidad and Tobago

Carib Chief Headress, Santa Rosa Community Center

Artifacts, Santa Rosa Community Center, Arima, Trinidad and Tobago

Replica of Carib Hut, Santa Rosa Community Center

Cacique Hyarima Memorial, Arima, Trinidad and Tobago

Notes

Chapter One

The Encounter of Religions in a New World

1. Patrick Taylor, Ed., *Nation Dance: Religion, Identity, and Cultural Differences in the Caribbean* (Bloomington, IN: Indiana University Press, 2001).

2. *Ibid.,* p. 2.

3. *Ibid.*

4. *Ibid.,* pp. 11–12.

5. Dale Bisnauth in his historical study of the religions of the Caribbean estimates that the Arawaks originated from the area of Orinoco basin in South America, settling at various periods in the Lesser Antilles; the Bahamas in approximately 1000 C.E.; Cuba around 800 C.E.; Jamaica about 750 C.E., and Puerto Rico and Hispaniola about 250 C.E. The Caribs he pinpoints as having originated in Brazil around the Amazon River, settling in Trinidad for a period and then moving further northward following pretty much the same routes as the Arawaks (*History of Religions in the Caribbean,* Kingston, Jamaica, Kingston Publishers Limited, 1989, p. 1). George Brandon, *Santeria from Africa to the New World: The Dead Sell Memories* (Bloomington, IN: Indiana University Press, 1993) cites the Ciboney, "a northern Amerindian group," as the first humans to reach Cuba and the first to have contact with the Europeans when they entered the land, p. 37.

6. See William C. Tremmel, *Religion: What Is It?* 2nd ed. (New York: Holt, Rinehart and Winston, 1984); Michael Barnes, *In the Presence of Mystery: An Introduction to the Story of Human Religiousness,* Revised ed. (Mystic, CT: Twenty-Third Publications, 1984); Rudolf Otto, *The Idea of the Holy* (New York: Oxford University Press,1958); William James, *The Varieties of Religious Experience* (New York: New American Library, 1958, 1902); Mircea Eliade, *The Sacred and the Profane* (New York: Harcourt, Brace and World, 1959).

7. *Varieties of Religious Experience,* pp. 58–59.

8. P. 2.

9. *Ibid.,* pp. 2–3.

10. *Ibid.,* p. 4. Barnes cites Robert Bellah, "Religious Evolution," *American Sociological Review,* Vol. 39 #3 (June 1964), pp. 348–374.

11. *Ibid.,* pp. 10–18.

12. *Ibid.,* pp. 18–19.

13. *Ibid.,* p. 21.

14. Rivera, Magaly, "Welcome to Puerto Rico: Glossary," http: //welcome .topuertorico.org /glossary/index.shtml, visited August 8, 2004.

15. Much has been written along with oral speculation about cannibalistic practices of the Caribs, which is why they were dubbed with the name that means cannibal. Kim Johnson makes some clarifications regarding the origin of the name and the truth of the actual practices. "The English used 'Caribbees,' 'Charibs' or 'Caribs,' the French used 'Caraibes' and, for those on the mainland, 'Galibis.' Fr. Raymond Breton, who lived amongst the Indians in Dominica from 1641 to 1655, said, however, that the men called themselves 'Callinago' and the women called themselves 'Callipunam.' Today, among anthropologists, the favored name is 'Kalina' but those still living in St. Vincent call themselves 'Garifuna.'" As to the cannibalistic tendencies, Johnson asserts: "For all its seeming detail Spanish knowledge of Kalina culinary habits was actually negligible, far more so than that of the French. It is true that the Kalina [Caribs] and the Lokono [the name the Arawaks called themselves] raided each other's settlements for captives or revenge. And there was practiced by both tribes, some degree of ritual cannibalism. In the 17th century account of Adriaan van Berkel who lived with Lokono in Berbice, and the 16th century account of Luisa Navarrete who was a Kalina 'slave' in Dominica, both tribes after successful raids killed one or two male captives in a victory ritual and put pieces of their flesh into the pot. An arm or a leg was preserved to remind them of their hatred of the enemy. That was more or less the extent of it. There has never been found any archaeological evidence as would indicate widespread and systematic cannibalism, evidence such as scorched human bones, bones with knife or saw cuts or which are unnaturally fractured, bones widely scattered," Kim Johnson, "Taino: The Story of the 'Caribs and Arawaks," Part 4, http://www.raceandhistory.com/Taino/, accessed September 23, 2004.

16. http://welcome.topuertorico.org/glossary/index.shtml, accessed August 8, 2004.

17. "Caribs," http://members.tripod.com/prejudice/caribs.htm, accessed September 23, 2004, pp. 2–4.

18. *Ibid.,* p. 4. See also Dale Bisnauth, *History of Religions of the Caribbean,* pp. 5–10.

19. "Taino, The Story of the Caribs and Arawak, Part I," http://www.raceandhistory.com / Taino/, September 23, 2004, p. 2: "If you were to go to Santo Domingo today people would tell you that their Amerindian ancestors were the 'Taino.' Actually, Indians of Greater Antilles did not call themselves 'Taino,' no more than they called themselves 'Arawak'—that name was given them in 1935 by Sven Loven, a Swedish archaeologist, from the word denoting in the Indian language the ruling class of their society.—(1) But let us not quibble: seeing as we do not know what the Greater Antilleans called themselves, we shall make do with Taino. If the people of the Greater Antilles were not Arawaks, neither did they passively accept Spanish [degradations]. Most of us are familiar with the story of Hatuey, the chief who organized to fight the Spanish and who was, when captured, burnt at the stake. Repent and go to heaven, they told him as they lit the fire. If there are Spaniards in heaven I would rather go to hell, he replied. Nor was Hatuey the only defiant one. There were several others, men like Guarocuya (Enrique) in Hispaniola, Uroyoan in Borinquen (Puerto Rico) and Guama in Cuba, who confronted the strange, terrifying European weapons—the man-eating dogs, the guns, the mounted soldiers,the naval galleons—with great courage and determination."

20. Rene Bermudez Negron, "The Arawaks," *300 Years of Spanish Presence*, http://community .wow.net/300history/01/07.html, p. 1, accessed September 24, 2004; also, Bob Corbett, "Pre-Columbian Hispaniola—Arawak/Taino Native Americans," http:/www.webster.edu /~corbetre/haiti/history/precolumbian/tainover.htm, accessed September 24, 2004; AD. F. Bandelier, Transcribed by M. Donahue, "Arawaks," *New Advent Catholic Newsletter*, http:/www.newadvent.org/cathen/01680c.htm, pp. 4–5, accessed September 24, 2004; Johnny Dahl, "The Arawaks—Caribbean Islands," http://www.en.original-people. eu.org /arawaks-caribbean.shtml, pp. 1–2, accessed September 24,2004; http://www.blackstudiess. ucsb.edu/antillians/arawaks.html, accessed September 24, 2004; and Dale Bisnauth, *History of Religions in the Caribbean,* p.12.

21. "The Arawaks—Caribbean Islands," p. 2.

22. Rene Bermudez Negron, pp. 1–2.

23. "Pre-Columbian Hispaniola—Arawak/Taino Native Americans," p. 3.

24. Negron, p. 2.

25. Edwin Miner Sola, "Mythology and Religion," *Diccionario Taino Illustrado* (Puerto Rico: Ediciones Servilibros, First Book Publishing of P. R., 2002), pp. 32–34. See also *History of Religions in the Caribbean*, pp. 2–5.

26. Negron, pp. 4–5.

27. *History of Religions in the Caribbean*, p. 12.

28. *Ibid.*; Ben Corbett speaks to the issue of the problem of numbering the Arawaks on the Island of Hispaniola and the number subjected to Genocide on this Island alone. He says that the number varies among Spanish historian/observers from 3,000,000 to 4,000,000 (seemingly much over-estimated) to more modern scholarly estimate of from 100,000 to 400,000, "Pre-Columbian Hispaniola—Arawak/Taino Native Americans," p.5.

29. "Pre-Columbian Hispaniola—Arawak/Taino Native Americans," p. 5.

30. Johnny Dahl, "The Arawaks—Caribbean Islands," p. 3.

31. Johnny Dahl, "The Arawaks—Caribbean Islands," p. 3.

32. *History of Religions of the Caribbean*, p. 12.

33. "Caribs," http://members.tripod.com/prejudice/caribs.htm, pp. 5–10.

34. Lee, Simon, "The Caribs of Dominica," http://www.geocities.com/Athens/Agora/3820 carib.html pp. 2 and 3, accessed September 23, 2004.

35. *History of Religions in the Caribbean,* pp. 15 and 16.

36. *Ibid.,* p. 29.

37. *Ibid.*

38. Leslie G. Desmangles, *The Faces of the Gods: Vodou and Roman Catholicism in Haiti* (Chapel Hill: The University of North Carolina Press, 1992), pp. 18 and 19.

39. *History of Religions in the Caribbean,* p. 32.

40. *Ibid.,* pp. 33–77.

41. *Ibid.,* pp. 35–77.

42. *Ibid.,* pp. 47–55.

43. *Ibid.,* pp. 57–59.

44. *Ibid.,* pp. 61, 62, 63, 64.

45. *Ibid.,* pp. 63–64.

46. *Ibid.,* pp. 80–81.

47. *Ibid.,* pp. 81–82.

48. *Ibid.,* pp. 82–83.

49. Leonard Barrett, *Soul-Force: African Heritage in Afro-American Religion* (Garden City, NY: Anchor Press, 1974, p. 16.

50. *Ibid.,* p. 17.

51. Bisnauth, pp. 83–84.

52. *Ibid.,* pp. 84, 85, 86; Barrett, pp. 17–24.

53. Bisnauth, pp. 86 and 87.

54. *Ibid.,* pp. 87 and 88.

55. *Ibid.,* pp. 88, 89, 90, 92; Barrett, pp. 23, 25, 55, 58–59, 60–61. Barrett asserts: "We have ample literature on the Caribbean and South America to prove that the cultural institution that survived best in the New World was the African traditional religion. However much it was modified, we now know that it was strong enough to outlast slavery. African traditional religion has come down to our day in such forms as Cumina in Jamaica, Shango in Trinidad, Santeria in Cuba, Vodun in Haiti, and Candomble in Brazil....Some writers believe that the tribe that was most active in fighting against slavery was the tribe whose rituals became routinized within the society, and that the rituals of other tribes were added on to this basic structure as they were felt to be necessary for the solidarity of the various peoples in their struggle. Other writers believe that because witchcraft became the most potent weapon in slavery, the tribe whose witchcraft proved the strongest, became the dominant religion of the society." Barrett points out that he believes both theories to be true, pp. 60 and 61.

56. Barrett, p. 79.

57. *Ibid.,* p. 80.

58. George Brandon, *Santeria from Africa to the New World,* p. 41.

59. Leslie G. Desmangles, *The Faces of the Gods,* p. 121.

60. Rebecca B. Bateman, "Africans and Indians: A Comparative Study of the Black Carib and Black Seminole," in Norman E. Whitten, Jr. and ArlenenTorres, Eds., *Blackness in Latin America and the Caribbean,* Vol. I (Bloomington, IN: Indiana University Press, 1998, pp. 200–222), p. 201.

61. *Ibid.,* p. 151; see also Andrea E. Leland and Kathy L. Berger, *The Garifuna Journey* (Hohokus, NJ: New Day Films, 1998).

62. *Ibid.* See also "Caribs," http://members.tripod.com/prejudice/carib.htm, accessed September 23, 2004, pp. 5–10.

63. Kamau Brathwaite, "Nanny, Palmares & the Caribbean Maroon Connexion" in E. Kofi Agorsah, Ed., *Maroon Heritage: Archaeological, Ethnographic and Historical Perspectives* (Barbados: Canoe Press, 1994), pp. 119–138.

64. Abraham H. Khan, "Identity, Personhood, and Religion in Caribbean Context," in Patrick Taylor, Ed., *Nation Dance* (Bloomington, IN: Indiana University Press, 2001), p. 149n. See also Dale Bisnauth, pp. 140–141.

65. Petronella Breinburg, "Communicating with Our Gods: The Language of Winti," in Patrick Taylor, *Nation Dance,* p. 37.

66. Khan, p. 149n.

67. *Ibid.,* p. 150n.

Chapter Two

The Present Setting of Caribbean Religious Interactions

1. Bisnauth, pp. 101, 104, 108–110.

2. *Ibid.,* pp. 110, 113, 114.

3. *Ibid.,* pp. 115, 116, 120, 121, 123.

4. *Ibid.,* pp. 123–24.

5. *Ibid.,* p. 165.

6. *Ibid.,* p. 96.

7. *Ibid.,* p. 97.

8. *Description topographique physique, civile et historique de la partie francaise de L'Isle de Saint-Dominique* (Philadelphia, 1797), I, 44–59; referenced in Barrett, *Soul-Force*, p. 99.

9. Barrett, p. 100.

10. *Ibid.*, pp. 100–102.

11. Maya Deren, *Divine Horsemen: The Voodoo Gods of Haiti* (New York: Chelsea House, 1970), p. 116, quoted in Barrett, *Soul-Force*, p. 103.

12. *Ibid.*, pp. 103–104.

13. Bisnauth, p. 166.

14. *Ibid.* See also Albert J. Raboteau, *Slave religion: The "Invisible Institution" in the Antebellum South* , Updated Edition (New York: Oxford University Press, 2004), pp. 25–27.

15. *Ibid.,* pp. 166–170.

16. *Ibid.,* p. 170. Leslie G. Desmangles, *The Faces of the Gods* (Chapel Hill: University of North Carolina Press, 1992), has somewhat different views of the origins and functions of Haiti's Simbi and Azaka. He admits the possibility of Azaka's derivation from the Arawaks, but asserts the Kongo source as the origin of Simbi, pp. 121 and 128.

17. Desmangles, p. 63.

18. Bisnauth, p. 172. What Bisnauth is saying here about Oluron surviving in Trinidad may be true of earlier periods, but in present-day Orisa (Shango) in Trinidad, the Yoruba Supreme Being Olurun is used and the highest deity, as I observed in all the ceremonies I attended in Port of Spain, San Juan, and other places in Trinidad and Tobago in November/December, 2004.

19. *Ibid.,* pp. 172–73.

20. Raboteau, pp. 27–28.

21. Raboteau, pp. 27–29. See also Frances Henry, *Reclaiming African Religions in Trinidad: The Socio-Political Legitimation of Orisha and Spiritual Baptist Faiths* (Jamaica, W.I.: The University of the West Indies Press, 2003).

22. Bisnauth, pp. 178–79.

23. Barry Chevannes, "New Approach to Rastafari" in Barry Chevannes, Ed., *Rastafari and Other African—Caribbean Worldviews* (London: Macmillan, 1995), pp. 20–42.

24. Abraham H. Khan, "Identity, Personhood, and Religion in Caribbean Context," in Patrick Taylor, Ed., *Nation Dance*, pp. 138–152.

25. *Ibid.,* p. 147.

26. Reference is to Rex Nettleford, *Inward Stretch, Outward Reach: A Voice from the Caribbean* (London: Macmillan, 1993).

27. Khan, p. 145.

28. Hesdie Zamuel, "Popular Religions and Ecumenism," in Burton Sankeralli, Ed., *At the Crossroads: African Caribbean Religion and Christianity* (St. James, Trinidad and Tobago, WI: Caribbean Conference of Churches, 1995, pp. 6–12), p. 11.

29. Bisnauth, p. 141.

30. *Ibid.,* pp. 141, 142, 150.

31. *Ibid.,* pp. 150, 151. Bisnauth states: "The worship of Kali Mai, the consort of Shiva [, the Destroyer, one of the three major Hindu trimurti of deities, including Vishnu, the Preserver, and Brahma, the Creator], was very much in evidence in the early 1900s. It was I times of crisis, the failure of crops or the occurrence of sickness, that pujas to the Black Mother were celebrated. Thus, in 1919–20 in Guyana, there was a Kali Mai revival on the Essequibo Coast. That period saw the outbreak of an influenza epidemic in the colony in which, in Essequibo alone, about a thousand East Indians died. Hindu priests said that this was because the gods, in particular Kali, were angry with the immigrants for having forsaken the faith of their fathers. Great pujas were held at which sacrifices were made to Kali" (p. 151).

32. *Ibid.,* pp. 154–55.

33. *Ibid.,* p. 159.

34. *Ibid.,* p. 160.

35. *Ibid.,* pp. 161, 163.

36. H. O. B. Wooding in "The Constitutional History of Trinidad and Tobago," *Caribbean Quarterly,* Vol. 6, Nos. 2 and 3, p. 147, quoted in Bisnauth, *History of Religions in the Caribbean,* pp. 195–96.

37. Bisnauth, pp. 195–96.

38. *Ibid.,* pp. 198–200.

39. *Ibid.,* pp. 200–201.

40. *Ibid.,* pp. 208–209; quotation is from H. V. P. Bronkhurst, *British Guiana and Its Labouring Population,* p. 202.

41. Bisnauth, pp. 208, 209, 210, 211, 212, 213, 214, 215.

42. See George Brandon's *Santeria from Africa to the New World,* pp. 80–81 in regard to this situation as it existed in Cuba.

Chapter Three

Challenges of Non–Christian Spirituality to Christian Spirituality in the Caribbean

1.   *Nation Dance*, p. 3.

2.   *Ibid.*

3.   *Creole Religions: An Introduction from Vodou and Santeria to Obeah and Espiriitsmo* (2003).

4.   *Ibid.*

5.   *Ibid.,* p. 7.

6.   *Ibid.,* pp. 7–9. The authors make reference to Andrew Apter, "Herskovits's Heritage: Rethinking Syncretism in African Diaspora," *Diaspora: A Journal of Transnational Studies* 1.3 (1991): 235–260.

7.   Althea Prince, "How Shall We Sing the Lord's Song in a Strange Land? Constructing the Divine in Caribbean Contexts," in Patrick Taylor, *Nation Dance*, pp. 25–31. p. 28.

8.   *Ibid.*

9.   See Olmos and Paravisini-Gebert, *Creole Religions*, p. 7.

10. Bisnauth, pp. 211–212.

11. *Ibid.,* p. 214.

12. *Ibid.,* pp. 214–215.

13. *Ibid.,* p. 215.

14. Frederick Ivor Case, "The Intersemiotics of Obeah and Kali Mai in Guyana," in Patrick Taylor, Ed., *Nation Dance* (Bloomington, IN: Indiana University Press, 2001), pp. 40–53.

15. *Ibid.,* p. 43.

16. *Ibid.,* pp. 40–41.

17. *Ibid.,* p. 41.

18. *Ibid.,* pp. 42–43.

19. *Ibid.,* p. 44.

20. Her experiences are presented in her autobiography: *The Altar of My Soul: The Living Traditions of Santeria* (New York: The Ballantine Publishing Group, 2000).

21. Espiritismo is a system of worshipping ancestors, having its origin in France.

22. Vega, p. 28.

23. Vega, pp. 30, 32, 34.

24. *Ibid.*, pp. 35, 37.
25. *Ibid.*, pp. 76–79.

26. *Ibid.*, pp. 109–110.

27. *Ibid.*, pp. 249–50.

28. *Ibid.*, pp. 250–52.

29. *Ibid.*, p. 206.

30. *Ibid.*, pp. 206–207.

31. *Ibid.*, p. 207.

32. Taylor, p. 18.

33. *Ibid.*, p. 74.

34. *Ibid.*, pp. 73–74.

35. Miguel F. Brooks, Trans. And Editor, *Kebra Nagast (The Glory of Kings)* (Kingston, Jamaica, WI: Kingston Publishers Limited, 1995), p. xiii. See also Patrick Taylor, " Sheba's Song: The Bible, the *Kebra Nagast,* and the Rastafari," *Nation Dance,* pp. 65–78.

36. Taylor, p. 75; see also Dale Bisnauth, pp. 185–193; and Leonard E. Barrett, *The Rastafarians* (Boston: Beacon Press, 1997), pp. 80–95.

Chapter Four

Issues of Religio–Social and Cultural Manifestations Found in Caribbean Religions: Cuban Santeria and Haitian Vodou, Brazilian Candomblè and Trinidadian Shango

1. Margarite Fernandez Olmos and Lizabeth Paravisini-Gebert Eds., *Sacred Possessions: Vodou, Santeria, Obeah, and the Caribbean* (New Brunswick, NJ: Rutgers University Press, 1997), p. 2.

2. Brandon, pp. 1–2.

3. Brandon, pp. 11–13.

4. Ford, p. 146.

5. Brandon, pp. 13–17.

6. Brandon, pp. 46–47.

7. Raboteau, pp. 22–23.

8. Brandon, pp. 69–73; see also Raul Canizares, *Walking the Night: The Afro-Cuban World of Santeria* (Rochester, VT: Destiny Books, 1993), pp. 24–25.

9. Raboteau, p. 21.

10. Miguel Barnet, p. 26.

11. Brandon, pp. 74–75.

12. *Creole Religions of the Caribbean,* pp. 50–51.

13. *Ibid.,* p. 62.

15. *Ibid.*

16. Raboteau, p. 25; Raboteau quotes Michel Laguerre, "An Ecological Approach to Voodoo," in *Freezing the Spirit,* Vol. 3, No. 1 (1974), p. 11.

17. *Ibid.,* p. 25; quotations are from Alfred Metraux, *Voodoo in Haiti* (New York: Schocken Books, 1972), pp. 34–35. See also Desmangles, pp. 25–28.

18. See *Soul-Force*, p. 99.

19. *Ibid.,* p. 100.

20. *Ibid.,* p. 109.

21. Desmangles, pp. 34–35. Desmangles uses as source Roger Bastide, *African Civilisations in the New World* (New York: Harper and Row, 1971), pp. 51, 53.

22. Bastide, p. 53.

23. Desmangles, pp. 34, 35, 36, and 37.

24. Ralph Korngold, *Citizen Touissaint* (New York: Macmillan Press, 1943), p. 33, quoted in *Soul-Force,* p. 101.

25. *Soul-Force,* p. 101.
26. *Creole Religions,* p.102.

27. Joseph M. Murphy, *Working the Spirit: Ceremonies of the African Diaspora* (Boston: Beacon Press, 1994), p. 10.

28. *Ibid.,* p. 30; Murphy quotes Ira Lowenthal, "Ritual Performance and Religious Experience: A Service for the Gods in Southern Haiti," *Journal for Anthropological Rresearch* 34 (1978): 393.

29. Murphy, pp. 38–39.

30. Hesdie Zamuel, "Popular Religions and Ecumenism," in Burton Sankeralli, Ed. *At the Cross-roads: African Caribbean Religion and Christianity* (St. James, Triinidad and Tobago: Caribbean Conference of Churches, 1995), p. 6.

31. *Ibid.,* pp. 6–7.

32. W. A. Visser't Hooft, *No Other Name* (London: 1963), p. 11, quoted in Zamuel, p. 8.

33. A. Oepeke, quoted in Hooft, p. 11 and Zamuel, p. 8.

34. *Ibid.,* pp. 8–11.

35. Chung Hyun Kyung, "Come Holy Spirit, Renew the Whole Creation," Keynote Address, in *Signs of the Spirit: Official Report of the Seventh Assembly,* edited by M. Kinnamon (Geneva, Switzerland: W.C.C., 1991), pp. 38–39, 46, quoted in Hans Ucko, "Syncretism—A Challenge to an Ecumenical Discussion on Gospel and Culture," in *At the Crossroads,* edited by Burton Sankeralli (St. James, Trinidad and Tobago: Caribbean Conference of Churches, 1995), pp. 30–31.

36. *Ibid.,* p. 31.

37. *Ibid.,* pp. 32–34.

38. *Ibid.,* pp. 35, 36, 37, 38, 39, 40.

39. *Ibid.,* pp. 44–45.

40. See Brandon, pp. 107, 114–115.

41. See Murphy, pp. 57–58, and 215–16n; also Robert A. Voeks, *Sacred Leaves of Candomble: African Magic, Medicine, and Religion in Brazil* (Austin, TX: University of Texas Press, 1997), pp. 60–61.

42. See Pearl Eintou Springer, "Orisa and the Spiritual Baptists Religion in Trinidad and Tobago," in *Crossroads,* Ed. By Burton Sankeralli (St. James, Trinidad and Tobago: Caribbean Conference of Churches, 1995), pp. 89–91, 96–97.

43. Voeks, *Sacred Leaves of Candomblé,* "Note on Orthography," front matter.

44. Voeks, pp. 54–55, and 63.

45. Voeks, p. 51. Voeks references E. Carneiro, *Candombles da Bahia* (NP: Editora Technoprint), 1967 [1948], pp. 63–65; and P. Verger, *Orixas* (Sao Paulo: Corrupio, 1981), pp. 28–29.

46. See Olmos and Paravisini-Gebert, *Creole Religions,* p. 25; Desmangles, pp. 94–95.

47. Voeks, pp. 53–54. Voeks says that Carneiro "lists seventeen types [nacoes] of Candomble extant in the 1930's," citing Carneiro 1967 (1948), p. 59.

48. Voeks, p. 63.

49. Murphy, p. 53; he cites Ruth Landes, *The City of Women* (New York: Macmillan, 1947).

50. Murphy, pp. 48--49; Murphy cites Carneiro, pp. 61–62.

51. Murphy, pp. 50, 51.

52. Murphy, pp. 52–53; the Carneiro quotation is from Landes, p. 36.

53. Maria Margarita Castro Flores, "Religions of African Origin in Cuba: A Gender Perspective," in *Nation Dance,* edited by Patrick Taylor (Bloomington, IN: Indiana University Press, 2001), p. 54.

54. Mercy Amba Oduyoye, *Daughters of Anowa: African Women and Patriarchy* (Maryknoll, NY: Orbis Books, 2000), p. 128.

55. *Ibid.,* p. 214.

56. Flores, pp. 54–55.

57. *Ibid.,* p. 55.

58. *Ibid.,* pp. 57, 58–60.

59. Voeks, pp. 89–90.

60. Murphy, p. 45.

61. Voeks, pp. 158–59.

62. *Ibid.,* p. 159.

63. Murphy, p. 47; Murphy quotes Mikelle Smith Omali, *From the Inside to the Outside: The Art and Ritual of Bahian Candomblé* (Los Angeles: Museum of Cultural History, UCLA Monograph Series No 24, 1984), p. 18.

64. Murphy, p. 49.

65. Voeks, pp. 63, 65, 67, and 68.

66. Pearl Eintou Springer, "Orisa and the Spiritual Baptist Religion in TT," in *Crossroads: Afro-Caribbean Religions and Christianity* (St. James, Trinidad and Tobago: Caribbean Conference of Churches, 1995), pp. 85–108.

67. *Ibid.,* pp. 89, 90, and 91.

68. Bisnauth, pp. 171–74.

69. Springer, pp. 96–97.

70. Bisnauth, pp. 173–74.

71. Springer, pp. 92 and 87.

72. Springer, pp. 91–92.

73. *Ibid.*, p. 87.

74. *Ibid.*, pp. 103–104.

75. *Ibid.*, pp. 103–106.

76. *Ibid.*, pp. 86 and 98.

Chapter Five

Crucial Issues in Obeah and Rastafari

1. Leonard Barrett, *Soul Force*, pp. 21–22, 61–62; also Karla Gottlieb, *"The Mother of Us All": A History of Queen Nanny Leader of the Windward Jamaican Maroons* (Trenton, NJ: Africa World Press, 2000), p. 10.

2. Gottlieb, p. 10; see also Barrett, pp. 64 –66. It should be noted that the Koromantyns were imported to all the islands of the British West Indes.

3. Barrett, p. 31; Barrett asserts that "the fear of African witchcraft became a potent weapon against the slave regime, and the means by which revolutions against oppression were fomented," p.31.

4. *Ibid.*, p. 63.

5. Bisnauth, pp. 90–91, 172–73 and 177–80.

6. Barry Chevannes, "New Approach to Rastafari," in *Rastafari and Other African-Caribbean Worldviews,* Edited by Barry Chevannes (London: Macmillan Press LTD, 1995), pp. 20–42.

7. Karla Y. E. Frye, "'An Article of Faith': Obeah and Hybrid Identities in Elizabeth Nunez-Harrell's *When Rocks Dance,"* in *Sacred Possessions: Vodou, Santeria, Obeah, and the Caribbean,* Edited by Margarite Fernandez Olmos and Lizabeth Paravisini-Gebert (New Brunswick, NJ: Rutgers University Press, 1997), p. 198. See also Olmos and Paravisini-Gebert, *Creole Religions of the Caribbean,* pp. 131–140; Jean Besson, "Religion as Resistance in Jamaican Peasant Life: The Baptist Church, Revival Worldview and Rastafari Movement," in *Rastafari and Other African-Caribbean Worldviews,* edited by Barry Chevannes (London: Macmillan Press LTD, 1995), pp. 56–57; Barrett, *Soul-Force,* pp. 64–69.

8. *Beyond the Limbo Silence,* pp. 82–83.

9. *Ibid.*, pp. 90, 91, 108–109.

10. *Ibid.*, p. 137.

11. *Ibid.*, p. 160.

12. This was the historical case of Andrew Goodman, Michael Schwerner, and James Chaney, who were killed in one of the most brutal civil rights murders of the period. *Ibid.*, pp. 220–21.

13. *Ibid.,* p. 258.

14. *Ibid.,* pp. 268–75, 280–81, 297.

15. *Ibid.,* pp. 273, 274, 275, 282–84, 289.

16. *Ibid.,* pp. 289–91.

17. *Ibid.,* p. 310.

18. Frye, p. 197. The fragmentation of Trinidadian society after Emancipation has be pointed out earlier in the text. See Bisnauth, pp. 195–96.

19. Frye, pp. 200–201.

20. *Ibid.,* pp. 205–206.

21. *Ibid.,* p. 210.

22. *Ibid.*

23. *Ibid.*

24. Olmos and Paravisini-Gebert, *Creole Religions of the Caribbean,* pp. 133–34.

25. *Ibid.,* p. 136.

26. Gottlieb, p. 10. See also Lucile Mathurin Mair, *The Rebel Woman in the British West Indies During Slavery* (Kingston, Jamaica, WI: Institute of Jamaica Publications Limited, 1975), pp. 1–2.

27. I was so moved by this generous gesture that it became a spiritual experience for me. It reminded me of the expression Howard Thurman has for true brotherhood/sisterhood: "Thou has seen thy brother, thou has seen thy God," *Conversations with Howard Thurman,* BBC, 1977. I was also reminded of the anonymous poem, "Foot Prints."

28. Barrett, *Soul-Force,* p. 21.

29. *Ibid.,* 63, 64, and 65.

30. *Ibid.,* p. 96.

31. *Ibid.*

32. *Ibid.,* pp. 97, 112, 113.

33. Barrett, pp. 126, 123. See also Jean Besson, pp. 51 and 53.

34. *Crossroads,* pp. 126–27.

35. *Ibid.,* pp. 128, 130, and 131. This quotation is exceptionally long because it shows more vividly in the language of the speaker what issues one branch of Rasttas sees as crucial in their

religious conception and practice. It is also reflective of issues common to the Rasta tradition.

36. Attrose Music Ltd. , 2003.

37. Sizzla, VP Records, 2002.

38. Putumayo, Dan Storper, Executive Producer, Sara Re, Project Coordinator, (NY: Putumayo World Music, 1998).

39. Balford Henry, Descriptive Introduction to the album.

40. *Ibid.*

Chapter Six

Crucial Issues in Haitian Vodou

1. Lucien Dakoudi Camera; editor, Pascal Degboue (Princeton, NJ: Films for the Humanities, 1992).

2. Barrett, pp. 72–73.

3. See Barrett, pp. 82 –83. Also Olmos and Paravisini-Gebert, *Creole Religions,* pp. 119, 122, 123; Murphy, p. 10; Katherine Dunham, *Island Possessed* (Chicago: University of Chicago Press, 1969).

4. Murphy, p. 10.

5. *Soul-Force,* p. 82.

6. Murphy, p. 17.

7. Desmangles, p. 3.

8. *Ibid.*

9. *Ibid.*

10. *Ibid.,* pp. 3–4.

11. *Ibid.,* Desmangles explains elsewhere that Bondye is the source of the human community, the Higher Principle. Bondye is "the insurer of universal order and the source of all human

    actions." Therefore, the "highest wisdom consists not only in recognizing the wholeness of the universal order as contained in Bondye, but also in affirming that same wholeness in the human community. All of life belongs to Bondye. He summons it into being and preserves it," p. 96.

12. *Ibid.,* pp. 6 and 7.

13. *Ibid.,* pp. 8–11.

14. *Ibid.,* p. 11.

14. Zora Neale Hurston, *Tell My Horse* (Berkeley, CA: Turtle Island Foundation, 1937, 1983), pp. 169–178.

15. *Ibid.,* p. 179.

17. See Barrett, *Soul-Force*, pp. 100–101; Bisnauth, pp. 170–71; Raboteau, pp. 25–27; Murphy, pp. 10–12; Desmangles, pp. 28–37; and Olmos and ParavisinGebert, *Creole Religions,* pp. 103–104.

18. Desmangles, pp. 12–14.

19. Bisnauth, p. 170. Desmangles disagrees with Bisnauth on origins of some of these, especially Simbi, whose origin he pinpoints as being the Kongo, p. 128.

20. Desmangles, pp. 29, 33 and 34.

21. *Ibid.,* p. 34; Desmangles cites D. Geggus, "The Haitian Revolution," in *The Modern Caribbean,* edited by Franklin W. Knight and Colin A. Palmer , pp. 21–50 (Chapel Hill: University of North Carolina Press, 1989), p. 29.

22. Desmangles, pp. 29 and 30.

23. *Ibid.,* pp. 36 and 47.

24. Murphy, p. 12.

25. *Ibid.,* p. 17

26. *Ibid.,* pp. 17–18.

27. *Ibid.,* pp. 17–18.

28. *Ibid.,* pp. 18–19. Katherine Dunham, *Island Possessed* (New York: Doubleday, 1969) calls this "prize or price of eyes," p. 98.

29. *Creole Religions,* p. 108.

30. *Ibid.*

31. *Ibid.,* p. 126.

32. Murphy, pp. 27–28.

33. Desmangles, pp. 64–65; Desmangles cites W. Davis, *Passage of Darkness: The Ethnobiography of the Haitian Zombie* (Chapel Hill: University of North Carolina Press, 1988), pp. 39–40.

34. *Ibid.,* p. 65.

35. *Ibid.,* pp. 66, 67, 68.

36. *Ibid.,* pp. 68–70.

37. Murphy, p. 38.

38. *Ibid.,* pp. 38–39.

39. *Ibid.,* p. 42.

40. *Ibid,* p. 43. See also Maya Deren, *Divine Horsement: The Living Gods of Haiti* (New York: Thames and Hudson, 1953), pp. 235; and Dunham, pp. 131f.

42. *Ibid.,* p. 95. See also Karen McCarthy Brown, "Systematic Remembering, Systematic Forgetting: Ogou in Haiti" in *Africa's Ogun: Old World and New,* edited by Sandra T. Barnes, pp. 65 - -89 (Bloomington: Indiana University Press, 1989), pp. 70 –75.

43. See Ronald Chilcote, ed., *Cuba, 1953–1978: A Bibliographical Guide to the Literature* ,2 vols (White Plains, NY, 1986), p. 113; also Judith Bettelheim, ed., *Cuban Festivals: A Century of Afro-Cuban Culture* (Princeton, NJ: Markus Wiener Pub., 2001), pp. 173–75.

44. Casa del Caribe, Santiago de Cuba, 2003.

45. *Ibid.*

46. Josh Zimmer, "Haitians hope, celebrate," *St. Petersburg Times,* 2 January 2004, p. 1B; also Associated press, "Haiti celebrates bicentennial," *St. Petersburg Times,* 2 January 2004, p. 11A.

47. Ogou Feray is the head of all the soldier Ogou in Haiti. In describing a ritual devoted to Ogou Feray, Karen McCarthy Brown states: " A Vodou altar is the repository of the history of a people. In addition to images of spirits of ancestors, it contains earthenware pots called *govi* in which reside the protective spirits of the ancestors. ....Ogou Feray is ...ensconced at the head of a vast battalion of spirits and ancestors, firing the cannon and launching a revolution with memories of all his 'children,'" Brown, p. 72.

48. Desmangles, p. 152.

49. Brown, p. 73.

50. See Maya Deren, p. 132.

51. Desmangles, p. 153.

52. *Ibid.*

53. Laennec Hurbon, "Current Evolution and Relations between Religion and Politics in Haiti," in *Nation Dance,* pp. 118–137, edited by Patrick Taylor (Bloomington: Indiana University Press, 2001).

54. *Ibid.,* pp. 121–122, 123.

55. *Ibid.,* pp. 124–125.

Chapter Seven

Crucial Issues in Cuban and Puerto Rican Santeria and Trinidadian Shango/Orisa

1.   *Creole Religions of the Caribbean,* pp. 19–20.

2.   Magaly Rivera, "Welcome to Puerto Rico, 2004," http://welcome.topuertorico.org/ peo-ple.shtml, accessed 8/8/04.

3.   *Creole Religions of the Caribbean,* p. 21.

4.   Media and Editorial Projects Limited, 2003, "Discover Trinidad and Tobago," http://www.meppublishers.com/discover/welcome/index.php?topic=about_tnt, accessed, 8/30/04, p. 1.

5.   *Ibid.*

6.   Springer, pp. 90–91.

7.   David Scott, "The Sovereignty of the Imagination: An Interview with George Lamming," *Small Axe,* no. 12 (September 2002): 172.

8.   *Ibid.*

9.   Springer, p. 91.

10. Judy Raymond, "Forward Home—Andre Revisited," *Caribbean Beat,* no. 61 (July/August 2004), p. 5, http://www.meppublishers.com/online/caribbean-beat/archive/ arti-cle.php?id=cb61-2-98, accessed 30 August 2004.

11. *Ibid.*

12. 1998, 2001, http://www.centrellink.org/fntt/Resurgence.html, accessed 23 September 2004.

13. Maximilian C. Forte, "A Brief Account of the Colonial History of Arima's Carib Commu-nity," 1998, 2001, http://www. Centrelink.org/fntt/History.html, accessed 23 September 2004, pp. 1 and 3.

14. Forte, "The Carib Resurgence," pp. 1 and 2.

15. *Ibid.,* p. 3.

16. Maxmilian C. Forte, "The Relationship of the Caribs of Arima with the Tainos of Puerto Rico and the USA," 1999, 2001, <httpp://www.centrelink.org/fntt/Tainos.html>, accessed 23 September, 2004.

17. *Ibid.,* p.1.

18. *Ibid.,* p. 2.

19. *Ibid.*

20. "Discover Trinidad and Tobago: Trinidad," http://www.meppublishers.com/online/discover/trinidad/index.php?topic=calendar, accessed 30 August 2004, p. 1.

21. *Ibid.,* p. 1–2.

22. *Ibid.,* pp. 2–3.

23. Brandon, p. 126.

24. Brandon, p. 54; see also Kenneth F. Kipler, *Blacks in Colonial Cuba 1774–1899,* Latin American Monographs, 2nd Series (Tallahassee: Center for Latin American Studies, University of Florida, 1976).

25. Brandon, pp. 68 –68; see also Verena Martinez-Alier, *Marriage, Class and Color in Nineteenth Century Cuba: A Study of Racial Attitudes and Sexual Values in a Slave Society* (London: Cambridge University Press, 1974), pp., 96, 98, 71, 91–99).

26. Brandon, pp. 80, 81, 82; See also Raul Canizares, *Walking with the Night: The Afro-Cuban World of Santeria* (Rochester, Vermont: Destiny Books, 1993), pp. 121–33. Canizares distinguishes U.S. and Cuban classifications of the black and of black and white and points to the prime importance of race relations in the development of Santeria. "Race relations strongly influenced the development of Santeria in Cuba; to understand Santeria it is important to understand the black-white dynamics of Cuban society," p. 128.

27. *Ibid.,* pp. 83–84. See also Canizares, pp. 121–122.

28. *Ibid.,* p. 85; see also Roberto Nodal, "The Social Evolution of the Afro-Cuban Drum," *Black Perspectives in Music,* 11, no. 2 (Fall 1983), 157–77, p. 160; also Fernando Ortiz, "Los cabildos afro-cubana" (Afro-Cuban Cabildos), *Revista Bimestre cubana* 26, 1921, 5–39, p. 30.

29. Canizares, pp.74–76; *Creole Religions of the Caribbean;* Brandon, pp. 85–86.

30. Brandon, pp. 86 –87.

31. Canizares, p. 77.

32. Brandon, p. 67.

33. *Ibid.,* pp. 88 and 90.

34. *Creole Religions of the Caribbean,* p. 177.

35. *Ibid.,* pp. 178, 179, 181, 183–84.

36. *Ibid.,* pp. 185–87.

37. *Ibid.,* p. 90.

38. "Translator's Preface," in *Cuban Festivals A Century of Afro-Cuban Culture,* ed. By Judith Bettel Heim (Kingston, Jamaica: Ian Randle Pub., 2001, and Princeton, New Jersey: Markus Wiener Pub., 2001), p. xiii.

39. Stubbs, p. xiii; Brandon, p. 91.

40. Brandon, p. 91. See also, Canizares, p. 132.

41. Brandon, pp. 91–92.

42. Brandon, p. 92. See also Jorge Duany, "Reconstructing Cubanness: Changing Discourses of National Identity on the Island and in the Diaspora during the Twentieth Century," in *Cuba, the Elusive Nation: Interpretations of National Identity*, pp. 18–42, ed. By Damián J. Fernández and Madeline Cámara Betancourt (Gainesville: University Press of Florida, 2000), pp. 22–24.

43. Stubbs, p. xiv.

44. Canizares, p. 132.

45. Brandon, p. 93.

46. In *Cuba, the Elusive Nation: Interpretations of National Identity,* pp. 43–59, ed. By Damián J. Fernández and Madeline Cámara Betancourt (Gainesville: University Press of Florida, 2000).

47. *Ibid.,* p. 43.

48. *Rituals and Spells of Santeria (*Bronx: New York: Original Publications, 1984), p. 35. See also Diedre Badejo, *Òsun SÈÈGÈÍ: The Elegant Deity of Wealth, Power, and Femininity* (Trenton, New Jersey: Africa World Press, 1996), pp. 67–86.

49. Canizares, pp. 65–66; Canizares draws from a version of this myth found in Mercedes Cros Sandoval, *La religion afrocubana* (Madrid: Playor, 1975), pp. 11–12. See also *Creole Religions of the Caribbean,* p. 46.

50. Maria Elena Diaz, p. 43. For further discussion of the Chinese eclusion practice, see Frank F. Scherer, "Sanfancón: Orientalism, Self-Orientalization, and 'Chinese Religion' in Cuba," in *Nation Dance*, pp. 153–70, ed. By Patrick Taylor (Bloomington: Indiana University Press, 2001), pp. 164–66.

51. See Maria Diaz, pp. 50–52.

52. C. Peter Ripley, *Conversations with Cuba,* (Athens, Georgia: The University of Georgia Press, 2001), pp. 183–84. See also, Brandon, pp. 51–52.

53. Diaz, pp. 49–50.

54. *Ibid.,* pp. 50–51. Diaz based her analysis on "Juan Moreno's notarized testimony given in Santiago del Prado on April 1, 1687, Investigation of the Virgin's Apparition. Fols. 12v-18v, Archivo General de Indias, Santo Domingo 363."

55. *Ibid.,* pp. 51–52.

56. *Ibid.,* pp. 53 –54.

57. *Ibid.,* p. 55.

58. Maureen Warner-Lewis, *Guinea's Other Suns: The African Dynamic in Trinidad Culture* (Dover, Mass.: The Majority Press, 1991), p. 139n.

59. *Ibid.,* pp. xix –xx.

60. *Ibid.,* pp. 54–55.

61. *Ibid.,* pp. xx, 54. In an explanatory note Warner-Lewis states: "More than any other sector of the balck Trinidad population, African Creoles are acutely aware of the close affinity between African and Indian cultures," p. 60n.

62. "Across the Waters, Practitioners Speak: Eva Fernandez Bravo, Yvonne B. Drake, and Delores Seiveright," in *Nation Dance*, ed. By Patrick Taylor (Bloomington: Indiana University Press, 2001), pp. 17–24.

63. Queen Mother Bishop Yvonne B. Drakes, "My Spiritual Journey," *Nation Dance*, pp. 19–21, ed. by Patrick Taylor (Bloomington: Indiana University Press, 2001), p. 20.

64. *Ibid.*

65. *Ibid.,* pp. 19–20.

66. Archbishop Doctor Delores Seiveright, "The Shouters National Evangelic Spirtual Baptist Faith," in *Nation Dance*, pp. 21–24, ed. by Patrick Taylor (Bloomington: Indiana University Press, 2001), pp. 21–22.

67. *Ibid.,* p. 22.

68. *Ibid.,* p. 21.

69. *Ibid.,* p. 22.

70. *Ibid.,* pp. 24 and 23.

71. *Ibid.,* p. 24.

Chapter Eight

Crucial Issues in Jamaican Religions

1. Leonard E. Barrett, Sr., *The Rastafarians* (Boston: Beacon Press, 1997), pp. 2, 16.

2. *Ibid.,* pp. 31, 32, 34, 38, and 63.

3. Besson, p. 47.

4. *Soul-Force,* p. 124.

5. Chevannes, pp. 7–8.

6. *The Rastafarians,* p. 22.

7. Edward Seaga, *Revival Cults in Jamaica,* Reprint from *Jamaica Journal,* vol. 3, no. 2 (June 1969) (Kingston, Jamaica: The Institute of Jamaica, 1882), p. 4.

8. *Creole Religions of the Caribbean,* pp. 148–49.

9. *Ibid.,* p. 4.

10. *Ibid.,* p. 4.

11. *Ibid.,* p. 5.

12. *Creole Religions of the Caribbean,* pp. 147–48.

13. *Ibid.,* pp. 148–49.

14. Seaga, p. 5.

15. Besson, pp. 56, 60, 73–74.

16. Barry Chevannes, "Introducing the Native Religions of Jamaica," in *Rastafari and Other African-Caribbean Worldviews,* pp. 1--99 (London: Macmillan Press, 1995), p. 1.

17. *Creole Religions of the Caribbean,* p. 154; the authors' explanatory note on Ethiopianism declares: "Rastafarian notions of an ancestral homeland is based on a complex set of notions known as Ethiopianism, an ideology derived from biblical refences to all black peoples as Ethiopians. These references underscore the African peoples' proud cultural heritage, shown to predate European civilization. Ethiopianism has been used to express the political, cultural, and spiritual aspirations of blacks throughout the Diaspora since the eighteenth century. As a unifying metaphor for African brotherhood, it has provided the basis for shared notions of destiny and identification between African peoples," pp. 230 –31n. See also Leonard Barrett, *The Rastafarians,* pp. 68–80.

18. Rex Nettleford, "Introduction," *Dread: The Rastarians of Jamaica,* by Joseph Owens (Kingston, Jamaica: Sangster, 1976, Reprint 1989), p. xii.

19. Joseph Owens, *Dread: The Rastafarians of Jamaica,* pp. 6–7.

20. Owens, p. 7.

21. Owens, pp. 7–8.

22. Chevannes, "Introducing the Native Religions of Jamaica," pp. 16–17.

23. *Creole Religions of the Caribbean,* pp. 156–57. See also Barry Chevannes, "New Approach to Rastafari," in *Rastafari and Other African-Caribbean Worldviews,* pp. 20–42, edited by Barry Chevannes (London: Macmillan, 1995), pp. 26–31.

24. *Ibid.,* pp. 157–58.

23. Barrett, *The Rastafarians,* p. 129; known as marijuana Mary Jane) in some contexts, from the Spanish Mexican origin, the herb's technical name is said to be *Cannabis sativa,* "a name given to it by Linnaeus in 1753, and was known by the Hindus for centuries as Indian hemp or Bhang. It seemed to have been used in India not only commercially for making rope, but also for religious meditation," p. 128.

24. *Creole Religions,* p. 163.

25. Chevannes, pp. 17–18. See also Berrett, *The Rastafarians,* pp. 120–25; *Creole Religions,* pp. 165–66.

26. *The Rastafarians,* p. 124.

27. Chevannes, p. 18. See also *The Rastafarians,* pp. 136–45.

28. *The Rastafarians,* pp. ix–x.

29. *Ibid.,* p. 226.

30. *Ibid.,* pp. 227–28.

31. *Ibid.,* pp. 229–31.

32. Chevannes, "Introducing the Native Religions of Jamaica," p. 12.

33. *Ibid.,* p. 13. The term Bobo Ashanti or Bobo Shanti is used also for the group. One source says it is "derived from from Bobo, which stands for Black and Ashanti, which is the fierce African tribe from Kumasi, Ghana. It is believed that most of the slaves brought to Jamaica were from the Ahanti tribe and are the ancestors of many Jamaicans. The late Prince Emanuel Charles Edwards founded the Bobo Shanti order in Jamaica in the 1950's. The new Bobo Shanti order leader is Trevor Stewart," ("The Rastafarian Orders/Sects," *Jamaica Culture,* 2003 http://www.jamaicans.com/culture/rasta/rasta_sects.htm, accessed 11/16/04).

34. *The Rastafarians,* p. 225.

35. Barry Chevannes and Maureen Warner Lewis of the University of the West Indes were among the main presenters at that meeting in March 1996. They arranged for our field trip to the settlement.

36. *Creole Religions,* p. 232; the authors reference Dianne M. B. Stewart, "The Evolution of African-Derived Religions in Jamaica, Ph.D. dissertation, Union Theological Seminary, 1997, p. 144.

39. *The Rastafarians,* p. 182.

40. *Ibid.,* p. 182. See also, Barry Chevannes, *Rastafari: Roots and Ideology* (Syracuse: Syracuse University Press, 1994), pp. 172–74.

41. Prince Emmanuel Edwards, *Black Supremacy in Righteous of Salvation* (Bull Bay P. O. St. Andrews, Jamaica: Ethiopia Africa International Congress, n.d.), pp. 52 and 53. One source describes this book as "easily the most important Bobo publication...probably dates from the period 1978- and later, but...contains many older texts from the 60s. The booklet is called the 'second bible' by many Bobos," ("Information about the Bobo Ashanti," http://home.student.uu.se/haha2581/ht/boboinfo.html, p. 2, accessed 11/16/04.

42. *The Rastafarians,* p. 184.

43. *Rastafari: Roots and Ideology,* pp. 180–8.

44. I am not sure when they abandoned the practice, but the members told our group that they no longer smoked ganja as a part of their rituals.

45. One source reports his death as having occurred in 1994 (*The New West Indian,* Nov.-Dec. 2003 <http://www. awigp.com/default.asp?numcat=lku>), accessed 11/16/04). Prince Edwards's son, Jesus Emmanuelle Edwards, is reported as having inherited the throne in the Bobo Dread Church ("rasta culture," big Upradio, http://www.bigupradio.com/bobo-ashanti.jsp, accessed 11/16/04.

46. Ethiopian African Black International Congress, *The Black Christ Salvation with Joy and Peace Internationally* Jerusalem School Hymn Book (St. Andrews' Jamaica, N.D.).

47. "The Rastafarian Orders/Sects," p. 1.

48. "Rasta Culture," p. 4.

49. "bobohills," http://www.nettilinja.fi/~hsaarist/bobohills.html, p. 1, accessed 11/16/04.

50. Mozella G. Mitchell, *New Africa in America* (New York: Peter Lang, 1992), pp. 88–142. See Genesis 12:1–2; Joshua 15:1, 20; 17:2; 19:1, 17, 24.

51. *Ibid.,* pp. 92–93.

52. "Introducing the Native Religions of Jamaica," p. 11.

53. "New Approach to Rastafari," pp. 26–27.

54. *Soul-Force,* p. 193.

55. "A New Approach to Rastafari," pp. 30 –31.

56. Besson, pp. 55–55. Basically, the the author sees the African continuity here, but asserts rightfully that it is a continuity that exists within the context of Caribbean culture-building. We should recall the spiritual significance of land in the African background. "Essentially, access to land meant in Africa openness to God, to the ancestors, to nature, the validation of one's human and divine connections. In the communal nature of life in Africa, there was the unbroken bond between the living, the dead, and the yet unborn. And access to the ancestral lands was an integral part of that connectedness," Mitchell, p. 134.

57. Besson, pp. 53, 54, 55–56.

58. *Ibid.,* p. 56.

59. *Ibid.,* pp. 63, 64, 65.

60. *Ibid.,* p. 66.

61. Barry Chevannes, "The Phallus and the Outcast: The Symbolism of Dreadlocks in Jamaica," in *Rastafari and Other African-Caribbean Worldviews,* pp. 97 –126, edited by Barry Chevannes (London: Macmillan Press, 1995), pp. 117–19. Diedre Bádéjo in her study of Òsun in Nigeria discovered the view that a woman's power is most potent during her menstruating years. "Indeed, in a spiritually charged environment, menses is a manifestation of *àse* [ache]. Perhaps this explains the exclusion of women in some male-dominated secret societies until after menopause," p. 91.

62. "The Symbolism of Dreadlocks in Jamaica," pp. 120–23.

63. Kingston, Jamaica: Jamaica Media Productions, 1991, 1992.

64. *Ibid.,* Cover description.

65. *Joseph,* pp. 40, 47–48.

Chapter Nine

Crucial Issues in Jamaican Religions

1. Swami Prabhavananda, *The Sermon on the Mount According to Vedanta* (New York: New American Library, 1963), pp. xi, xiii.

2. *Conversations with Howard Thurman,* Part 2. Videocassette hosted by Landrum Bolling (San Francisco: The Howard Thurman Educational Trust, 1978).

3. Mozella G. Mitchell, "Religion and the Discovery of Self: Howard Thurman and the Tributaries of the Deep River," in *The Religion Factor: An Introduction to How Religion Matters,* pp. 84 –95, edited by William S. Green and Jacob Neusner (Louisville, Kentucky: Westminster John Knox Press, 1996), p. 86.

4. *Conversations with Howard Thurman,* Part 2.

5. *Conversations with Howard Thurman,* Part 1.

6. *Creole Religions of the Caribbean,* pp. 2 and 3.

7. Bisnauth, p. 165.

8. Brandon, pp. 68 and 69. See also Vera Martinez-Alier, *Marriage, Class and Color in Nineteenth Century Cuba: A Study of Racial Attitudes and Sexual Values in a Slave Society* (London: Cambridge University Press, 1974), pp. 71, 91–99.

9. See Frances Henry, *Reclaiming African Traditions in Trinidad, The Socio-Political Legitimation of the Orisha and Spiritual Baptist Faiths* (Jamaica, West Indies: The University of West Indies Press, 2003), pp. 108–36.

10. Interviews, Port of Spain, Santa Cruz, and San Juan, Trinidad and Tobago, West Indies, November 22-December 3, 2004.

11. Interview, Port of Spain Trinidad and Tobago, November 24, 2004.

12. "Orisa and Spiritual Baptist Religion in TT," pp. 87 –88.

13. *Dread: The Rastafarians of Jamaica,* pp. 114 and 115.

14. *Ibid.*, pp. 254 –55.

15. Richmond, Indiana: Friends United Press, 1976.

16. Howard Thurman, *Jesus and the Disinherited* (Richmond, Indiana: Friends United Press, 1976), pp. 11–12.

17. *Ibid.,* p. 29.

18. Frances Henry, pp. 108, 109.

19. Henry, p. 110. See also George Brandon, pp. 104–120.

20. Interview, Port of Spain, Trinidad and Tobago, W. I., 183183183 November 24, 2004.

21. Henry, pp. 133 and 134. See also Molefi Kete Asante, *Kemet, Afrocentricity and Knowledge* (Trenton, N. J.: Africa World Press, 1990).

22. Henry, pp. 108–35. Also *Eniyan Wa, Commemorative Brochure 2004: Gelede, Egungun & African Celebrations—T & T* (Princess Town, Trinidad, 2004). I attended the Seventh Egungun Festival, held at the Eniyan Wa Shrine at Nohar Road, Tableland, Trinidad, W. I., Sunday, November 28, 2004. Its theme was "Egungun Festival of Thanksgiving—The Way We Were." I was invited and hosted by Iyalorisha Amoye, Priestess of Yemoja, who was the organizer and director of the event. Babalorisha Clarence Forde, the head of the Orisa community in Trinidad and Tobago, led in honoring the ancestors and gave a brief welcome to the participants. The establishment of this festival in Trinidad over the past decade or so is very significant in the self-totalization process in that it brings to the people of the African heritage there a vital link to the Yoruba culture in Nigeria, where the Egungun is celebrated annual as a necessary part of the traditional culture in observance of the death of important elders in the society.

23. Henry, p. 136.

24. Robert B. Fisher, *West African Religious Traditions: Focus on the Akan of Ghana* (Maryknoll, New York: Orbis Books, 1998), pp. 138–42, and 133. See also Lamin Sanneh, *Translating the Message: The Missionary Impact on Culture* (Maryknoll, N. Y.: Orbis Books, 1990).

25. Fisher, pp. 163–64.

26. Sanneh, p. 159, quoted in Fisher, pp. 164–65.

27. Fisher, p. 166.

28. *Ibid.,* pp. 166, 170.

29. Kofi Appiah-Kubi, "Indigenous African Christian Churches: Signs of Authenticity, in *African Theology en Route,* edited by Kofi Appiah-Kubi and Sergio Torres, 117–25 (Maryknoll, N. Y.: Orbis Books, 1979), cited in Fisher, p. 172.

30. Fisher, pp. 170, 171.

31. Lamin Sanneh, *West African Christianity: The Religious Impact* (Maryknoll, N. Y.: Orbis Books, 1983), quoted in Fisher, pp. 172 –73.

32. Henry, p. 133.

33. Oludumare and Olorun are names used variously for the Creator God. Obatala is deity of truth, and Orunmila (variously Orula, Orunla, Ifá) is god of truth, divination, etc.

34. Interview with Babalorisa Sam Phills, Port of Spain, Trinidad and Tobago, December 2, 2004.

35. *Ibid.*

36. See Frances Henry, p. 127.

37. Interview, December 2, 2004. Baba Phills spoke of the progress that is being made in the direction of exposing people to Orisha (Yoruba) religion and culture, such as the teaching of Yoruba language classes by a native Nigerian at the University of the West Indies in St. Augustine, near Port of Spain. He himself has been taking students coming to Trinidad to study the culture on tours, filed trips to see all the different Yoruba traditions in the country. He stated that they can do much more if they have their own facility where students can live and learn for periods of weeks and months.

38. *Ibid.*

39. *Ibid.*

40. At this juncture in the interview an struck Port of Spain (5.0 on the Richter Scale), and in the few seconds the hotel building rocked from side to side as though it were floating on water, Baba Phills stopped talking in response to questions and whispered prayers aloud, looking upward. Continuing as the quike subsided, he uttered in relief, "That was a big tremor indeed!" I was astonished to realize that I had indeed experienced an earthquake for the first time in my life.

41. *Ibid.*

42. Baba stated that his group fell apart in New York City when the members were detracted from their course by New York brothers and sisters who led them into local activities and interests. He did not follow suit, he said, because he was there for a cause, which was to promote the Independence Movement of Trinidad, which was not achieved until 1962. Their last big concert was performed with a man named Vincent from Haiti, who established a building in Harlem at 135th Street and Lenox Avenue, name Damballah-Wedo (after the snake god of the Fon religion of Dahomey (Benin presently) known as Vodun). The building has the image of a huge snake on top. He changed his own name to the African name Nana Baruku.

43. Interview with Mr. Rawle Gibbons, St. Augustine, Trinidad and Tobago, West Indies, November 30, 2004.

44. Interview with Pearl Eintou Springer, San Juan, Trinidad and Tobago, December 2, 2004.

45. The Ooni of Ifé, Nigeria, is the spiritual Head of the Orisa religion worldwide, similar to the Pope in Christianity or the DaLai Lama in Tebetan Buddhism.

46. *Ibid.* Frances Henry describes and documents fully the reclamation process and events of the Orisha people in her book discussed earlier in this chapter.

47. Baba Erin Folami is one of the leaders of the Orisha community of Trinidad and Tobago who is very much involved with recovery of the true dignity and place of African tradition against the political and social and religious encroachment of other cultures. His perspective is Afro-centric, as discussed by Henry in her book, Reclaiming African Religions in Trinidad (discussed earlier in this chapter). Folami is also a part of the teaching staff of the Osun Abiadama School established by Iyalorisha Patricia McCleod, head of the Ile Eko Shango-Oshun Shrine in Santa Cruz, Trinidad and Tobago, where Dr. Althea and Mr. Eddie LeCointe are members. Kambiri Osunreyeke conducts the Oshuna Centre especially for the restoration of African values among women located at St. James outside Port of Spain.

48. Clyde W. Ford, *The Hero with an African Face: Mythic Wisdom of Traditional Africa* (New York: Bantam Books, 1999), p. 52.

49. *Ibid.*, pp. 52–53.

50. Cambridge: Cambridge University Press, 1992.

51. Ford, p. 145.

52. Joseph Owens, Dread: The Rastafarians of Jamaica (Kingston, Jamaica: Sangster, 1976), p. 172.

53. *Ibid.*, p. 173.

54. Rex Nettleford, "Introduction," to *Dread* by Joseph Owens, pp. vii–xix (Kingston, Jamaica: Sangster, 1976), pp. xiv–xvi.

Bibliography

Apter, Andrew. "Herskovits's Heritage: Rethinking Syncretism in African Diaspora." *Diaspora: A Journal of Transnational Studies* 1, no. 3 (1991): 235–260.

Agorsah, E. Kofi, ed. *Maroon Heritage: Archaeological, Ethnographic and Historical Perspectives.* Kingston, Jamaica, West Indies: Canoe Press, The University of the West Indies, 1994.

Appiah-Kubi, Kofi. "Indigenous African Christian Churches: Signs of Authenticity." In *African Theology en Route*, edited by Kofi Appiah Kubi and Sergio Torres, 117–25. Maryknoll, N.Y.: Orbis Books, 1979.

Asante, Molefi Kete. *Kemet, Afrocentricity and Knowledge.* Trenton, N.J.: Africa World Press, 1990.

Bádéjo, Diedre. *Ósun Séégési: The Elegant Deity of Wealth, Power, and Feminity.* Trenton, N.J.: Africa World Press, 1996.

Bandelier, AD. F., Transcribed by M. Donahue. "Arawaks." *New Advent Catholic Newsletter.* http://www.newadvent.org/cathen/01680c.htm, accessed September 24, 2004.

Barnes, Michael H. *In the Presence of Mystery: An Introduction to the Story of Human Religiousness.* Mystic, Conn.: Twenty-Third Publications, 1985.

Barnes, Sandra T. *Africa's Ogun: Old World and New.* Bloomington: Indiana University Press, 1989.

Barnet, Miguel. *Afro-Cuban Religions*, translated from the Spanish by Renata Ayorinde. Princeton, N.J.: Markus Wiener Publishers, 2001.

Barrett, Leonard E. *Soul-Force: African Heritage in Afro-American Religion.* Garden City, N.Y.: Anchor Books, 1974.

———*The Rastafarians: Sounds of Cultural Dissonance.* Boston: Beacon Press, 1988.

Bastide, Roger. *African Civilisations in the New World.* New York: Harper and Row, 1971.

Bellah, Robert. "Religious Evolution." *American Sociological Review* 39, no. 3 (June 1964): 348--374.

Besson, Jean. "Religion as Resistance in Jamaican Peasant Life: The Baptist Church, Revival Worldview and Rastafari Movwment." In *Rastafari and Other African-Caribbean Worldviews*, edited by Barry Chevannes, 43–76. London: Macmillan Press, 1955.

Bettelheim, Judith, ed. *Cuban Festivals: A Century of Afro-Cuban Culture.* Princeton, N.J.: Markus Wiener Publishers, 2001.

Bisnauth, Dale. *History of Religions in the Caribbean.* Kingston, Jamaica, West Indies: Kingston Publishers, 1989.

"bobohills." <http://www.nettilinja.fi/~hsaarist/bobohills.html>, accessed November 16, 2004.

Braithwaite, Kamau. "Nanny, Palmares and the Caribbean Maroon Connexion." In *Maroon Heritage: Archaeological, Ethnographic and Historical Perspectives*, edited by E. Kofi Agorsah, 119--138. Barbadoes, British West Indies: Canoe Press, 1994.

Brandon, George. *Santeria from Africa to the New World: The Sell Memories.* Bloomington: Indiana University Press, 1993.

Bronkhurst, H. V. P. *British Guiana and Its Labouring Population*, 202.

Brooks, Miguel F., ed., comp., trans. *A Modern Translation of the Kebra Nagast (The Glory of Kings).* Kingston, Jamaica, West Indies: Kingston Publishers, 1995.

Brown, Karen McCarthy. "Systematic Remembering, Systematic Forgetting: Ogou in Haiti." In *Africa's Ogun: Old World and New*, edited by Sandra T. Barnes, 65–89. Bloomington: Indiana University Press, 1989.

Canizares, Raul. *Walking with the Night: The Afro-Cuban World of Santeria.* Rochester, Vermont: Destiny Books, 1993.

"Caribs." http://members.tripod.com/prejudice/caribs.htm, accessed September 23, 2004.

Carneiro, E. *Candombles da Bahia.* NP: Editora Technoprint, 1967.

"Casa del Caribe," Descriptive Flyer, Santiago de Cuba, 2003.

Chevannes, Barry, ed. *Rastafari and Other African—Caribbean Worldviews*. London: Macmillan Press, 1995.

———.*Rastafari: Roots and Ideology*. Syracuse: Syracuse University Press, 1994.

Chilcote, Ronald, ed. *Cuba, 1953–1978: A Bibliographical Guide to the Literature*, **2 vols**. White Plains, N. Y.:, 1986.

Corbett, Bob. "Pre-Columbia Hispaniola-Arawak/Taino Native Americans."

Dahl, Johnny. "The Arawaks – Caribbean Islands." http://www.en.original-people.eu. org/arawaks-caribbean.shtml, accessed September 24, 2004. http://www.webster.edu/ ~corbetre/haiti/history/pre-columbian/tainover.htm, accessed September 24, 2004.

Davis, W. *Passage of Darkness: The Ethnography of the Haitian Zombie*. Chapel Hill: University of North Carolina Press, 1988.

Deren, Maya. *Divine Horsemen: The Voodoo Gods of Haiti*. New York: Chelsea House, 1970.

De Saint-Mery. Description topographique physique, civili et historique de la partie francaise de L'Isle de Saint-Domingue. Philadelphia, 1797.

Desmangles, Leslie G. *The Faces of the Gods: Vodou and Roman Catholicism in Haiti*. Chapel Hill: University of North Carolina Press, 1992.

Diaz, Maria Elena. "Rethinking Tradition and Identity: The Virgin of Charity of El Cobre." In *Cuba, the Elusive Nation: Interpretations of National Identity*, edited by Damián J. Fernández and Madeline Cámara Betancourt, 43–59. Gainesville: University Press of Florida, 2000.

"Discover Trinidad and Tobago: Trinidad." http://www.meppublishers.com/online/discover/ discover/trinidad/index.php?topic:calendar, accessed August 30, 2004.

Doval, Teresa De La Caridad. *A Girl Like Che Guevara*. New York: Soho Press, 2004.

Drakes, Queen Mother Yvonne B. "My Spiritual Journey"; Archbishop Doctor Deloris Seiveright. "The Shouters National Evangelic Spiritual Baptist Faith." In *Nation Dance*, 19–21; 21–24. Bloomington: Indiana University Press, 2001.

Drewal Margaret T. *Yoruba Ritual: Performers, Play, Agency*. Bloomington: Indiana University Press, 1992.

Dudley, Shannan. *Carnival Music in Trinidad: Experiencing Music, Expressing Culture*. New York: Oxford University Press, 2004.

Dunham, Katherine. *Island Possessed*. Chicago: University of Chicago Press, 1969.

Edwards, Prince Emmanuel Charles The 7th. *Black Supremacy in Righteousness of Salvation: Jesus Negus Christ*. St. Andrews, Jamaica, West Indies: Ethiopia Africa Black International Congress, n.d.

Eliade, Mircea. *The Sacred and the Profane*. New Harcourt, Brace and World, 1959.

Eniyan Wa. *Commemorative Brochure 2004: Gelede and African Celebrations—T and T* Princess Town, Trinidad and Tobago, West Indies.

Fisher, Robert B. *West African Religious Traditions: Focus on Ghana*. Maryknoll, N.Y.: Orbis Books, 1998.

Flores, Maria M. Castro. "Religions of African Origin in Cuba: A Gender Perspective." In *Nation Dance*, edited by Patrick Taylor, 54–62. Bloomington: Indiana University Press, 2001.

Folami, Erin. Interview, Port of Spain, Trinidad and Tobago, West Indies, November 24, 2004.

Fontaine, Nasio. *Reggae Power*, Compact Disc. Attrose Music, 2003.

Ford, Clyde W. *The Hero with and African Face: Mythic Wisdom of Traditional Africa*. New York: Bantam Books, 1999.

Forte, Maximillian C. "A Brief Account of the Colonial History of Arima's Carib Community," 1998, 2001. http://www.Centrelink,org/fntt/History.html, accessed September 23, 2004.

———."The Carib Resurgence from 1973 to the Present." http://www.centrellink.org/fntt /Resurgence.html, accessed September 23, 2004.

————."The Relationship of the Caribs of Arima with the Tainos of Puerto Rico and the USA," 1999, 2001. http://www.centrelink.org/fntt/Tainos.html, accessed September 23, 2004.

Frye, Karla Y. E. "'An Article of Faith': Obeah and Hybrid Identities in Elizabeth Nunez-Harrell's *When Rocks Dance.*" In *Sacred Possessions: Vodou, Santeria, Obeah, and the Caribbean,* edited by Margarite F. Olmos and Lizabeth Paravisini-Gebert, 195–215. New Brunswick, N. J.: Rutgers University Press, 1997.

Geggus, D. "The Haitian Revolution." In *The Modern Caribbean,* edited by Franklin W. Knight and Colin A. Palmer, 21–50. Chapel Hill: University of North Carolina Press, 1989.

Gibbons, Rawle. Interview. St. Augustine, Trinidad and Tobago, West Indies, November 30, 2004.

González-Wippler, Migene. *Rituals and Spells of Santeria.* New York: Original Publications, 1984.

————. *The Santeria Experience.* Bronx, N.Y.: Original Publications, 1982.

Gottlieb, Karla. "*The Mother of Us All": A History of Queen Nanny, Leader of the Winward Jamaican Maroons.* Trenton, N. J.: Africa World Press, 2000.

Hannah, Barbara Blake. *Joseph: A Rasta Reggae Fable.* Kingston, Jamaica, West Indies: Jamaica Media Productions, 1991.

Helg, Aline. *Our Rightful Share: The Afro-Cuban Struggle for Equality, 1886–1912.* Chapel Hill: The University of North Carolina Press, 1995.

Henry, Frances. *Reclaiming African Religions in Trinidad: The Socio-Political Legitimation of the Orisha and Spiritual Baptist Faiths.* Kingston, Jamaica, West Indies: The University of the West Indies Press, 2003.

Holloway, Joseph E. ed. *Africanisms in American Culture.* Bloomington: Indiana University Press, 1991.

Hooft, W. A. Visser't. *No Other Name.* London, 1963.

Hurbon, Laennec. "Current Evolution and Relations Between Religion and Politics in Haiti." In *Nation Dance,* edited by Patrick Taylor, 118–137. Bloomington: Indiana University Press, 2001.

Hurston, Zora Neale. *Dust Tracks on a Road.* New York: Harper Perennial, 1991.

————. *Tell My Horse.* Berkeley, Calif.: Turtle Island, 1983.

"Information About the Bobo Ashanti." http://home.student.uu.se /haha2581/ ht/ boboinfo .html, accessed November 16, 2004.

Jamaica Culture, 2003. "The New Rastafarian Orders/Sects." http://www.jamaicans.com /culture/rasta sects.htm, accessed November 16, 2004.

James, William. *The Varieties of Religious Experience.* New York: Modern Library, 1929.

Jenkins, Carol L. "The Garifuna *dugu*"; Rebecca B. Bateman. "A Comparative Study of the Black Carib and Black Seminole." In *Blackness in Latin America and the Caribbean,* Volume 1, edited by Norman E. Whitten, Jr. and Arlene Torres, 149–167; 200–222. Bloomington: Indiana University Press, 1998.

Jerusalem School Hymn Book, *The Black Christ Salvation: with Joy and Peace Internationally.* St. Andrews, Jamaica, West Indies: Ethiopia Africa Black International Congress, n.d.

Johnson, Kim. "Taino: The Story of the Caribs and Arawaks," https//www.race and history .com/Taino/, accessed September 23, 2004.

Karade, Baba Ifa. *The Handbook of Yoruba Religious Concepts.* Boston: Weiser Books, 1994.

Khan, Abraham H. "Identity, Personhood, and Religion in Caribbean Context"; Breinburg, Pertonella. "Communicating with Our Gods: The Language of Winti." In *Nation Dance,* edited by Patrick Taylor, 130–151; 32–39. Bloomington: Indiana University Press, 2001.

Kipler, Kenneth F. *Blacks in Colonial Cuba 1774–1899, Latin American Monograph,* 2nd Series. Tallahassee: Center for Latin American Studies, University of Florida, 1976.

Korngold, Ralph. *Citizen Toussaint.* New York: Macmillan Press, 1943.

Kyung, Chung Hyun. "Come Holy Spirit, Renew the Whole Creation." In *Signs of the Spirit: Official Report of the Seventh Assembly*, edited by M. Kinnamon. Geneva, Switzerland: W. C. C., 1991.

Laguerre, Michel, "An Ecological Approach to Voodoo." *Freezing the Spirit 3, no. 1* (1974): 11.

Landes, Ruth. *The City of Women*. New York: Macmillan, 1947.

Lee, Simon. "The Caribs of Dominica." http://www.geocities.com/Athens/Agora/3820/carib.html, accessed September 23, 2004.

Leland, Andrea E. and Kathy L. Berger. *The Garifuna Journey*. Hohoku, N. J.: New Day Films, 1998.

Lowenthal, Ira. "Ritual Performance and Religious Experience: A Service for the Gods in Southern Haiti." *Journal of Anthropological Research* 34(1978): 393.

Mair, Lucille M. *The Rebel Woman in the British West Indies During Slavery*. Kingston, Jamaica, West Indies: Institute of Jamaica Publications, 1995.

Martinez-Alier. *Marriage, Class and Color in Nineteenth Century Cuba: A Study of Racial Attitudes and Sexual Values in a Slave Society*. London: Cambridge University Press, 1974.

Media and Editorial Projects Limited. "Discover Trinidad and Tobago 2003." http://www.meppublishers .com/ discover/ welcome / index.php? topic= about tnt accessed August 30, 2004.

Metraux, Alfred. *Voodoo in Haiti*. New York: Schocken Books, 1972.

Mitchell, Mozella G. "Religion and the Discovery of Self: Howard Thurman and the Tributaries of the Deep River." In *The Religion Factor: An Introduction to How Religion Matters*, edited by William Scott Green and Jacob Neusner, 84--96. Louisaville, Ky.: 1996.

———. *Spiritual Dynamics of Howard Thurman's Theology*. Bristol, Ind.: Wyndham Hall Press, 1985.

———. *New Africa in America*. New York: Peter Publishers, 1994.

Murphy, Joseph M. *African Spirits in America*. Boston: Beacon Press, 1993.

———. *Working the Spirit: Ceremonies of the African Diaspora*. Boston: Beacon Press, 1994.

Nahum, Roger et al. *Dance, Voodoo, Dance*. Princeton: Films for the Humanities, 1992.

Negron, Rene Bermudez. "The Arawaks," *300 Years of Spanish Presence*. http://community. wow.net/300history/01/07.html, accessed September 24, 2004.

Neihardt, John G. *Black Elk Speaks: Being the Life Story of a Holy Man of the Oglala Sioux*. New York: Pocket Books, 1959.

Nettleford, Rex. "Introduction." In *Dread: The Rastafarians of Jamaica*, by Joseph Owens, vii–xix. Kingston, Jamaica, West Indies: Sangster, 1976.

———. *Inward Stretch, Outward Reach: A Voice from the Caribbean*. London: Macmillan, 1993.

The New West Indian (November-December 2003, http://www.awigp.com/ default.asp? numcat=1ku, accessed November 16, 2004.

Nodal, Roberto. "The Social Evolution of the Afro-Cuban Drum." *Black Perspectives in Music* 11, no. 2 (Fall 1983): 157–77.

Nunez, Elizabeth. *Beyond the Limbo Silence*. Seattle: Seal Press, 1998.

Oduyoye, Mercy Amba. *Daughters of Anowa: African Women and Patriarchy*. Maryknoll, N.Y.: Orbis Books, 2000.

Olmos, Margarite Fernández, and Lizabeth Paravisini-Gebert. *Creole Religions of the Caribbean: An Introduction from Vodou and Santeria to Obeah and Espiritismo*. New York: New York University Press, 2003.

———, eds. *Sacred Possessions: Vodou, Santeria, Obeah, and the Caribbean*. New Brunswick, N.J.: Rutgers University Press, 1997.

Omali, Mikelle S. *From the Inside to the Outside: The Art and Ritual of Bahian Candomblé*. Los Angeles: Museum of Cultural History, UCLA Monograph Series, 1984.

Ortiz, Fernando. "Los cabildos afro-cubana." *Revista Bimestre cubana* 26 (1921): 5–39.

Otto, Rudolph. The Idea of the Holy. New York: Oxford University Press, 1958.

Owens, Joseph. *Dread: The Rastafarians of Jamaica*. Kingston, Jamaica, West Indies: Sangster's Book Stores, 1976.

Parrinder, Geoffrey. *In the Belly of the Snake: West Africa over Sixty Years Ago*. Peterborough: PE3 7PG, Methodist Publishing House, 2000.

Pérez, Louis A. Jr. *Cuba: Between Reform and Revolution*, 2nd ed. New York: Oxford University Press, 1995.

Phills, Sam. Interview. Port of Spain, Trinidad and Tobago, West Indies, December 2, 2004.

Prabhavananda, Swami. *The Sermon on the Mount According to Vedanta*. New York: New American Library, 1963.

Prince, Althea. "How Shall We Sing the Lord's Song in a Strange Land? Constructing the Divine in Caribbean Contexts"; Frederick Ivor Case. "The Intersemiotics of Obeah and Kali Mai in Guyana." In *Nation Dance*, edited by Patrick Taylor, 25–31; 40–53. Bloomington: Indiana University Press, 2001.

Raboteau, Albert J. *Slave Religion: The "Invisible Institution" in the Antebellum South*. New York: Oxford University Press, 2004.

"rasta culture." bigUpradio. http://www.bigupradio.com/bobo-ashanti.jsp, accessed November 16, 2004.

Raymond, Judy. "Forward Home—Andre Revisited." *Caribbean Beat*, no. 61 (July/August 2004): 5 http://www.meppublishers.com/online/caribbean-beat/archive/article.php?id=cb61-2–98, accessed August 30, 2004.

Ripley, C. Peter. *Conversations with Cuba*. Athens, Ga.: The University of Georgia Press, 1999.

Rivera, Magaly. "Welcome to Puerto Rico: Glossary." http://welcome.topuerto rico.org /glossary /index.shtml, accessed August 8, 2004.

Sandoval, Mercedes Cros. *La religion afrocubana*. Madrid: Playor, 1975.

Sankeralli, Burton, ed. *At the Crossroads: African Caribbean Religion and Christianity*. St. James, Trinidad and Tobago, West Indies: Caribbean Conference of Churches, 1994.

Sanneh, Lamin. *The Missionary Impact on Culture*. Maryknoll, N.Y.: Orbis Books, 1990.

———. *Piety and Power: Muslims and Christians in West Africa*. Maryknoll, N.Y.: Orbis Books, 1996.

———. *West African Christianity: The Religious Impact*. Maryknoll, N.Y.: Orbis Books, 1983.

Scherer, Frank F. "Sanfancón: Orientalism, Self-Orientalization, and 'Chinese Religion' in Cuba." In *Nation Dance*, edited by Patrick Taylor, 153–170. Bloomington: Indiana University Press, 2001.

Scott, David. "The Sovereignty of the Imagination: An Interview with George Lamming." *Small Axe: A Caribbean Journal of Criticism* 6, no. 2 (September 2002): 72–200.

Seaga, Edward. *Revival Cults in Jamaica*, Reprinted from *Jamaica Journal* 3, no. 2 (June 1969). Kingston, Jamaica, West Indies: The Institute of Jamaica, 1882.

Sizzla. *Black Woman and Child*, Compact Disc. Kingston, Jamaica, West Indies: Crage Music and Jam Rec, 2002.

Sohl, Robert and Aubrey Carr, eds. *The Gospel According to Zen: Beyond the Death of God*. New York: New American Library, 1970.

Solá, Edwin Miner. *Diccionario Taino Illustrado*. San Juan, Puerto Rico: Primero Impresión, 2002.

Soyinka, Wole. *Myth, Literature, and the African World*. Cambridge: Cambridge University Press, 1992.

Springer, Pearl Eintou. Interview. San Juan, Trinidad and Tobago, West Indies, December 2, 2004.

———. "Orisa and the Spiritual Baptist Religion in Trinidad and Tobago." In *At the Crossroads*, edited by Burton Sankeralli, 85–108. St. James, Trinidad and Tobago, W. I.: Caribbean Conference of Churches, 1995.

Stewart, Dianne M. B. "The Evolution of African-Derived Religions in Jamaica," Ph.D. Dissertation. New York: Union Theological Seminary, 1997.

Storper, Dan, Executive Producer. *Reggae Around the World*, Compact Disc. New York: Putumayo World Music, 1998.

Stubbs, Jean. "Translator's Preface." In *Cuban Festivals*, edited by Judith Bettelheim, xiii–xviii. Princeton: Markus Wiener Publishers, 2001.

Taylor, Patrick. *Nation Dance: Religion, Identity, and Cultural Difference in the Caribbean.* Bloomington: Indiana University Press, 2001.

Thurman, Howard with Landrum Bolling. *Conversations with Howard Thurman.* San Francisco: BBC, 1977.

———. *Jesus and the Disinherited.* Richmond, Ind.: Friends United Press, 1981.

Tremmel, William C. *Religion: What Is It?* 2nd ed. New York: Holt, Rinehart and Winston, 1984.

Ucko, Hans. "Syncretism: A Challenge to an Ecumenical Discussion on Gospel and Culture." In *At the Crossroads*, edited by Burton Sankeralli, 33–45 . St. James, Trinidad and Tobago, W. I.: Caribbean Conference of Churches, 1995.

Varger, P. *Orixas.* Sao Paulo: Corrupio, 1981.

Vega, Marta Moreno. *The Altar of My Soul: The Living Traditions of Santeria.* New York: The Ballantine Publishing Group, 2000.

Voeks, Robert A. *Sacred Leaves of Candomblé: African Magic, Medicine, and Religion in Brazil.* Austin: University of Texas Press, 1997.

Warner-Lewis, Maureen. *Guinea's Other Suns: The African Dynamic in Trinidad Culture.* Dover, Mass.: The Majority Press, 1991.

Waters, Mary-Alice, ed. *From the Escambray to the Congo: In the Whirlwind of the Cuban Revolution, Interview with Victor Dreke.* New York: Pathfinder, 2002.

Williams, Claudette M. *Charcoal and Cinnamon: The Politics of Color in Spanish Caribbean Literature.* Gainesville: University Press of Florida, 2000.

Wooding, H. O. B. "The Constitutional History of Trinidad and Tobago." In *Caribbean Quarterly* 6, nos. 2 and 3, 147.

Zamuel, Hesdie. "Popular Religions and Ecumenism." In *At the Crossroads: African Caribben Religion and Christianity*, edited by Burton Sankeralli, 6–12. St. James, Trinidad and Tobago, West Indies: Caribbean Conference of Churches, 1995.

Zimmer, Josh. "Haitians hope, celebrate," 1B, and Associated Press, "Haiti celebrates bicentennial," 11A. *St. Peters*

Index

Foreign Words and Phrases

Martin Luther King, Jr. Memorial Studies in Religion, Culture, and Social Development

Mozella G. Mitchell, General Editor

This series is named for Martin Luther King Jr., because of his superb scholarship and eminence in religion and society, and is designed to promote excellence in scholarly research and writing in areas that reflect the interrelatedness of religion and social/cultural/political development both in American society and in the world. Examination of and elaboration on religion and sociocultural components such as race relations, economic developments, marital and sexual relations, inter-ethnic cooperation, contemporary political problems, women, Black American, Native America, and Third World issues, and the like are welcomed. Manuscripts must be equal to a 200 to 425 page book and are to be submitted in duplicate.

For additional information about this series or for the submission of manuscripts, please contact:

Peter Lang Publishing, Inc.
Acquisitions Department
29 Broadway, 18th floor
New York, New York 10006

To order other books in this series, please contact our Customer Service Department:

800-770-LANG (within the U.S.)
(212) 647-7706 (outside the U.S.)
(212) 647-7707 FAX

Or browse online by series at:

www.peterlang.com